The Russian Invasion of Ukraine, February–December 2022

To the Men and Women of the Ukrainian Armed Forces in their fight for liberty and to Command Sergeant Major William Clark Jr., (Ret.), California National Guard, for his dedication and perseverance in helping create a professional Ukrainian Non-Commissioned Officers Corps.

In Memoriam
MG(Ret), Willian H Wade III.

The Russian Invasion of Ukraine, February–December 2022

Destroying the Myth of Russian Invincibility

John S Harrel

Pen & Sword
MILITARY

First published in Great Britain in 2023 by
Pen & Sword Military
An imprint of Pen & Sword Books Limited
Yorkshire – Philadelphia

ISBN 978 1 39903 176 9

Typeset by Mac Style
Printed in the UK by CPI Group (UK) Ltd, Croydon, CR0 4YY.

Pen & Sword Books Limited incorporates the imprints of After
the Battle, Atlas, Archaeology, Aviation, Discovery, Family History,
Fiction, History, Maritime, Military, Military Classics, Politics,
Select, Transport, True Crime, Air World, Frontline Publishing, Leo
Cooper, Remember When, Seaforth Publishing, The Praetorian Press,
Wharncliffe Local History, Wharncliffe Transport, Wharncliffe True
Crime and White Owl.

For a complete list of Pen & Sword titles please contact

PEN & SWORD BOOKS LIMITED
47 Church Street, Barnsley, South Yorkshire, S70 2AS, England
E-mail: enquiries@pen-and-sword.co.uk
Website: www.pen-and-sword.co.uk
or
PEN AND SWORD BOOKS
1950 Lawrence Rd, Havertown, PA 19083, USA
E-mail: Uspen-and-sword@casematepublishers.com
Website: www.penandswordbooks.com

Contents

List of Abbreviations

AAA	Anti-Air Artillery
ADA	Air Defence Artillery
APC	Armoured Personnel Carrier
BMP	IFV used by Ukraine and Russia
BMD	Air Droppable IFV
BOS	Battlefield Operating System
BTG	Battalion Tactical Group
BTR	APC used by Ukraine and Russia
C2	Command and Control
CAB	Combined Arms Battalion
DPR	Donetsk People's Republic
EW	Electronic Warfare
ENG	Engineer
HIMARS	High Mobility Artillery Rocket System
HQ	Headquarters
IFV	Infantry Fighting Vehicle
LPR	Luhansk People's Republic
MANPAD	Man Portable Air Defence Weapon
MLRS	Multiple Rocket System
MOD	Ministry of Defence
NLAW	Fire and Forget Light Anti-Armor Weapon
OC	Ukrainian Operational Command
OK	Russian Operational Command
RAF	Russian Armed Forces
RU	Russia
TAC	Tactical Command Centre
TOC	Tactical Operation Centre
UA	Ukraine
UAF	Ukrainian Armed Forces
NGU	Ukrainian National Guard
VDV	Russian Airborne Forces
VKS	Russian Air and Space Force

Map Symbols

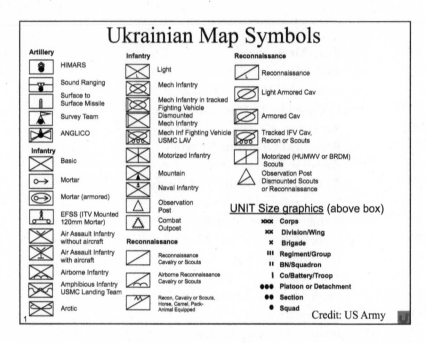

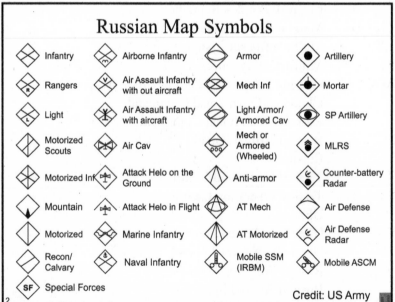

List of Maps

List of Charts

List of Photographs

Acknowledgements

Credit for turning my newsletters on the Russian Invasion of Ukraine to friends and family into a book belongs to my friend and pen pal Philip Sidnell, Commissioning Editor for Pen & Sword. Setting a short timeline for the book, Phil also served as the first line editor for the completed manuscript. The proof-reader and copy editor was Tony Williams, who had the challenging job of standardizing the spelling of English translations of Cyrillic place names into consistent standardized form. In addition, his attention to detail caught subtle errors, ensuring a better book. The eye-catching cover was the work of Dominic Allen. He was able to demonstrate the violence of war, while ensuring the cover was suitable for all audiences. I would like to thank Olivia Camozzi-Jones for guiding me though the marketing process. The ramrod for this project was Matt Jones. Matt had been the project manager for my previous books and has the skills to keep the project on track.

The photographs were compiled from Ukrainian government sources, Militarnyi (Defence industry of Ukraine), US and UK military and other open sources. Special mention should go to bloggers Preston Stewart (US), Paul Lewandowski (US), Deny Davydov (UA), Arthur Rehi (Estonian), Peron (Australian), Institute of the Study of War (US), Rochan Consulting (Poland), Deep State Ukrainian Map (UA) and Colonel Markus Reisner (Austrian) for their insights and reporting of the events in Ukraine and Russia in real time. Their analysis was validated as the invasion played out; more accurate, insightful and in depth than the 'news' as reported by the mainstream media.

Final credit for this book goes to US Colonel (Ret) Linda Harrel, Staff Judge Advocate, for her editing skills, transforming this work from a US Army War College staff study into a readable account of the political and military analysis of the first year of the illegal Russian invasion of Ukraine.

Introduction: 'Welcome to Hell'

Why did Russia invade Ukraine? How has Ukraine defended itself against the rampaging 'Bear'? How did the strategic narcissism of the West and NATO and their initial appeasement of Putin's imperial ambitions contribute to the cause of the war?[1]

The genesis of this book was a series of essays written for friends and family explaining details and implications of Russia's unlawful invasion of Ukraine on 24 February 2022. Having trained with the Ukrainian Army and National Guard in the 1990s and 2006, the author formed relationships with Ukrainian soldiers, soldiers whose sons and daughters now fight on the front line.[2] Having commanded Ukrainian soldiers in 2005 while peacekeeping in Kosovo, the author has an obvious bias for the Ukrainian cause, but seeks to provide an unbiased coverage of the first year of Putin's 'Special Operation'.

The more complicated aspects of twenty-first century warfare have been presented in basic terms, focused on the political, strategic, and operational level of the war, including weapon capabilities and tactics.

The primary armament of the T-64, T-72, T-80 and T-90 series of main battle tanks, fielded by both sides, is the Soviet 125mm tank gun. The 125mm tank round can penetrate the frontal armour (where the armour is the thickest) of all tanks on the Ukrainian battlefields making model and upgrade comparisons moot. As will be seen, the more important characteristic was whether the tanks could fire ammunition other than the old 125mm Soviet rounds. The level of training and motivation of the crew is more important than the tank model. If either side scored a solid hit on the front armour of an opposing tank it was disabled or destroyed. Most of the heavy weapons and equipment employed by both sides during the first eleven months of the war, from trucks to aircraft, were upgraded Soviet-era equipment.

The ability to correctly identify deployed Russian combat units was problematic. During the Second World War, Ukraine was the site of some of the largest land battles in history. Hundreds of thousands of men fought and died in a single battle. Troop density in Putin's 'Special Operation', on these same battlefields has been reduced to only thousands of soldiers. A few hundred Russian soldiers have fought under the same army and division banners that once heralded thousands of combatants into battle. The media often referred to the presence of a Russian combat unit such as the 1st Guards Tank Regiment, implying that a force of 3,000 soldiers was engaged (with 90 tanks, 40 APCs, and 18 howitzers). In fact, there was only a battalion tactical group from that regiment of 500–900 troops (with only 30 tanks, 10 APCs and 18 howitzers) participating in the referenced operation. The media often referred to a formation with its historic title, ie 1st Guards Tank Regiment, and followed that title with a notation of '1 BTG', or one battalion tactical group. In other words, big names but little battalions. Another misconception was the reported presence of a Russian 'combined-arms or tank army', that in reality was only a division-size formation (that is 7–14 battalions as opposed to an army with 50 or more battalions).

Generally, military ground forces are divided into three types of units: combat, combat support and combat service support. Combat units are tanks and infantry, direct action special forces and arguably attack helicopters i.e., units that close with the enemy and destroy them by fire, manoeuvre, and close combat. Combat support units provide fire support and operational assistance to combat elements. They include artillery (tubed, rocket and missiles), air defence artillery, close air support, electronic warfare attack and defence, cyber-attack and defence, intelligence, military police, etc. Combat service support units include legal, administration, finance, ordnance, quartermaster, and transportation units, providing logistical support from company to army level. At the basic level an infantry company consists of approximately 120 soldiers and 6 officers, divided into a command group, 3 infantry platoons (combat), a mortar platoon (combat support) and small administration, maintenance and supply sections (combat service support).

A combined-arms army will have more combat support and combat service support soldiers than combat soldiers. As an example, the Russian invasion force included nearly 200,000 soldiers of which only 65,000 were considered combat troops, with the remaining 135,000 troops providing combat support and combat service support.

Neither Ukraine nor Russia have yet to publish an official account and what has been published thus far was often fake news or propaganda designed to mislead the reader. Eyewitness reports provided colour, but accuracy suffered, depending on the babushka's understanding of her observation. As an example, civilians reported that in the morning '170 Russian boys and their vehicles drove toward the city; that night 18 returned without their vehicles'. What was apparently witnessed was the destruction of an entire Russian tank battalion. Often more accurate were the many unclassified reports from think tanks, military professionals on YouTube, newspaper/internet articles, press releases and interviews of military personnel. Particularly helpful were the daily YouTube reports of Paul Lenwandowski (US Army Combat Veteran), *Combat Veteran Reacts*; Deny Davydov (Ukrainian commercial pilot), daily reports; Artur Rehi's (former Lithuanian soldier), daily reports; Ukrainian Group's (probably Ukrainian MoD) daily reports *War In Ukraine Explained*, and the daily updated map of military operations and analysis, author identified only as 'Perun'. Three think tanks, Institute for the Study of War, Five Coat Consulting, and Atlantic Council Rochan Consulting also provided valuable information.

The first part of this book provides the background for the war, how modern technology impacted twenty-first century high intensity warfare, how terrain and weather impacted military operations, and a comparison of the combatants. The war, or as characterized by Putin this 'Special Operation', can be divided into four phases. During Phase 1 (24 February–7 April 2022) Putin attempted a blitzkrieg (lightning war) to overturn the Ukrainian government and capture key Ukrainian cities and regions. Putin apparently envisioned a short one- or two-week operation to accomplish his objectives. Russia did indeed capture the Black Sea coast, up to and including the important port city and regional capital of Kherson, within two weeks of his assault. However, after months of heavy fighting the Russian Army was defeated in detail before Kyiv and fought to a standstill before Kharkiv and the Donbas.

During Phase 2 (8 April–6 September 2022), the Russians massed troops against the Donbas and fought an artillery attrition war, expending massive numbers of men and material for little gain. While Russia was focused on the Donbas, Ukraine received, but husbanded material reinforcement from the West in preparation for a counteroffensive.

In Phase 3 (6 September–1 November 2022), Ukrainian Armed Forces launched a two-pronged counteroffensive, regaining all Kharkiv Oblast and recapturing the city of Kherson, as well as the west bank of the Dnipro River. The Russians then focused their main offensive to capture the fortified city of Bakhmut by frontal assault.

Finally in Phase 4 (1 December 2022–January 2023) the Russians continued their frontal and shallow flanking attack on Bakhmut. Only in the beginning of January 2023 did the Russians temporarily halt their futile frontal attacks of Bakhmut and attempt wider flanking attacks against the weaker parts of the Ukrainian defensive line.

Unlike any prior war in history there was literally a daily flood of data from the war. Using modern technology, civilians and soldiers from both sides posted details about battles and skirmishes. This war was like a football field where observers could monitor the live-time action.

It is important to realize that the spelling of transliterated Cyrillic words in this book has adopted Ukrainian spelling. Examples: Kharkiv instead of Kharkov, Kyiv instead of Kiev, Dnipro River instead of Dnieper River, etc. Russians and Ukrainians both use the term 'battalion tactical group' or 'BTG' yet they refer to different tactical formations. To the Russians a BTG is a small, combined-arms infantry/tank battalion with an attached artillery battalion. Ukrainians use the term to refer to a combined-arms battalion of infantry and tanks, or in NATO parlance a 'task force'. To prevent confusion where appropriate, Ukrainian mixed infantry and tank battalions are referred to herein as combined-arms battalions or (CABs).

Does Putin have an exit plan? His initial demands, based on an easy expected victory were that Ukraine recognize Russia's 'annexation' of Crimea, Ukraine sign a declaration stating it would not apply for NATO membership, Ukraine would demilitarize and finally, Ukraine would recognize the Donetsk People's Republic (formerly Donetsk Oblast) and Luhansk People's Republic (formerly Luhansk Oblast) as sovereign states with their pre-2014 borders. Putin's desired end state is a Ukraine politically aligned with the Kremlin, militarily neutral and partnered with Russian armed forces (ie dependent upon Russia for defence), and most importantly the establishment of transparent borders to facilitate cultural and economic integration of Ukraine into the Eurasian Economic Union (EAEU). In other words, the re-establishment of the former Soviet Empire, under the economic dictatorship of Russian Oligarchy and suppression of the developing liberal democracy in Ukraine.[3] Ukraine rejected all these demands.

Chapter 1

A Short History of Ukraine

Outside of Eastern Europe, the history of Ukraine is rarely studied as part of a public-school curriculum. The word 'Ukraine' derives from the Slavic and Hungarian words for 'borderland'. Ukraine's oral history begins with the founding of Kyiv. Legend has it that Kyiv was founded in 482 CE. The city was an East Slav trading centre supported by trade along the Dnipro River, flowing from its confluence with the Pripyat River (marshlands) in what is today modern Russia and Belarus. Since late antiquity the steppe tribes and the Slavic tribes of the Boreal Forest engaged in trade where the modern city of Kyiv is currently located.[1]

Prior to the legendary founding of the city, during the Copper, Bronze and Iron Ages, forest tribes traded with nomads including Scythians, Sarmatians and Goths. Archaeological evidence suggests that Kyiv was founded as a trade centre during the sixth or seventh century.[2]

Scandinavian Vikings established the Kyivan-Rus state during the ninth century.[3] Scandinavian traders and raiders were active in Eastern Europe as early as the eighth century.[4] In 882, Rus Viking Oleg, ruler of Novgorod, captured Smolensk and Kyiv. Due to Kyiv's strategic location Oleg established it as the capital.[5] A Slavic-Rus elite ruled the developing town. In 988 Christianity was introduced and Kyiv became the centre of what would become Orthodox Christianity.[6] By the eleventh century the Rus principalities controlled an area from the Baltic Sea to the Black Sea. To put these events in perspective, Moscow was not founded by the Rus until 1147.[7]

After the founding of the principality of Moscow, the fledgling Russian identity followed a parallel course of development with Ukrainian culture. The Kyivan-Rus was the dominant culture until the Mongol invasion of Moscow, which sent it on a separate ethnic course. The developing culture in Ukraine would be referred to as 'Ruthenian.'[8]

Between the tenth and twelfth centuries, the Ruthenian and other Rus principalities were engaged in a series of wars with nomadic tribes such as the Khazars, Pechenegs, and Polovtsians. Weakened by wars with competing principalities and nomads, Kyiv was ultimately unable to resist the Mongol invaders in the thirteenth century. In 1238 a Mongol army stormed and sacked Kyiv, killing most of its inhabitants.[9] Kyiv never fully recovered from the Mongol destruction and the capital of the Ruthenian principality was moved to Lviv.

The Ruthenian capital was heavily influenced by the Poles while Russian Novgorod and Moscow drifted toward an identity highly influenced by the Mongols. The tsars ruled in Moscow while Ruthenian kings ruled in Lviv.[10]

In the fourteenth century, the Ruthernian Kingdom was partitioned into the Kingdom of Poland and the Grand Duchy of Lithuania. Kyiv functioned as a fortress and small market town. The regional culture remained Ruthernian which became the foundation of modern Ukrainian culture. The western-orientated Lithuanian-Ruthenian nobles fought with the Mongol-dominated Grand Duchy of Moscow.[11] Despite its decline as an important trading centre, Kyiv remained an influential Eastern Orthodox Christian stronghold.[12] In 1569, the Grand Duchy of Lithuania merged into the Polish-Lithuanian Commonwealth.[13]

During the sixteenth and seventeenth centuries the Commonwealth and Moscow engaged in a series of wars. Bands of warriors within the Commonwealth known as the Zaporizhzhia Host from the Cossack Hetmanate (an area that would become Ukraine) were led by 'hetmen' (military leaders). In 1618, Hetman Petro Sahaidchny attempted to capture Moscow. While he failed, his campaign resulted in a peace treaty wherein Moscow ceded territory to the Commonwealth.[14]

In 1648 Hetman Bohdan Khmelnytsky rebelled against the Commonwealth, captured Kyiv, and organized the first Ukrainian Cossack state. In 1654 he signed the Treaty of Pereyaslav with Tsar Alexey I and brought Ukraine into the Russian Empire.

During the seventeenth century the Commonwealth decayed as Austria and Russia pushed its frontiers back. The Russian Empire expanded into the Tartar-controlled Crimea, and Cossacks and Ukrainian peasants moved into the newly acquired lands. This expansion continued and by the nineteenth century the Russian Empire extended into Siberia and across the Bering Sea to Alaska, with forts and trading posts as far south as northern California. During this period of expansion, Ukraine developed and maintained their distinctive identity.[15]

During the Russian Civil War at the end of the First World War, a Ukrainian independence movement established a short-lived autonomous region. However, after the Bolsheviks gained power this independent region was absorbed into the USSR.[16] Stalin's first Five Year Plan established Soviet control over Ukraine's rich agricultural lands and grain exports. The land in question had previously been owned and operated by Ukrainian small farmers.

In the early 1930s these small farmers were forced off their land and made to work on Soviet collective farms. The wealthier farmers, known as 'kulaks' were declared enemies of the state and were forced off their land, imprisoned or executed. Over 4,000 local protests were recorded and were brutally suppressed by the Red Army and secret police. Brutal laws and regulations created famine conditions by confiscating all food stuffs and preventing Ukrainians from leaving the region. It is estimated that 3.9 million Ukrainians were intentionally murdered by starvation, amounting to the Soviet genocide known as the 'Holodomor'. Stalin's policies achieved his objective of enforced collectivization. Ukrainian nationalism was suppressed. The Ukrainian Autocephalous (independent) Orthodox Church was destroyed and prosperous peasants eliminated.[17] Despite the horrors of the Holodomor, Ukrainian nationalism was not eliminated. A dramatized depiction of this atrocity can be found in the 2019 movie *Mr. Jones*, depicting a Welsh journalist's investigation in the early 1930s.[18] This well-acted but disturbing drama depicts Stalin's regime of terror and the West's narcissism in wilfully ignoring the genocide for economic and political gain.

Seeking to achieve independence and preserve the Ukrainian language, religion and culture, two political groups developed in Western Ukraine: the moderate Ukrainian National Democratic Alliance (UNDO) and the radical Organization of Ukrainian Nationalists (OUN).[19] In 1942 OUN formed the Ukrainian Insurgent Army (UPA) and fought both the Soviet Union and Nazi Germany.[20]

Despite Stalin's crimes against Ukrainians, they fought bravely against the invading Nazis. Some initially welcomed the Germans as liberators, but Nazi policies soon turned Ukrainians against the invaders.[21]

After the war, the UPA continued to resist Soviet occupation for fourteen years. The Red Army finally suppressed the insurgency in the mid-1950s.[22] However, the insurgency remained active in the undeveloped forests of Western Ukraine, explaining why horse-mounted Soviet Cavalry Divisions were maintained in the Soviet order of battle until 1955.[23]

Most in the West are unaware of the Ukrainian fight for post-Second World War freedom. In 1997, a group of California Army National Guard officers training outside Lviv (with Partnership for Peace) toured a museum dedicated to the many churches destroyed during the Second World War. As the matron led the group to display cases of Orthodox relics and icons, she related the story of the insurgency. The items in the museum were from several villages destroyed by Red Army counter-insurgency operations. The villages and their fields once occupied the land where the Lviv training base stood.

The big surprise was that these Ukrainian villages had been destroyed by the Soviets between 1947–1950, not during the war.[24]

It should be noted that at the Yalta Conference in 1945 it was agreed between the Allies that the Soviet Union and the Soviet Republics of Ukraine and Belarus would be admitted as full voting members of the United Nations. The Soviet Republic of Ukraine remained a voting member of the United Nations General Assembly between 1945–1991.

In 1954, Khrushchev transferred Crimea to Ukraine. Despite the official announcement of linked culture and economic ties, the transfer was associated with Khrushchev's need for political allies against then-Soviet Prime Minister Georgii Malenkov. Malenkov had emerged as the leader of the Soviet Union after Stalin died in 1953. Khrushchev was courting support from Oleksiy Kyrychenko as the First Secretary of the Communist Party of Ukraine.[25] Khrushchev won the political fight and Crimea was transferred to Soviet Ukraine.

After the dissolution of the Soviet Union in December 1991, Ukrainians chose to become an independent republic. Following their own destiny, while acknowledging a shared historical relationship with Russia, Ukraine specifically rejected inclusion into a post-Soviet Russian state.[26] The newly independent Ukraine faced Russian interference in its political and economic development. This threat pushed Ukraine closer to the West and on 8 February 1994 Ukraine joined NATO's Partnership for Peace.[27]

Chapter 2

Partnership for Peace

After the collapse of the Soviet Union and Warsaw Pact, NATO sought avenues on which to build cooperation with the new democratic political and military leadership of the former Soviet Republics and Warsaw Pact members.[1] To facilitate this cooperation, in 1994 NATO established the 'Partnership for Peace' programme (PfP). The programme invited former Soviet Republics and Warsaw Pact members to establish relations at their own pace while developing democratic institutions and interoperability with NATO.[2] While not specifically mentioned in NATO literature, the goal of most former Soviet Republics and Warsaw Pact members was admission to NATO as full members, for protection against a resurgent Russia.

A derivative 'State Partnership for Peace' programme (SPfP) evolved from a 1991 US European Command decision to set up a 'Joint Contact Team' comprised of US reserve soldiers and airmen interacting with corresponding military personnel from former Soviet Republics and Warsaw Pact countries. A subsequent US National Guard Bureau programme paired National Guards from several US States with former Soviet Republics and Warsaw Pact members. This extremely successful programme evolved into a key security development tool. It facilitated cooperation across all aspects of civil-military affairs.[3]

The National Guard in the US is an unusual military force. In many countries, like Ukraine, the 'National Guard' functions as an internal security force, often separate from the national armed forces. The National Guard of the various US states and territories are direct descendants of colonial British militias. Each colonial governor had the authority to call out every able-bodied man between the ages of 15 and 60 to defend the colony from attack by indigenous natives, pirates, the French, or Spanish. In addition to defence of the colony, expeditionary forces could be formed to strike enemies of the king outside the colony. During the eighteenth century, the French fortress city of Louisburg was captured twice by British expeditionary forces, comprised primarily of colonial militias.

Modern US State National Guards are the combat reserve of the United State Army and Air Force. The President and Congress have at their disposal approximately thirty Army National Guard combat brigades and hundreds of support units. Similarly, the Air Force is supported by the Air National Guard of each state. Simultaneously, each National Guard of a specific state like California for example, is under the command of its governor. When commanded by the state governor the National Guard is in 'State Status' and may be utilized for law enforcement and emergency services. In California, again for example, the National Guard has four 'seasons': Fire, Flood, Civil Disturbance and Earthquakes. Trained, armed and equipped by the Federal Government for its wartime mission, the National Guard is well equipped for domestic emergencies.

The National Guards of the fifty states and four territories are uniquely suited for the role of mentors to emerging democracies. At each level its part-time members ('weekend warriors') are pulled from all walks of life, ie firefighters, police officers, attorneys, state and local government officials, farmers, teachers, truck drivers, cooks, tradesmen etc.

On 8 February 1994, Ukraine and Hungary became the fifth and sixth countries to join SPfP.[4] The California National Guard was paired with Ukraine. Initially, generals and colonels from each country met in California and then in Ukraine to develop the programme based upon Ukraine's priorities. After goals and objectives were established subject matter experts were exchanged. Ukrainian officers attended the National Interagency Counter-Drug Institute at Camp San Louis Obispo, California where they were exposed to the concept of civil control of the military during domestic emergencies. In 1997, large peacekeeping field exercises commenced in the Yavoriv training base in Ukraine.

Senior officers from both California and Ukraine realized they had to build trust between their subordinates. Field-grade officers from both countries had trained their entire military career to fight each other. This became an obvious obstacle to overcome. A series of social events had been arranged during a planning session at Yavoriv. Two former Soviet officers were grouped with two California Guard officers by branch: tankers with tankers, infantry with infantry etc. An English-speaking Ukrainian officer cadet was assigned to each group of four as interpreter. On the dinner table were four bottles of vodka, a plate of black bread and butter (to better absorb the vodka).

The party started friendly enough. Toasts were offered to everything from family to tanks. After the first bottle of vodka the diners were somewhat belligerent, claiming their tanks were better and would have destroyed their counterpart on the battlefield. After the second bottle of vodka, the parties realized they had all been stationed in Germany and spoke German, albeit badly. The young translator cadets were soon dismissed and sent to bed.

By the third bottle of vodka, it was discovered that everyone toasting came from the working class and had more in common with each other than with elite political leaders. By the fourth bottle of vodka, lifelong friendships had been forged.[5] This series of 'bonding social events' helped cement relations on an individual level and eventually shaped the partnership for peace between California and Ukraine.

Over the decades since 1994, NATO, US Army and Air Force, and the California National Guard, worked to improve Ukraine's ability to defend itself and develop interoperability with NATO. Ukrainian military and police have participated in joint peacekeeping missions in the Republic of Congo, Cyprus, South Sudan, Abyei, Mali, Afghanistan, Iraq and Kosovo.[6] During the first decade of the twenty-first century a combined Polish-Ukrainian battalion was assigned to Multi-National Brigade East, commanded by a US brigade headquarters. During most of the rotations, the headquarters was formed from an Army National Guard division or brigade headquarters with a Ukrainian riot police unit assigned to the NATO HQ.

In 2020 Ukraine applied to and was accepted into NATO's Enhanced Opportunity Partner Program to develop interoperability between NATO members and non-member partners.[7] This programme improved the Ukrainian armed force's ability to act in conjunction with NATO members and equipment during on-going peace operations around the world.[8]

The success of SPfP was acknowledged by all participants and after 2015 it was expanded so that additional US State National Guards were assigned to rotate to Ukraine to conduct combat arms training. Until November 2021, the California National Guard continued to participate in SPfP and in field exercises in Ukraine. Once the threat of Russian invasion became imminent, the California National Guard was ordered home, along with most US military personnel. However, as late as 10 February 2022, the Florida Army National Guard had 160 soldiers from the 53rd Infantry Combat Team (Task Force Gator) deployed at Yavoriv training centre in Ukraine under the auspices of the PfP.[9]

As Russia invaded, California Governor Gavin Newsom authorized the State Military Department, Office of the Adjutant General to establish a special emergency operations centre, to continue round the clock contact with the Ukrainian Ministry of Defence and their National Guard (Ministry of the Interior). Within the rules, regulations, and limited funding of the SPfP programme, the California National Guard was only authorized to fly humanitarian supplies, body armour and helmets aboard US Air Force transport aircraft that were not fully loaded. Known as 'Space A' (Space Available) or low priority, these supplies were flown to Poland and then forwarded to Ukraine. The humanitarian supplies were donated by many organizations and the protective equipment was surplus donated by California and Colorado Police, Sheriff, and Fire Departments. Two airlifts reached Poland before the Federal Government assumed support for Ukraine, dwarfing California's efforts. The initial expansion of providing humanitarian aid and supplies was notably facilitated by California Congressman Adam Schiff.[10]

Additional support was provided by the California National Guard in facilitating early and direct individual contact between Ukrainian officials and other countries. Having served all through Europe, the Middle East, Africa and Afghanistan, the California National Guard was able to help its SPfP partner access additional aid through a chain of personal individual military contacts since the official military chain of contact had been disrupted by the Russians. Individual introductions were made via personal cell phones with countries having stockpiles of Soviet artillery and rocket ammunition. The ammunition was shipped to Ukraine via Poland.[11]

Chapter 3

Ukraine: Terrain and Weather

Combat in the Ukrainian theatre of operation is greatly influenced by terrain and climate. An army that recognizes and respects these natural forces can successfully conduct combat operations by taking advantage of these extreme conditions. Whether Napoleon's nineteenth century Grand Army or the twentieth century German Wehrmacht or the twenty-first century Russian Army, invaders must contend with Ukraine's major terrain and weather obstacles.

In early spring and late autumn, the two *rasputitsas* (muddy seasons) historically render unpaved roads in Ukraine into bottomless mud pits, with the countryside becoming a quagmire. The *rasputitsas* are caused by heavy rains in the autumn and last approximately four weeks, from the end of September through October. In the spring, the same muddy conditions reappear caused by the winter thaw and rain lasting approximately six weeks, starting in April.

Historically, winter in most parts of Russia and Ukraine lasts five to six months. The temperature in December 2021–Febuary 2022 can fall as low as –5 Celsius (23 Fahrenheit), with the spring 2022 *rasputitsa* beginning in late March.[1] Due to global warming, the spring 2022 *rasputitsa* came early, and the ground did not freeze in February, hampering the Russian operational plan. As Putin's 'Special Operation' commenced, muddy conditions confined Russian mechanized, motorized, and logistic operations to all-weather roads. The quagmire significantly contributed to Russia's defeat during the Battle of Kyiv.

Historically, Ukrainian winters are extremely cold with heavy snowfall and icy conditions. The extreme cold reduces the efficiency of men, animals, and machines. Ice causes weapons to jam and cold temperatures freeze recoil fluids. Engines freeze when turned off and metal becomes brittle. Soldiers become paralyzed by extreme cold and survival often depends on whether there is available shelter from the elements. Russians and Ukrainians are well aware of the extreme winter conditions in their home countries. Uniforms and equipment are designed for these extreme conditions. Summer weather dries out the dirt and gravel roads but dust and sand clog filters, creating continuous maintenance problems.

The Ukrainian road network has generally been upgraded since the Second World War with major paved highways linking cities, and secondary all-weather roads linking towns and villages. However, thousands of miles of dirt and gravel roads remain. These unimproved roads quickly turn into impassable quagmires when travelled by armoured vehicles and heavy supply trucks. Most modern army wheeled vehicle fleets are equipped with tyres that can be deflated for better traction in muddy or sandy conditions, if they are maintained.

The Ukrainian rail network links the country's cities and is a critical supply link, transporting raw materials and agricultural products to the Black Sea ports. The internal rail supply lines allowed Ukraine to quickly shift heavy equipment and supplies to any front. The road network supplemented the rail system. Due to redundancy of the road network, the Ukrainian Armed Forces (UAF) was not over-reliant on the easily targeted rail system to supply their troops.

Most of Ukraine consists of fertile rolling steppes and plateaus. Mountains arise in the west, the Carpathians, and in the Crimean Peninsula. The Dnipro and Southern Bug, both major rivers, constituted formidable military obstacles to any attack by Russia into Ukraine from the north, northeast, and southeast. However, the eastern Ukrainian border did not benefit from such a defensive obstacle and as a result Ukraine was required to heavily fortify the Donbas along its border with Russia, and the Republics of Donetsk and Luhansk. The small east-flowing Siversky-Donets River protected the northern flank of Ukrainian Donbas defences.

The Dnipro River divides Ukraine in half, running north to south, emptying into the Black Sea west of the Crimean Peninsula. Militarily, the cities of Kherson, Zaporizhzhia, Dnipro, Kremenchuk and Kyiv were key to defending the Dnipro River Valley. An invasion force advancing north or south along the Dnipro cannot bypass these cities. The cities can be quickly transformed into bastions from which defenders can interdict lines of communication and supply. The cities must be captured, blockaded, or besieged by an advancing army.

The southern edge of the Pripyat Marshes created a maze of swamps and small rivers along Ukraine's border with Belarus and Russia. These natural conditions protected Kyiv from potential attack originating in the north and advancing south along both sides of the Dnipro River. Aggressors attacking Kyiv from the northwest must isolate the cities of Kharkov and Sumy, advance 500km/310 miles through the steppes and successfully cross the Dnipro.

The central axis of advance began in the recently annexed Russian states of Donetsk and Luhansk. The route was roughly 400km/248 miles of open terrain without any major strategic obstacles prior to arriving at the city of Zaporizhzhia on the Dnipro River. Since 2015, Ukrainians had fortified and garrisoned this contested region. Russian and proxy forces had to penetrate this fortified zone before advancing into central Ukraine.

There were two Russian axes of advance from Crimea. The first axis headed west along the Black Sea coast to Odesa, while the eastern axis led to Mariupol. The Odesa axis required the crossing of the Dnipro and Southern Bug rivers, both major military obstacles. Bridges crossing these rivers became strategic objectives. The axis toward Mariupol lacked any significant military obstacle.

Fully aware of the impact of Ukrainian weather on military operations, Russian leadership nevertheless ordered the invasion in late winter, surprisingly ignoring the predictable impact of the spring *rasputitsa*. As previously stated, the ground did not freeze in February 2022. Russian heavy wheeled support and supply vehicles were confined to the limited improved road system along both sides of the Dnipro River. The mud was a combat multiplier for Ukrainian defence and contributed to preventing Russia from capturing or encircling Kyiv from east or west in the early weeks of the war. 'General Mud' derailed the Russian timetable.

Chapter 4

Twenty-first Century Warfare

A basic understanding of twenty-first century warfare will help understand the first year of Putin's 'Special Operation', the first 'near peer' conflict involving one of the top three world powers (US, Russia, and China) since the Korean War (1950–53). During the Korean War the US and United Nations opposed North Korea and China, backed by the Soviet Union. There had been great technological developments since the end of the Second World War and the beginning of the Korean War.

In 1950, jet aircraft ruled the sky. Helicopters provided aerial assault and casualty evacuation, and nuclear attack was a real threat. Hawks in Washington advocated nuclear bombing of Chinese industrial centres in Manchuria. Despite these advances, the war was fought to a stalemate by 'boots on the ground', in the end fighting much like that of the First World War of attrition.

The traditional definition of 'war' is a conflict carried on by the force of arms or a period of armed hostility.[1] Carl von Clausewitz summed up: 'war is merely the continuation of policy by other means.'[2] In the twenty-first century, Russia merged an aggressive expansionist policy into a 'hybrid war', weaponizing traditional economic and political activities. Over the past two decades the Kremlin had engaged in 'hybrid warfare' to achieve its goal of recreating the Russian Empire and extending its political/economic influence throughout Europe.[3] Information technology in the twenty-first century empowered Russia to propagandize and disrupt the dissemination of truth if and when it helped achieve its goal.

Hybrid warfare is a strategy utilizing political warfare with conventional, irregular and cyberwarfare. Its tactics include fake news, propaganda, foreign political and electoral intervention as well as conventional warfare. By combining kinetic and subversive operations aggressors seek to avoid attribution. Conventional forces may be deployed in special operations that fall below the threshold of high-intensity conflict.[4]

Hybrid warfare is a whole governmental approach that seeks to integrate all instruments of national power through campaigns that blur the traditional division between strategy and policy.[5] Russian hybrid warfare is rooted in its national goal of expanding its economy and influence throughout the world.[6]

Russian cyber interference in the American elections in 2016 and 2020 is an example of weaponizing the internet.[7] Russia's hybrid warfare included cyberspace operations, perception management, deception, electronic warfare, political pressure, preclusion, legal action, proxies, and non-state actors ('little green men' or mercenaries) all seeking to and continuing to cause disruption of the normal course of governmental activity. A student of Sun Tzu will realize these activities are not new; successful generals, kings and emperors have employed these strategies for centuries. However, new information and cyber technology has made them more effective.

There are three levels of war: strategic, operational, and tactical. As the chart below demonstrates, linked tactical and operational actions achieve strategic goals.[8] The media often uses these terms interchangeably, causing confusion.[9] Strategy combines national objectives with the military capacity to achieve its goals.[10]

Operations deal with the organization of campaigns, planning and employing tactical forces to achieve strategic objectives. Tactics employ direct action in battles and smaller engagements to achieve military objectives. As depicted in the chart below, a tactical militia patrol destroys supply trucks that potentially result in disrupting the Russian supply line. Lack of supplies resulted in Russia losing the Battle of Kyiv, thwarting the Kremlin's strategic goal of eliminating

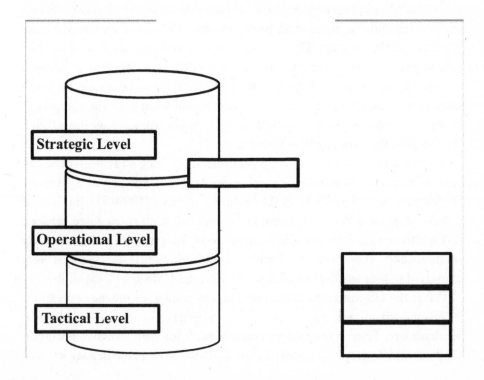

Ukrainian political leadership. In the cyber world, the strategy may be to disrupt the government of an opponent and assume control, or at least exert great influence on the actions of that government. The operation may be to interfere with an election, while the tactic would be publishing a false message on social media to the effect that illegal aliens were voting by mailed ballots. In the first example the 'operation' occurred in the context of actual combat, while the second 'operation' occurred, and continued in hyperspace.

The seven warfighting systems are: command and control, fires, force protection, information, intelligence, logistics and manoeuvre. Each has been greatly enhanced by twenty-first century technology.

Historic sections of command and control (C2) now include command, control, communications, computers, cyber defence/attack, surveillance, intelligence/reconnaissance, and electronic warfare. For simplicity these functions are reduced to the acronym C5ISR/EW. It does not take a graduate of a senior executive war college to realize that to effectively execute C5ISR/EW a commander needs a large, specialized staff. Small cells assigned to perform individual elements can be found at company, battalion, and brigade headquarters, but the overall work of the section is complex and must be completed at a division level.

Despite the complicated nature of modern combat and its expansion into the electronic and cyber spectrum, a command headquarters is most efficient when controlling no more than three subordinate combat manoeuvre units (infantry and/or armour). The more manoeuvre units greater than three that a headquarters seeks to control, the more inefficient its operations become. This is referred to as the 'Rule of Three'. When a commander (and his staff) attempt to command and control too many battalions at once the complexity of the operation becomes overwhelming.[11] Major armies have mistakenly drifted away from this combat-tested rule.

There has been debate in the US Army about shifting away from division-centric combat units to brigade combat teams. The US deployed a division-centric force to defeat the Iraqi Army during the first (1990–91) and second (2003–2004) Gulf Wars.[12] It shifted to a semi-brigade-centric force between (2006–2016) to counteract the insurgency in Iraq and to facilitate yearly rotations and ground control. Each of the US three-brigade divisions were converted to four smaller brigades, with improved C5ISR/EW capability.

While the US shifted to smaller brigades to combat insurgency operations it maintained all ten Army and eight National Guard combat division headquarters. They continued to conduct high intensity combat operation exercises and developed state-of-the-art C5ISR/EW-capable headquarters.

An offensive operation is divided into phases: shape, deter, dominate and seize. The attacker shapes the battlefield for success by manoeuvring forces to advantageous positions before launching a decisive ground attack, while using fire to attrite, fix, and isolate the enemy. Security operations keep or inhibit the enemy from acquiring information about friendly forces. Contact with enemy forces before decisive operations is deliberate and designed to shape the optimum situation for success.[13] During the deter phase the combatant takes action to prevent or stop the defender from implementing his proposed action. By dominating the offensive, the combatant takes control of the fight. If all phases of the offensive operation are successfully executed the objective is seized.

The key to twenty-first century offensive operations is the interrelation between tempo, fatigue, and reaction to unexpected events. Tempo is the relative speed and rhythm of a military operation with respect to the enemy. Controlling tempo is necessary to retain the initiative. A rapid tempo reduces time in which the enemy can react.[14]

Operational tempo is the ability of a force to integrate warfighting functions to achieve an objective. As an example, Russia's inability to balance sustainment (supply) with movement and manoeuvre lead to a slow operational tempo, resulting in defeat before Kyiv. In contrast, the Ukrainian-Kharkov counteroffensive demonstrated effective coordination of warfighting functions at a high tempo, resulting in the recapturing of Izym. The Russian 1st Guards Tank Army's operational tempo was slow to react, despite having sufficient armoured forces to counter the Ukrainian assault. The 1st Guards Tank Army's C2 and intelligence could not process the flood of enemy information in a timely manner which would have allowed the commanding general to manoeuvre to contain the Ukrainian blitz.

Fatigue is a limiting factor on tempo. An implemented sleep plan is required to sustain an offensive beyond seventy-two hours. In the absence of adequate rest, even the most disciplined, motivated force will become fatigued and ineffective.

An unpredictable event, known as a 'black swan', can derail the offensive tempo. The classic example of a black swan is Operation Market Garden in 1944 (portrayed in the book/movie *A Bridge Too Far*). An undetected German panzer battle group had established an assembly area near the British paratroopers' drop zone. Despite the bravery and skill of British and Polish paratroopers falling into the drop zone, they found themselves in the midst of heavy fighting instead of surprising the enemy. This black swan had a devastating impact and resulted in the loss of the Battle of Arnhem and the failure of Operation Market Garden.

During Russia's current 'Special Operation', the muddy ground did not freeze. Invading Russians presumably assumed that the ground would be frozen and would support the weight of their tracked and wheeled vehicles. The muddy ground, their black swan, derailed the Russian operational tempo, leading to defeat at the Battle of Kyiv.

Control of the aerospace environment is critical to twenty-first century warfare. Satellites circling the planet provide communication, jamming, intelligence collection, control of large drones, targeting for modern weapons and ground command and control. The US, China and Russia dominate space, while Ukraine totally lacks military satellite capabilities. After the Russian invasion, the US, other allies, and private companies (notably SpaceX) provided Ukraine with satellite capabilities that not only levelled the playing field but afforded Ukraine with an operational advantage.

The US has held air superiority in every conflict dating back to the Korean War. Air power has been a significant enabler of US military forces. As a result, NATO members developed air doctrine that complemented and duplicated US efforts. To counter NATO's air power, the Soviet Union and twenty-first century Russia invested in air defence capabilities on the tactical, operational, and strategic level. Post-Soviet countries, such as Ukraine, inherited air defence capabilities consisting of direct fire cannon, rockets, missiles, and electronic warfare to protect ground units and cities up to a 300km/186-mile radius. A carefully planned air campaign is required to defeat this Soviet-style integrated air defence system. NATO air and missile forces required two weeks to achieve air superiority against this type of Soviet system in the first Gulf War.

Ukraine and Russia, both post-Soviet states, have maintained their integrated ground air defences to control the sky over their cities, key infrastructure, and combat forces.[15] Neither have invested in the type of aircraft, weapons and training required to defeat a Soviet-style integrated ground air defence. Ground air defence for both countries at the tactical and operational level consisted of a range of weapons, from man portable (MANPADs) to self-propelled missile launch vehicles, some of which are still equipped with auto cannon as a secondary anti-aircraft system. At the strategic level, missile systems are either in fixed or semi-fixed positions. Tactical and operational vehicles include targeting radars for acquisition and engagement capabilities.[16]

The twenty-first century saw the introduction of unmanned aerial vehicles (UAVs) into civilian and military life on a massive scale. In the uncontested air space during the Global War on Terrorism, the US utilized expensive strategic drones, like the Global Hawk to loiter for hours at high altitudes, providing intelligence and targeting information to ground forces. Operational drones like the Predator hunted targets at lower levels to conduct precision strikes against high-value targets and terrorist leaders. Small, hand-launched, tactical UAVs provided intelligence and targeting information for company, troop, battalion, and squadron operations. However, UAV swarms deployed to strike targets were not fully developed until the Russian invasion of Ukraine in 2022. The UAVs used during the Global War on Terrorism were similarly used by Russia and Ukraine but were referred to as drones. Military drones provided a relatively cheap air force without the danger of losing a pilot. The pilots could be located half a globe away, or out of harm's way in a control centre in the next oblast, in a tactical vehicle or in a fox hole a few metres from a target.

Military strategic and operational drones, while cheap compared to a jet aircraft, were nonetheless expensive. An American RQ-4 Global Hawk cost $99 million, while an MQ-1 Predator cost around $40 million, not including its Hellfire missile. However, the Turkish Bayraktar TB2 drone cost a mere $5 million, while 100 MAML smart micro munitions cost an additional $15 million. More cost effective, the Iranian Shahed-136 kamikaze drone cost just $20,000. In comparison a Patriot anti-air missile cost $4 million.

The US armed forces utilized tactical drones to direct mortar and artillery strikes in the late twentieth century but a human observer or second electronic sensor was always relied upon to verify the target. In the battle space over Ukraine both sides integrated drones into every phase of the fighting but did not verify the target with secondary sources. Extensive fleets of costly military UAVs, as well as cheap converted civilian drones, contended with air defences and jamming to locate, attack or direct fire onto enemy positions. Inexpensive gyrocopter observation drones helped fire teams (four soldiers) clear bunkers, while repurposed obsolete strategic drones struck Russian airfields 600km/372 miles from the Ukrainian border. Drones hovering over a battle provided commanders, whether fire team or battalion, a full real-time picture of the fight.[17]

Drone reconnaissance rendered massing ground forces for the attack problematic. The detection of traditional armoured and infantry massing for an attack was quickly neutralized by drone-directed massed artillery fire. Russia's 1st Tank Army's attempt to mass combat forces at Izyum, to cut off the Donbass, was defeated at Dovhenke (April-August 2022) by the Ukrainian 81st Airmobile Brigade, reinforced with Territorial units. Despite being heavily outnumbered, Ukrainian reconnaissance drones directed concentrated artillery strikes against massing Russian armour units.

At 0420 on 29 October 2022 the Russian Black Sea Fleet was attacked in Sevastopol harbour by a swarm of naval kamikaze drones. The *Admiral Makarov* and two other ships were damaged. Nine air and seven naval drones were intercepted by Russian defences.[18] With a navy slowly rebuilding a mosquito surface fleet, Ukraine had developed unmanned surface vessels (USVs) to counter Russia's Black Sea Fleet. These naval kamikaze drones were purchased by an internet 'crowdfunding campaign'. Handmade, each USV cost $250,000 and included its ground control station. The naval drones had a range of 800km/500 miles, a speed of 80kph/50mph, carried a payload of 400 pounds and could operate for 60 hours.[19] The lesson from this engagement is that twenty-first century technology could and did provide a defender with relatively inexpensive weaponry to damage/destroy expensive war ships.

Two of the most spectacular Ukrainian drone attacks of the war occurred on 5 December 2022 at two Russian strategic airbases, 600km/372 miles inside Russia. As crews were loading Russian long-range bombers with missiles, Ukrainian kamikaze drones hit the base, damaging the bombers, and destroying the ammo dump.[20] These strikes sent a message to Moscow and Washington. To Putin the message read: 'We could attack Moscow!'To Biden the message read: 'Ukraine can be trusted to strike only military targets inside Russia if the US provided long-range artillery missiles.'

The best defence against drones was jamming. Disrupting signals controlling drones was effective. The cheaper the drone the more effective. The $20,000 Iranian Shahed-136 depended on GPS or other satellite systems to navigate. Inexpensive commercial GPS jammers or spoofers deployed around targets proved effective. Large ground and air military jammers defended large areas. When and if the jammers failed, loitering attack drones with air-to-air missiles targeted faster UAVs, while Hellfire anti-tank missiles targeted slower UAVs.[21] Slow and low tactical drones were engaged by IFV chain guns, light machineguns, and riflemen.

Despite these innovations, battlefield success still depended on putting an infantryman's boots on the objective. All this technology would have been useless if Putin was unable to put boots on the ground. Combined-arms tactics is a method to secure the ground.

The theory is as simple as the child's game 'rock, paper, scissors'. Combined arms balances manoeuvre, fire power and logistics to achieve an objective. Manoeuvre includes tank and infantry formations of all types with their various supporting weapons, organized into company teams, battalion task forces and brigade combat teams. Fires include artillery of all types, air, and space support, whether it provides lethal or non-lethal effects on a target. Logistics feeds the other elements of the triad.

For manoeuvre to be successful, infantry and tanks must cross open ground to capture an objective, but fires, notably howitzers, rocket artillery and mortars prevent infantry from closing with the objective, while defending infantry and tanks stop tanks. For manoeuvre to be successful, infantry must be protected by either armoured personnel carriers (APCs) or infantry fighting vehicles (IFVs). APCs, whether wheeled or tracked are lightly armoured to protect an infantry squad/section (7–9 men) from small arms and shrapnel from artillery and mortars. The APC is basically an armoured battle taxi, armed with a heavy machinegun. The infantry dismounts close to the objective, to protect the tanks by clearing obstacles and urban areas. APCs normally take cover, providing fire support with their heavy machinegun. More modern APCs may carry an automatic grenade launcher or even an autocannon. Classic examples of APCs are the American M-113 series and Soviet/Russian and Ukrainian BTRs series vehicles.

Armour protection on the infantry fighting vehicles (IFVs) falls between APCs and tanks. Armed with autocannon (20mm NATO, 30mm Soviet/Russian) and anti-tank guided missiles (ATGMs), they are formidable combat vehicles. Carrying a squad of six, the squad and IFV complement each other's strengths and vulnerabilities, while protecting the tanks. On the defensive, the IFV's ATGM often out-ranges the enemy tank's main gun. Examples of IFVs are American M2/3 Bradleys, German Marders and Soviet/Russian/Ukrainian BMP-series vehicles. When working as a team, the tanks and armoured infantry (riding in APCs or IFVs) are very effective. Modern and twentieth-century main battle tanks use heavy armour and high velocity main guns (120mm NATO/125mm Soviet/Russian/Ukrainian) to destroy any enemy on the battlefield. Their speed and armour allow them to take advantage of gaps in a defence or blunt an enemy penetration. However, without infantry support, they are very vulnerable to various light and medium anti-tank weapons carried by light infantry.

The failure of the Russian tanks and infantry to properly execute combined-arms tactics led to excessive casualties and high armoured vehicle losses early in the war. As demonstrated by the Ukrainian counteroffensive in September 2022, well-executed combined-arms tactics with tanks and armoured infantry are critical to offensive manoeuvre.

While technology has altered warfare, the execution of basic principles of combat and success on the battlefield ultimately relies on sound independent judgment of well-trained officers and non-commissioned officers. The ability to adapt new technologies to combined-arm tactics remained the key to tactical and operational victory.

Chapter 5

Road To War

Two strategic objectives have historically driven the expanding Russian state since its inception; the need for an ice-free seaport and the need for buffer states along its borders to protect the Russian heartland from invasion. The Russian psyche contributes to a not-totally unfounded paranoid view of the world, and a belief that the West will eventually invade Mother Russia again and again. This fear, while discounted by modern commentators, is based in historical fact.

From the Russian point of view, with the notable exception of the Mongols, invaders emanate from Western and Central Europe. Teutonic Knights attempted to subdue the Russian and Ukrainian principalities in the thirteenth century. In the sixteenth and seventeenth centuries the Polish-Lithuania Commonwealth conquered almost all of Ukraine. In the eighteenth century Swedes attacked Tsar Peter the Great's Russian Empire. Perhaps most famously, Napoleon invaded Russia, capturing Moscow in the very cold winter of 1812. France and Great Britain attacked Crimea in the 1850s (Crimean War 1853–1856). In the First World War (1914–1918) Imperial Germany and Austria invaded Russia and occupied most of Ukraine up to the Volga River (1917–1918). In the Second World War (1939–1945) Germany and the Axis Powers invaded, nearly destroying the Soviet Union and killing more than twenty million Soviet citizens; this despite the Non-Aggression Pact signed by Stalin and Hitler. It is therefore not surprising that after the Second World War, Soviet-occupied Eastern Europe was incorporated into a Soviet 'sphere of influence' as a buffer zone to protect Mother Russia.

Most Western countries, NATO and EU members viewed the disintegration of the Soviet Union with 'strategic narcissism'; a tendency to view the world only in relation to the observer's interests and to assume that the future course of events depended primarily on the observer's decision or plans.[1] The West envisioned a future of friendship and cooperation with Russia.[2] NATO and EU members failed to take Russia's strategic plans, goals, and public statements at face value. The *siloviki*, i.e., politicians arising from the Russian Military Industrial Complex, FSB and full-time professional Interior Security troops, did not view Western assistance in the post-Soviet period as benign.

The offered aid to soften economic disintegration and the encouragement of former Soviet Republics to seek their independence was viewed as a threat and an attempt to reduce Russia to a third-rate power. The expansion of NATO did very little to ease Russia's concerns.[3] By the late 1990s Moscow commenced hostile cyber infiltration operations, stealing vast amounts of Western classified military data.[4]

The disintegration of the Soviet Union in the late 1980s and early 1990s stripped Russia of its buffer zone. Western political leaders believed the Russian/Soviet Empire had permanently disintegrated and hoped that expanded economic opportunities and democratic governmental principles would restrain Russian expansionist tendencies. The dream was short-lived and by the mid-1990s oligarchs had gained control of the Russian economy and suppressed the move toward democratic reforms. As early as the 1990s, Putin, a former KGB officer, publicly expounded on the reunification of the Russian Empire, and an end to American global hegemony.[5] Russian oligarchs and *siloviki*, acting more like robber barons or mafia dons, gained control. With control came great wealth and influence.[6] Former Warsaw Pact countries and Soviet Republics (Poland, Lithuania, Latvia, Estonia, Bulgaria, Rumania, Slovakia, Slovenia, Hungary, Czech Republic, Moldavia and Georgia) sought protection against future Russian expansion and oppression by joining NATO and the EU.

Moscow continued to consider the area that was once the Soviet Union its exclusive sphere of influence, critical for Russia's security.[7] Over the last thirty years expanding membership into NATO and the EU created the illusion of neutralizing the threat of future Russian resurgence. Poland and other former Warsaw Pact members developed into liberal democracies, greatly improving their standard of living and demonstrating the benefits of an open society, and directly threatening the rule of the Russian oligarchy and *siloviki*. Ukraine's establishment of a liberal democracy (on Russia's border) and its goal of joining NATO and the EU constituted a direct threat to Russian oligarchy/*siloviki* control over the region.[8]

To counter this threat in the twenty-first century, Putin sought to re-establish a protective buffer. Based on its twentieth century experience, Russia adopted a 'fear-equals-respect' mentality to intimidate perceived enemies with hostile rhetoric and sabre-rattling.[9] Russians believed that only a strong czar-like leader, such as Putin, could protect them from foreign invaders, provide domestic stability and command respect internationally.[10] Partly due to propaganda and a controlled media, Putin enjoyed 60 to 80 per cent approval ratings despite military setbacks during the invasion. Putin clearly sought to rebuild the Russian Empire into a world superpower. It is not by chance he selected the imperial double-headed eagle as the 'New Russian' coat of arms.

Initial political steps for the creation of a new Russian Empire were taken in the late 1990s with the formation of the Eurasian Economic Union (EEU). This union consisted of Russia, Armenia, Belarus, Kazakakstan and Kyrgyzstan. The EEU secured Russia's southern and eastern borders. Under Russian leadership all member countries were either dictatorships or ruled by oligarchies.[11] It should be noted that while Russia was distracted in Ukraine, the Armenia-Azerbaijan border war flared up again in September 2022.[12]

Putin viewed the former Soviet Republics as prospective members of the EEU rather than independent republics. His ultimate objective was to expand Russia's influence throughout Eurasia, from Lisbon to Vladivostok. Putin's goal was to achieve economic control over the post-Soviet states, eventually leading to a military alliance to counter NATO and eventually dismember it.[13] Putin had two incredibly powerful weapons in his arsenal: cheap gas and oil.

During the late twentieth and twenty-first centuries, Western and Central Europe took the lead in developing clean, and then green energy. The EU shifted from coal and nuclear power to natural gas. Europe, however, produced little natural gas while the Russian Caspian oil fields produced massive surpluses. The thought was not only would Europe obtain necessary fuel, but it would also assist Russia's economic development and would engage Russia as a partner in the European community. Russia took advantage of European narcissism, enticing and ultimately trapping Western and Central Europe into a dependency on Russian natural gas. Pipelines were constructed through Eastern Europe, notably through Belarus, Ukraine, and under the Baltic Sea. As dirty and dangerous sources of energy were reduced, the EU became increasingly dependent on Russian fossil fuel, providing Putin with a perfect opportunity to test EU and NATO resolve.

Germany was especially ensnared in this petrochemical trap and, to appease their Russian partner, vetoed NATO applications by both Ukraine and Georgia in 2008.[14] Chancellor Angela Merkel's administration stubbornly protected the German-Russian oil deal, despite Russia's invasion of Georgia in 2008 and its annexation of Ukrainian Crimea in 2014–15. This policy of appeasement empowered Putin's misbehaviour, directly leading to the invasion of Ukraine.[15]

Increasing conservative rhetoric across Western Europe fuelled Putin's propaganda machine as he sought to justify the invasion to suppress a claimed 'Nazification of Ukraine', echoing the very real historic threat Russia faced from Nazi Germany, not only of invasion but of ethnic cleansing. It is interesting to note that a popular Russian movie, *White Tiger* (released in 2012) contained a not-so-subtle anti-NATO, anti-West message. The movie portrays a three-year-long duel between a Russian tank commander and a phantom white Tiger tank. The Tiger tank is ultimately disabled and disappears; the war ends, and the Russian commander is seen waiting for its suspected reappearance. The final scene is a fictional conversation with Hitler justifying his actions and implying the war between Western Europe and Russia is never-ending. The film was very popular in Russia and was selected as the Russian entry in the Best Foreign Language Oscar category in 2013.[16]

The 'Nazification of Ukraine' claim is patently absurd. The president of Ukraine, Volodymyr Zelensky, is a Jew, obviously not a Nazi. But note, the Azov Battalion, a minority faction of the Ukrainian Territorial Militia, had publicly adopted a Neo-Nazi/White Supremacist ideology. This Ukrainian battalion successfully fought the Separatists during the Russian invasion of the Donbas in 2014–2015 and fought hard in the defence of Mariupol.[17] But it should also be noted that more than a few notable Russians have Nazi tattoos and proudly display other white supremacist symbols.[18]

Putin evoked the horrors of the Second World War and *Mein Kampf's* reference to Slavs as 'subhuman' (*untermenfch*). The slaughter of twenty million Soviets is not easily forgotten nor forgiven.[19] As Putin evoked memories of the Great Patriotic War he harkened to an illusory threat of repeated invasion. The Neo-Nazi sympathies of some members of the Azov Battalion certainly provided kindling for the fire.

Chapter 6

Putin Tests NATO and EU Resolve

Putin's first test of NATO and EU opposition to Russian expansion was little Georgia. There was an apparent issue over a pipeline that would have delivered non-Russian oil from the Caspian Sea to the Black Sea Coast, bypassing the Russian pipelines. Georgia was also seeking NATO membership and was a member of the Partnership for Peace programme.[1]

In April 2008, German Chancellor Angela Merkel's administration announced at the NATO summit in Bucharest that it would veto applications by both Ukraine and Georgia for NATO membership. Putin had been invited to the summit and arrived on 3 April 2008. Despite the efforts of President Bush and leaders of other NATO countries to dissuade Merkel, she remained firm in her veto and the issue was tabled until December 2008. France ultimately joined Germany in objecting to applications by Ukraine and Georgia, citing Russian concerns over NATO expansion eastward. Alexander Grushko, Russian Deputy Foreign Minister was reported saying that 'Georgia's and Ukraine's membership in the alliance is a huge strategic mistake which would have serious consequences for pan-European security'.[2] President Bush's strategic narcissism failed to consider Putin's world goals and the Russian (somewhat justified) paranoia about invaders from Central and Western Europe.[3] Merkel's actions unknowingly gave Putin the nod of approval for his first overt 'Special Operation'.

It is important to note that prior to February 2014 the expansion of NATO was not covertly aimed at countering Russia's potential or threatened expansion. NATO's enlargement was a broad policy to spread a liberal international order into Eastern Europe and make the entire continent more like Western Europe.[4] The Baltic states, Latvia, Lithuania, and Estonia joined NATO in 2004 as part of this broad policy. Like Georgia, all three former Soviet Republics shared a border with Russia. Unlike Georgia, the Baltic states did not compete with the export of Russia's petroleum products to Europe. NATO and the EU failed to understand that even though the purpose of an expansion of NATO was not to limit or restrict Russia, it was perceived as a direct threat by Russia to its system of government, as dangerous a threat as Napoleonic armies spreading 'liberty, equality and fraternity' in their wake.

Unaware of the pending Russian invasion into Georgia, President Bush and US military leaders adhered to their PfP and SPfP schedule. Ironically the US State of Georgia had been assigned to partner with the former Soviet Republic of Georgia. In July 2008, the State of Georgia sent its Army National Guard's 1st Battalion, 121st Infantry to conduct a three-week exercise at Vaziani Military Base in the former Soviet Republic. Soldiers and Marines from US, Georgia, Azerbaijan, Armenia, and Ukraine conducted joint manoeuvres in the surrounding area.[5] Russia invaded on 1 August 2008, just after the majority of the American, Azerbaijanian, Armenian and Ukrainian troops had departed Georgia. As Russian troops crossed the border, the rear party of the Georgia Army National Guard were still in the country.[6]

The Russia-Georgia War of 2008 was the first test of NATO and Western resolve to protect a former Soviet Republic that had applied, but had not yet been accepted into NATO. In five days, the Russian Army quickly defeated Georgia's Army before NATO could react. The following negotiated peace stripped the oblasts (districts) of Abkhazia and South Ossetia from Georgia. Russia quickly recognized them as independent countries on 25 August 2008. The invasion was condemned by the EU and NATO and some sanctions were imposed.

The sanctions imposed were ineffective and failed to alter the situation on the ground. While the Russian army eventually withdrew from Georgia, Abkhazia and South Ossetia were not returned. NATO and EU appeasement of the Russian aggression was based on reluctance to antagonize Russia over 'insignificant Georgia'.[7] The Russian oligarchy and Putin viewed the sanctions as a slap on the wrist. They had achieved all their military, political and economic objectives at little cost, essentially warning NATO and the EU that expanding into the Russian sphere of influence would have serious consequences.

Meanwhile, Ukraine had been making great strides in establishing a liberal democracy and a NATO-acceptable military force. Between 2008 and 2014, the partnership between the State of California, NATO, and Ukraine continued to improve the combat readiness of the UAF. In particular, the partnership between the 144th Fighter Wing California Air Guard and Ukrainian Air Force improved the latter's combat readiness. The improvements were in training, tactics, techniques, and procedures.[8]

Oddly enough, despite Ukraine's progressive tendencies toward a liberal democracy, a pro-Russian President, Viktor Yanukovych was elected in 2010. The election was judged fair by international observers. In October 2011, Yanukovych jailed his main rival, former Prime Minister Yulia Tymoshenko, on false charges of abuse of power.[9] After 2013, Yanukovych quickly eroded many of the democratic liberal reforms passed by Ukrainians who responded en-mass, in the November 2013 'Euromaidan' protests. Yanukovych was ousted from power and fled to Russia in February 2014.[10]

On 11 March 2014, from Rostov-on-Don in Russia, ousted President Yanukovych ordered the UAF not to obey 'criminal orders from the neofascists' in Kyiv.[11] Shortly after his message, on 18 March 2014 Russian special forces gained control of the political and strategic infrastructure in Crimea.

On or about 20 February 2014, Russian forces commenced military operations in preparations to occupy Crimea. On 26 February 2014, large scale exercises commenced along Ukraine's border. By early March 2014, Russia had massed 150,000 troops, 90 aircraft, 120 helicopters, 800 tanks and 1,200 other military vehicles, with 80 ships, all arrayed against Ukraine. All the pro-Moscow Ukrainian ministers followed Yanukovych and fled to Russia. The Ukrainian government was in disarray.[12]

On the night of 26 February 2014, Russian Spetsnaz (special forces) seized the Crimean Parliament, capturing the Sebastopol Airport and taking Belbek military airport the next day. The rest of the Crimean Peninsula was quickly occupied. A referendum held on 16 March 2014 resulted in overwhelming support for succession from Ukraine and annexation by Russia.[13]

The capture and annexation of the Crimean Peninsula went relatively smoothly for Russia, but maintaining ownership and control posed challenges. The peninsula does not provide sufficient fresh water for its population and infrastructure. The water required for survival and operations in the peninsula flows from the Dnipro River through a channel originating near the city of Kherson, in Ukraine.[14]

On 11 March 2014, Acting Ukrainian Minister of Defence Ihor Teniuk reported to the government that only 6,000 of the active army's 41,000 troops were combat ready. All brigades deployed their combat-ready combined-arms battalions to Eastern and Southern Ukraine to cover the expected Russian avenues of advance (Crimea, Sumy, Chernihiv, Kharkiv, Donetsk and Odesa).[15] By the end of March 2014, the Ukrainian Army was deployed to oppose pro-Russian separatists in the Donbas, and Russian attacks on the Kharkiv, Sumy and Crimea axes.[16]

With Yanukovych out, pro-Russian unrest, instigated and organized by Russian special forces and FSB (formerly KGB) erupted in the Donbas Oblast, Eastern Ukraine.[17] In April 2014, demonstrations escalated to open war in the Donbas between pro-Russian separatists and Ukrainian security forces. By July the separatists had surrounded two Ukrainian brigades that were pinned down by Russian artillery fire from across the border. To stabilize the situation, Ukrainian command selected Colonel Mykhailo Zabrodskyi and his 95th Air Assault Brigade to conduct an old-fashioned Cossack cavalry raid into the separatist rear.[18] The raiders crewed sixty to seventy tanks, IFVs and APCs and were assigned the mission of rescuing the encircled Ukrainian brigades and recapturing the Luhansk airport. On 13 July 2014, after breaking through the frontlines, the raiders raced 321km/200 miles through the enemy rear, leaving havoc in their wake.

The heaviest fighting occurred around the Luhansk airport. By 23 July 2014, Zabrodskyi had successfully destroyed supply dumps, disrupting separatist logistics. Finally short of ammunition, Zabrodskyi fell back to the relative safety of Kramatorsk.[19]

Lead by Russian special forces, the separatists failed to achieve their objectives, even when supported by heavy artillery firing from inside Russia. The raid forced Putin to provide additional support to the separatists by invading the Donbas with regular Russian military units. Additional force was apparently required to capture key objectives (infrastructure) and Russian BTGs crossed the border. With an insufficient number of battalions and brigades to hold the line, Ukrainians employed a mobile defence. As Russian BTGs advanced into the Donbas, Ukrainian battalions manoeuvred to attack their flank. Heavy fighting ensued until 2015, ultimately culminating in the cease fire Minsk II Agreement. Despite the agreement, a state of hostilities continued along the frontline until the February 2022 invasion.

The fighting in the Donbas (2014–2015) should have put Putin on notice that even lacking secure political leadership, Ukrainians would fiercely oppose Russian invaders. Zabrodskyi had attended the US Army Command and General Staff College at Fort Leavenworth, Kansas, class of 2005/2006. At the time of the raid, the Ukrainian 95th Air Assault Brigade had been fully trained in NATO combined-arms tactics. Despite the lack of Western combined-arms training, the remaining Ukrainian brigades and battalions performed well in combat, even in the face of heavy Russian artillery bombardment.

Despite its massive army, Russia fielded only 40,000 modernized troops, organized into 40 BTGs. These troops in theory fielded the best equipment, on par with NATO's, and had a higher ratio of regular (contract) to conscript soldiers, compared to the rest of the Russian Army.

NATO and the EU once again imposed some sanctions on Russia, but since Europe was dependent upon Russian fuel the sanctions did not affect the flow of petrochemicals. Repeated ineffective sanctions proved to be a form of appeasement. Putin once again achieved most of his military/political/economic objectives without significant cost.

NATO was now put on notice and was alarmed by Putin's imperial ambitions. Putin very much became a current, visible threat and the West began to understand that his aspirations would need to be seriously considered. Joint ventures and appeasement were not going to satisfy Putin's quest to recreate Imperial Russia.

Between 2014 and 2022, Ukrainians, Russians and separatists continued to skirmish along the line of contact. Ukrainians heavily fortified their positions in the Donbas expecting hostilities to commence at any time. With the mentorship of NATO under PfP and the California National Guard (pursuant to SPfP) the UAF concentrated on improving combat readiness within its military forces, as well as its National Guard's internal security force. Ukraine had worked to increase interoperability with NATO since becoming an 'Enhanced Opportunity Partner' in June of 2020. By February 2022, all ground combat battalions were trained to NATO standards in combined-arms operations.[20]

Generally, the West now saw Ukraine as a bulwark against Russian attempts to expand its influence into Europe. As a US senator during the Cold War, President Biden especially recognized the threat of Putin's Russia to Europe and world order.

In March and April 2021, the Russian Army began to mass men and material along its border with Ukraine and in Crimea.[21] On 14 June 2021, Biden issued a statement supporting Ukraine's entry into NATO. On 1 September 2021, President Zelensky visited Biden at the White House. Biden made it clear that the US was firmly committed to Ukraine's NATO aspirations. The US position was based in part on the US Ukraine Charter on Strategic Partnership signed by representatives of both countries on 10 November 2008.

The US Ukraine Charter on Strategic Partnership basically affirmed the importance of the relationship between the two countries as friends and strategic partners. The charter emphasized the countries' shared interests in expanding democracy and economic freedom, protecting security, and territorial integrity while strengthening the rule of law. Perhaps most important is the affirmation of the security assurances described in the Trilateral Statement by the Presidents of the US, Russian Federation and Ukraine, part of the Memorandum of Security Assurances in connection with the Treaty on the Non-Proliferation of Nuclear Weapons, signed by all parties on 5 December 1994.

Besides verbal threats and warnings, Putin, to coerce Biden and Zelensky, sent letters to both on 17 December 2022 demanding a written guarantee that: 1) Ukraine would not join NATO, 2) no offensive weapons would be stationed near Russia's borders, and 3) NATO troops and equipment moved into Eastern Europe since 1997 would be moved back to Western Europe.[22]

By December 2021, over 100,000 Russian troops had been deployed on three sides of Ukraine, including those inside Belarus. Yet as late as 20 February 2022, Russia continued to deny it would invade. As a prelude to the invasion, on 21 February 2022 Russia officially recognized the self-proclaimed separatist oblasts (Donetsk People's Republic and Luhansk People's Republic) as independent countries.[23] Following the proclamation Russian combat troops entered the new countries as peacekeepers.

In November 2021, US European Command had ordered California National Guard soldiers and airmen training in Ukraine to leave the country. Task Force Orion, 27th Infantry Brigade Combat Team, New York Army National Guard remained to complete training Ukrainian soldiers and remained in country until 10 February, 2022.[24] The California State Military Department, headquarters of the California National Guard, maintained almost daily contact with established counterparts inside the Ukrainian Ministry of Defence. Information received by General David Baldwin, Adjutant General of the State of California, indicating that Russia would invade, was passed to his Ukrainian contacts. Despite repeated warnings, the Ukrainian Ministry of Defence concluded Putin was bluffing. However, after Putin's 21 February 2022 speech the warning was finally heeded, and Ukrainian troops deployed from their barracks. The California rolodex of phone numbers for important commanders of the Ukrainian Ministry of Defence, Army and National Guard would become critical in the first few weeks of the war.[25]

Chapter 7

The Ukrainian Armed Forces (UAF)

Upon the disintegration of the Soviet Union, Ukraine inherited fourteen Soviet tank and motorized rifle divisions that had been stationed within its borders. For a short time, Ukraine was also in possession of former Soviet nuclear weapons and joined the top four nuclear powers in the world. Like Russia and other former Soviet Republics, it also inherited an extremely corrupt military infrastructure. Unlike Russia, its military leadership was dedicated to re-modelling its military up to NATO standards in anticipation of applying for membership.

For almost two decades, Ukrainian military leadership instituted reforms. Ukrainians sought to remedy governmental corruption and Russian influence to create a modern democracy

As Chief of Staff, Lieutenant General Valerii Zaluzhnyi lead the fight against the 2022 Russian invasion. Zaluzhnyi had trained to modern NATO standards and had successfully moulded a professional group of subordinate veteran combat leaders. As the '[b]est graduate of "Operational Strategic Level Training" he was awarded the Transition Sword of the Queen of Great Britain'. Contrary to Soviet and Russian training, NATO encouraged commanders of battalions and companies to fight in small, dispersed combined-arms teams. Field commanders were encouraged to think, plan, and take decisive action in response to battlefield conditions.[1]

To improve UAF fighting capabilities, Zaluzhnyi worked through his political leadership to convince the US and NATO to provide hundreds of millions of dollars in lethal military aid in 2017. The US Congress approved a $400 million aid package that included Stinger MANPADS (man-portable air defence systems) and 150 Javelin anti-tank missiles.[2]

Ukrainian Ground Forces

Ukrainian Ground Forces were divided into 6 branches: Army, Airborne and Air Assault, Naval Infantry (Marines), Territorial Defence, Special Forces and National Guard.

UAF active ground-manoeuvre forces were organized with 2 mountain assault, 9 mechanized, 2 tank (plus an independent tank battalion), and 4 motorized brigades. The Reserve contained 3 tank, 2 mechanized, 2 motorized and 2 artillery brigades.[3] The Air Assault Branch included 1 airborne mechanized brigade, with air droppable BMD IFVs, plus 1 artillery and 6 air assault mechanized brigades. The Naval Infantry, like the US Marines, fell under the Department of the Navy and consisted of 1 artillery, 1 rocket artillery and 3 motorized infantry brigades. The National Guard consisted of 1 motorized brigade and several light infantry combat units such as the Donbas and Azov battalions. As Russia invaded, the UAF fielded a total of 27 active-manoeuvre and 4 artillery brigades, supported by 5 reserve brigades. This was the equivalent of 68 Russian BTGs, plus sometimes as many as 62 additional CABs. The organization of the brigades was uniquely Ukrainian rather than carbon copies of NATO or Russian formations.[4]

Great Britain had been decisively engaged for years training the Ukrainian Special Forces regiments from the various branches. The elite British Special Boat Service (SBS) commandos trained Ukrainians in clandestine amphibious operations. Formed during the Second World War, the SBS were trained to take over ships, oil rigs and small islands by fast assault boats and helicopters. The Special Air Service (SAS) commando trainers, also formed during the Second World War, worked closely with Ukrainian commandos to improve tactics, techniques, and procedures.[5] As the war progressed Great Britain authorised 50 retired SAS and SBS experts to train Ukrainian commandos within Ukraine.[6]

Some analysts claimed that the Ukrainian ground forces equated to 68 Russian BTGs, and apparently the Russians made the same assumption.[7] At the start of the war, Ukrainian active ground forces fielded over 114 combined-arms battalions (CABs) and over 38 artillery battalions organic to manoeuvre brigades in its regular army. The CABs fought in brigade combat teams. Each brigade combat team coordinated the efforts of three to six various types of CABs: tank, motorized, mechanized, mountain, Marine or airborne.

The 25 Territorial Defence Brigades (hereinafter Territorials) were formed in 2015 as local militia units to provide local security and disaster assistance in their individual oblasts. Lightly armed, but with local knowledge of their home territory, they were a combat multiplier. Each Territorial contained six manoeuvre battalions, a mortar battery and limited combat service support. At the start of the war many battalions were at cadre strength but quickly filled their ranks with local volunteers. Once the ranks of the Territorials were full, excess volunteers were organized into hastily raised militias and a foreign legion.

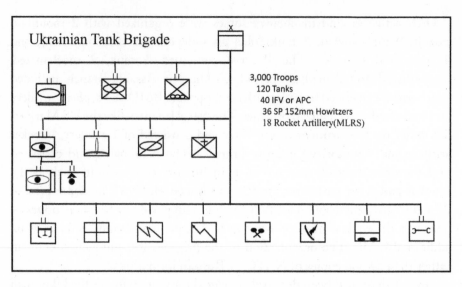

Ukrainian Tank Brigade

3,000 Troops
120 Tanks
40 IFV or APC
36 SP 152mm Howitzers
18 Rocket Artillery(MLRS)

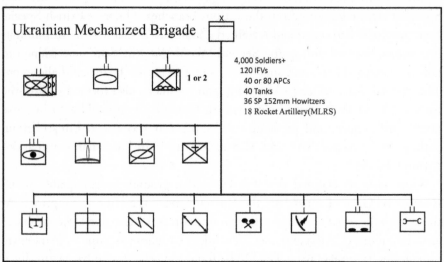

Ukrainian Mechanized Brigade

4,000 Soldiers+
120 IFVs
40 or 80 APCs
40 Tanks
36 SP 152mm Howitzers
18 Rocket Artillery(MLRS)

Legally, the entire population of Ukraine became a 'levée en masse' providing combat support and combat service support to the Regular, Reserves, National Guard, and Territorials. The UAF and the Ukrainian government had planned to augment their military force with a levée en masse to defend the major cities. A levée en masse refers to citizens that spontaneously take up arms to resist an invading army without having time to organize themselves into the regular armed forces.[8]

As Russian tanks rolled toward Kyiv, the Ukrainian parliament declared martial law and President Zelensky announced that Kyiv would issue weapons to anyone willing to protect Ukraine's sovereignty.[9] There were 18,000 assault rifles stockpiled in Kyiv at the time of the invasion and by 25 February 2022 they were all issued to members of the public.[10] Semi-organized militias were reported defending Kyiv, Kharkiv and Sumy as the cities were bombarded and the Russian armoured spearhead crossed the international border. Even the *babushka* (grandmother) who welcomed Ukrainian soldiers in her village became a combatant under the laws of warfare.[11] The abled bodied members of the *levée* were eventually incorporated into the UAF as augmentees or recruits to Regular, Territorial or National Guard battalions.[12]

Geographic Operational Commands (OCs) provided command and control of combat operations within the four regions of Ukraine. They combined the function of divisions and corps of a typical NATO force structure. OCs provided the combat support and combat service support to the manoeuvre brigades in their area of operations. Their organic combat support units included an artillery brigade, anti-air artillery, engineer, signal regiments, reconnaissance intelligence centre, signal intelligence centre and electronic warfare battalions. Their organic combat service support units included a maintenance regiment, logistics and transportation battalions.

At the start of the war, OC West (Lviv) contained 2 mechanized, 2 mountain (motorized), and 8 Territorial brigades. OC North (Kyiv) contained 2 mechanized, 1 motorized, 1 National Guard motorized, 1 tank and 7 Territorial brigades. In addition, the 12th Independent Tank Battalion was stationed in this area of operations. OC East (Donbas) had 4 mechanized, 1 tank and 5 Territorial brigades. OC East brigades were dug in, holding the

front line against Russian and separatist attacks from the Donbas to the Black Sea. OC South (Kherson and Odessa) contained 3 motorized, 1 mechanized and 5 Territorial brigades. The 8 Reserve brigades provided Ukraine's strategic reserve.

Training Level

Prior to 2014, the UAF worked closely with NATO and the National Guards of various American states. After 2015, the Ukrainian military and political leadership realised the UAF needed better training to successfully oppose Russia. By the time of the invasion 26,000 Ukrainian soldiers had successfully completed various training programs.[13] Active Ukrainian battalions were trained in combined-arms tactics to NATO standards. Only a few brigades, including the 95th Air Assault Brigade and National Guard 4th Rapid Reaction Brigade met NATO standards for brigade combined-arms operations.[14] This did not mean the other active brigades were not combat ready for combined-arms operations on 24 February 2022, it only meant they had not been evaluated and certified by the NATO training teams. They received their evaluation in combat.

One of the most important military cultural changes enacted by Ukraine was to authorize and enable small-unit leaders to exercise individual initiative and allow them the freedom to improvise and make decisions in the field. This required 'pushing down' decision-making authority and creating leaders able to take action based on their commander's intent. Always important, these skills became particularly critical as Russia was soon able to jam all communications.

Ukrainian command and control (C2) and fire systems were a combination of NATO and improvised methods. Ukrainian Regular Army first line units, like the 95th Air Assault Brigade and 4th Rapid Reaction Brigade, operated like a NATO brigade.[15] Reserve, Territorial, and voluntary/militia units were comprised of a small number of regulars and did not receive NATO focused C2 training before the invasion. Trained officers assigned to lead these battalions found mixed levels of training. These units were manned with mobilized military technical specialists, without rank (not combat arms), reservists and recently raised militia. These units were highly egalitarian. Platoon order groups tended to be chaotic, with all members participating in decision making, often resulting in innovative solutions to tactical problems. While this informal process worked well at platoon and company level it was not effective at battalion and brigade level where a quick, clear orders process is required.[16]

Eight years of training also focused on building a non-commissioned officers (NCO) corps in all branches of the UAF. This paid significant dividends. UAF NCOs took the initiative to conduct small operations without wating for instructions from above. NCO initiative often resulted in making Ukrainian small units unpredictable, a real bane to enemy operational planning. The use of the Ukrainian NCOs greatly enhanced the combat capabilities of their land, sea, and air formations.[17]

UAF's development of an NCO corps started with SPfP, mentored by the California Army National Guard during the 1990s. Soviet-era generals were unconvinced of the value of an NCO corps. Creating and mentoring the Ukrainian NCO corps was a passion with Command Sergeant Major (Ret) William (Bill) Clark, Command Sergeant Major of the California National Guard. For almost ten years his tireless efforts helped convince emerging Ukrainian military leaders that the NCO corps was a valuable combat multiplier. After observing NCOs in action, Ukraine recognized their value and began to develop an NCO Corps. After the beginning of the Donbas War in 2014, the Ukrainian NCO Defence Education Enhancement Programme (DEEP) was accelerated.[18]

Problems with the Ukrainian force structure before the war resulted in a shortage of combat troops in sufficient ratio to the numbers of technical specialists. During the first few months of the war, first line combat troops and officers were seconded to Reserve and Territorial units in the defence. During an offensive these experienced combat troops were recalled to their infantry and tank formations to spearhead attacks. This solution resulted in a disproportionate number of casualities among Ukraine's best troops.[19]

The Ukrainian fire control system employed inexpensive drones to acquire targets for its artillery, firing 'dumb' artillery shells.[20] Masses of cheap civilian drones augmented military UAVs and enabled Ukrainians to locate targets and adjust fire for maximum damage. Ukraine produced its own high-precision laser guided artillery ammunition and civilian drones were modified to carry laser designators. During the first year of the war, it is estimated that Ukraine operated over 6,000 military and converted civilian drones of various types for command and control, target acquisition and attack missions.[21]

At the start of the war, the OCs lacked trained battle staff capable of integrating airspace, deep fires, logistics, intelligence and higher command and control for offensive operations.[22] Over the first five months of defensive combat, OC-East and OC-South developed staff with the skills to plan and execute division-sized offensive operations in the Kharkiv and Kherson sectors.

The Territorials were organized into 25 brigades and 150 battalions and were located in every oblast and major city. The branch consisted of 10,000

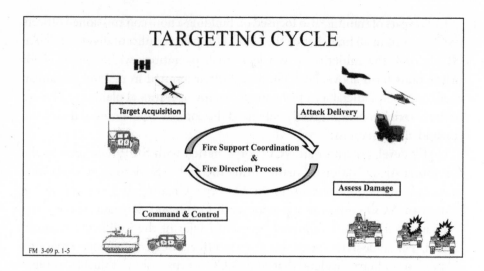

regular soldiers and up to 130,000 part-time volunteers. Volunteers were 18–60 years old, with a clean record, having passed medical and psychological examinations. The Territorials were light infantry formations, tasked with supporting the regulars by securing streets, guarding infrastructure and other supporting combat roles.

Over 60,000 women served in the TDF and UAF.[23] In the TDF women served in the ranks and as officers. Platoon commander Marii, age 41, a lawyer, led soldiers during the July 2022 Donbas battles. She joined the TDF in 2018. Her husband was also fighting in the Donbas but in a different unit.[24] Platoon commander Olga, call sign 'Witch', serving in the 241st TDF Brigade, was a lawyer, working on her PhD with a six-year-old son.

On 24 February 2022, the TDF armaments included NLAW and Javelin man-portable anti-tank missiles, and Stingers, along with their small arms. By 17 February 2022, 20 Kyiv City Council members had joined the local 112th Territorial Defence Brigade, and two months prior to the beginning of the war volunteers joined in large numbers.[25]

The Ukrainian National Guard (NGU) was a national gendarmerie and internal military force falling within the jurisdiction of the Ministry of Internal Affairs. Originally formed in 1991, it was later disbanded in 2002 as part of a governmental cost-saving initiative. During 2014 the NGU was reformed in response to the Russian invasion supporting the Donbas separatists. The mission of the Guard was to provide military units with police powers. During the 2022 Russian invasion they were incorporated into the Ukrainian ground forces.

Between 2014 and 2015, the volunteer and militia battalions were incorporated into the NGU. The NGU units fought against the pro-Russian separatists and Russians masquerading as separatists. During the fighting the Azov and Donbas battalions were the largest formations, fielding 900–1,000 fighters each.

At the beginning of the 2022 Russian invasion the NGU fielded several combat and police units. The combat units included the Azov Regiment, Donbas Regiment and 4th Rapid Reaction Brigade.

During May 2014 the Azov Regiment was organized in Mariupol. It fought as a paramilitary militia battalion under the command of Andriy Biletsky. It was incorporated into the Ukrainian National Guard on 11 November, 2014 as the Azov Regiment. Fighting as a regiment during the Russian invasion, in February 2023 it was authorized to expand into a brigade.[26]

In 2014 the Donbas Battalion was formed from Russian speaking Ukrainians opposed to the pro-Russian separatists. This highly effective combat unit was integrated into the NGU as the 2nd Special Purpose (Donbas) Battalion within the 15th NGU Regiment. The original battalion was demobilized in 2016 only to be reformed a few years later within the NGU.[27]

The 4th Rapid Reaction Brigade was established on 2 June 2015. It was organized as a motorized, combined-arms combat unit. The brigade was trained to NATO standard prior to the Russian invasion. During 2022, the brigade fought in the battles of Kyiv and Donbas.

International ethnic battalions have been incorporated into the UAF. The Georgian Legion was founded in 2014 with veterans from the country of Georgia. At least one anti-Putin Russian battalion has been formed.[28] The details about this unit were shrouded in secrecy to protect their families within Russia.[29] Formed during 2014–15 Donbas fighting, the Dzhokhar Dudayev (Chechen) and Sheikh Mansur (Chechen) battalions were the oldest of the Chechen volunteer units fighting for Ukraine.

As the Russian invasion unfolded, the call for volunteers resulted in the formation of the International Legion of Territorial Defence of Ukraine. By 6 March, 20,000 volunteers from 52 countries answered the call. Some of these volunteers were incorporated into existing ethnic battalions. However, the screening process and dissatisfaction with Ukrainian leadership (especially in Intelligence Directive Units) resulted in many volunteers leaving the programme and returning to their home countries.[30] Out of the remaining volunteers at least 11 battalions were formed within the Territorial organization.

Ukraine's Navy consisted of 15 ships, the largest of which was a frigate among other small combat and landing ships. This small naval force was augmented by land-based Neptune anti-ship missile batteries, with a range of 305km/190 miles and Turkish TB2 Bayraketar armed UAVs.[31]

The Ukrainian Air Force was well-trained, having participated in numerous NATO exercises over the past two decades.[32] Its mission was to protect the air space over Ukraine. Within that overarching mission, it was charged to conduct close air support (CAS) for ground and naval forces, provide air defence (against aircraft and missiles), establish air superiority, and disrupt Russian operations, communications, reconnaissance, and troop and cargo transport. Additionally, the Air Force was responsible for ground-based air defence and operated 516 mobile, short-, medium- and long-range surface-to-air missile (SAM) systems to protect Ukraine's key infrastructure and units from Russian air and missile attack.

In December 2021, Ukraine operated 125 combat aircraft (51 Mig-29s, 12 Su-24s, 17 Su-25s, 32 Su-27s), 3 reconnaissance aircraft, and 30 transport aircraft. Rotary wing squadrons operated 15 Mi-8 Transport Helicopters and 34 Mi-24 Hind attack helicopters.[33] Its fleet of UAVs included 72 RQ-11 Ravens and 54 Bayraktar TB2s.

Although it had the advantage of superior pilot training, Ukraine's Air Force was heavily outnumbered at the start of the war. Ukraine, like Russia, inherited the Soviet air defence doctrine. This doctrine sought to limit NATO's offensive air capabilities by an integrated air defence system. To implement this doctrine the Soviets developed high-, medium-, and low-altitude ADA (air defence artillery) systems.

The Ukrainian Air Force C2 organization mirrored the ground force OCs. There were four Air Command (AC) headquarters that corresponded with the ground force OCs' geographic boundaries. Each of the four ACs (East, West, North and South) provided the C2, maintenance and logistics for the air and helicopter squadrons in their area of operations.

Ukrainian pilots had participated in numerous NATO exercises. In 2011 and 2018 these pilots had trained with the F-16s of the California Air National Guard. Many were combat veterans of the Donbas fighting.[34]

Chapter 8

Russian Armed Forces

On paper, the Russian Army that invaded Ukraine was a formidable opponent. Putin's propaganda had convinced the world that Russian armed forces were invincible and would crush the Ukrainian armed forces, (UAF) in a matter of days. The twenty-first century Russian army is a direct descendant of the Soviet Red Army that marched into Berlin in 1945, enslaved Eastern Europe and enforced Moscow's rule over an empire for almost five decades. During the 1990s that army disintegrated, and the post-Soviet Russian military faced many challenges trying to maintain the remnants of the Soviet Empire for the new Russian Federation.

During the First and Second Chechen Wars (1994–2009) many problems surfaced within the post-Soviet Russian army.[1] Reverses on the battlefield and counter-insurgency operations during the guerrilla war (2000–2009) were countered by terror bombing of civilians and civilian infrastructure. Heavy bombardment of cities by artillery, missiles and aircraft became the norm. During the Russian intervention in Syria (September 2015–2022) Putin's air force conducted 19,160 sorties against civilian infrastructure. Between 2015–2016 over 2,000 civilians were killed in air strikes.[2] Amnesty International reported that the bombing of civilians by the Russian Air Force was deliberate.[3]

Russian military operations of the late-twentieth and early twenty-first century had clearly established a pattern. When Russia's military was unsuccessful on the battlefield, it reverted to terror tactics against civilians and civilian targets. Russian commanders who committed war crimes were not only not punished but were in fact rewarded. Putin awarded General Sergei Surovikin the 'Hero of Russia' medal in 2017 and promoted him to full general for the conduct of his air campaign in Syria.[4] This after Surovikin had committed war crimes as acknowledged by and reported by the international community.

A study of the Russian military reorganization in 2008 would take volumes, but it is noteworthy to focus on how it impacted the force structure that invaded Ukraine in 2022. Russia's Strategic Rocket Force, (RVSN) was reorganized, as was its Navy, but except for the Black Sea Fleet, it was not part of the invasion force.

The reform was felt at the military district level or in Second World War Russian parlance a 'front' or army group.[5] The Soviet Union was divided into sixteen military districts. District commanders were not responsible for operational control of units within their territory. In peace time that responsibility lay with ground and air force branch commanders. The 2010 reform gave district commanders operational control of most of the Ministry of Defence forces in their district, except for nuclear and certain strategic forces, such as the Strategic Rocket Force (RVSN), Airborne (VDV), GRU (military intelligence) and Spetsnaz (special forces) that remained under higher centralized command. The districts were renamed 'Operational Strategic Commands' (OSKs) and each was commanded by a four-star general.[6]

Significant modernization of Russian ground forces included a shift away from divisions to brigades. After studying the inherent problems with their post-Soviet army, the Russian military leadership decided to move from a division-centric basic manoeuvre unit to modular combined-arms brigades of 3,000 to 4,500 soldiers.

Each brigade was capable of independent action, providing its own organic support, and was typically based in a separate garrison. Each brigade trained its conscripts. The conversion to brigades reduced the bloated officer corps, eliminated cadre units, and reduced the overall Russian Army from 1,890 smaller organizations to 172 large units. The reduction in the officer corps allowed the consolidation of the 65 military academies to 10. In theory the resulting cost savings went into increased salaries and modernization of equipment.[7]

Divisions were reorganized into manoeuvre brigades, with a preponderance of motorized rifle brigades. Each of these consisted of three motorized rifle battalions and one tank battalion, an anti-aircraft artillery battalion, a sniper company, a recon battalion, an engineer battalion, and a signal battalion. Its organic combat service support units included a hospital command and MTO (logistics) battalion.

The Brigade Artillery Group (BrAG) was organized with two self-propelled howitzer battalions, a MLRS battalion and an anti-tank artillery battalion. The brigade headquarters controlled the radar platoon, a fire-control battery, an NBC company, an electronic warfare company, a UAV company, and an intelligence support platoon. Similar to a motorized rifle brigade, the tank brigade contained three tank battalions and one motorized rifle battalion. At full strength, a motorized rifle brigade contained 3,000 to 4,500 soldiers and a tank brigade of 3,000.[8] In terms of logistics, a single brigade was easier to support and transport than an old division. Brigades were often transported thousands of miles via rail to conduct training.

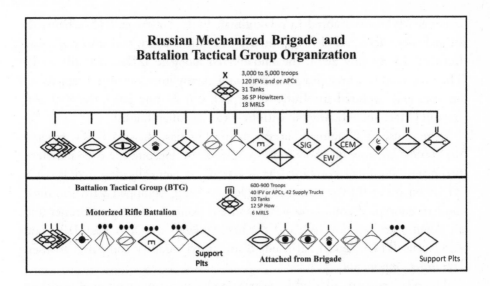

Russian Mechanized Brigade and Battalion Tactical Group Organization

While the idea of an ad hoc, independent combined-arms battalion serving as a forward detachment developed during the Second World War, its use as a fire support formation was only developed during the 2014–2015 war for the Donbas. The Battalion Tactical Group (BTG) was a combined-arms battalion (either motorized infantry- or tank-heavy) with an artillery battalion attached and sufficient combat service support companies to allow it to perform as an independent manoeuvre unit. Because of the Russian conscript system, at any one time, only a third of a brigade had completed training and was combat ready.

The companies in the BTG were based on a reinforced motor rifle battalion. They contained 40 combat vehicles (tanks, IFVs, and APCs). The artillery battalion contained 12 self-propelled howitzers, 6 multiple launch rocket systems (MRLS) and 62 ammunition and support supply trucks. The combat service support companies contained 22 support or logistics supply vehicles. Assuming 9 soldiers in each of the 27 infantry squads, there should have been 81 crewing the BMPs or BTRs, and 162 dismounted infantry. There were approximately 500 soldiers in the reinforced motorized battalion and 400 in the combat support and combat service support units. Tank BTGs had three tank companies and one motorized or mechanized company with similar combat support and combat service support units. Logistically, a BTG could sustain itself under combat conditions for 3 to 5 days.[9] The BTG's greatest weakness was its small number of dismounted infantry.[10]

The BTG concept was validated during fighting in the Donbas, where it supported Russian-led separatists in the Donetsk and Luhansk Oblasts. The BTGs initially provided fire support to Russian separatists. Eventually

Colonel Mykhailo Zabrodsky's Ukrainian 95th Air Assault (Mechanized) Brigade conducted an old-style Soviet Cossack Cavalry raid into their rear. Between 13–24 July 2014, the raid blitzed along a 321km/200mile route. The raid freed two brigades pinned behind enemy lines, destroyed separatists' logistics and captured the Luhansk airport. On 23 July 2014, the 95th Air Assault (Mechanized) Brigade withdrew to Ukrainian lines.[11]

In response to Ukrainian success in the Donbas, Russian BTGs entered the conflict in large numbers in November 2014. Despite the over-match in firepower, Ukrainian combined arms battalions tactically defeated Russian BTGs on more than one occasion. Despite being equipped with the most modern encrypted communications and electronic warfare gear, drones and air defence artillery [ADA], and the best tanks (T-80s and 90s), IFVs and APCs, the BTGs lacked sufficient dismounted infantry compared to their Ukrainian opponents.

The BTG concept allowed Russian brigades to maintain a tiered readiness with one third of its assets available to form an expeditionary force on short notice. It was not only a tool for combined-arms force projection, but a means of managing training and deployment challenges inherent to Russia's tiered readiness and mixed manning system.[12]

CAAs or tank armies exercised command and control over two or more motorized rifle/tank divisions or brigades. Unlike the Cold War and Second World War, Russian armies no longer commanded four or five divisions with over 100,000 soldiers. As Russia invaded Ukraine, Russian armies provided C2 for 6–15 BTGs. Based upon the twenty-first century reorganization, armies became the manpower and equipment equivalent of Cold War Soviet

21st Century Russian Command and Control

Post Soviet Command Structure	2008 Reformed Command Structure	February 2022 Invasion Command Structure
Ground forces HQ 2+ Armies	Operational Strategic Command 2+ Armies	Operational Strategic Command 2+ Armies
Combined Arms or Tank Army 2 to 4 Infantry or Tank Divisions	Combined Arms or Tank Army 3+ Maneuver Brigades	Combined Arms or Tank Army* (5 to 15+ BTG)
Division (3 to 4 Maneuver Regiments)	----	---
Regiment (4 Maneuver Battalions)	Brigade 3 to 4 Maneuver Battalions	---**
Maneuver Battalion	Battalion or Battalion Tactical Group	Battalion Tactical Group(BTG) *A few Division and Corps HQs **BDE C2 appeared in Mar-Apr.

Union divisions, while incorporating modern technology and enhanced organic support.

While each army had slight variations, most contained an army artillery group (AAG) of one or more artillery brigades, an air defence brigade, a reconnaissance brigade, an engineer regiment, an NBC regiment, a pontoon bridge brigade and a maintenance and transport logistic organization (MTO) brigade. Artillery battalions in the AAG were often attached as reinforcements to Brigade Artillery Groups (BrAG). Within the various brigades were signal, electronic warfare, and UAV/drone units. Russia's difficulty in securing logistics was its biggest handicap.

Lack of supply and the logistical infrastructure to move supplies to the front line hampered the BTGs' ability to manoeuvre. A modern tank averages 0.6 miles per gallon or 1 kilometre per 3.5 litres.[13] A Russian tank division (the equivalent of 12 BTGs with support vehicles) burned approximately 600,000 gallons (or 2,271,247 litres) of fuel per day.[14] The gas turbine engine in the T-80 series tank burned 642 litres of fuel to drive 100km/60 miles, while the T-72 series diesel engines burned 357 litres to drive the same distance.[15] The 1st Guards Tank Army's fuel consumption was probably 30 per cent higher due to the number of T-80s within its formations. During the invasion, this fuel was transported to the fighting lines in unarmoured fuel trucks.

Before the invasion, it was estimated that an engaged Russian CAA lacked sufficient trucks to meet its logistical requirements for more than 144km/90 miles beyond its rail head supply dump. For example, the resupply ammunition requirement for each multiple launch rocket system (MLRS) required one entire truck load each time it fired. If a CAA artillery group of 90 MRLS fired one volley per day, it would have required 90 trucks to reload the launchers. Each of the firing batteries included one supply truck per firing vehicle and launcher. The CAA needed to allocate 90 supply trucks to meet the firing batteries' trucks at an ammunition transfer point, multiple times a day, to allow the batteries to fire more than two bombardments a day. Ninety trucks equalled a quarter of the total number of cargo trucks assigned to a Russian CAA support brigade.[16] Denied use of Ukrainian rail lines, moving supplies from these dumps required a massive number of trucks.[17] Russian forward ammunition dumps were possibly the most dangerous places in the war zone. By doctrine, there is very vague guidance relating to the proper and safe storage of ammunition and fuel. Minimum safe areas are not defined and supplies such as munitions, food and fuel are not required to be segregated. Poorly trained conscripts made up the majority of logistics support soldiers and they were apparently unaware of the dangers of compiling supplies of different categories in close proximity.[18]

The Russian army brigades within the military districts were a mix of conscripts and contract soldiers. The elite Spetsnaz, Airborne, and Naval Infantry generally consisted of contract soldiers and were the best-trained soldiers in the Russian order of battle. The Russian Army was a conscript force, in the process of transforming into a partly professional force. Conscripts served a year and could range in age from 18 to 27 years. Each year, during the spring draft (April-July), 125,000 recruits were processed with an additional 125,000 being called up during the autumn draft (October-December). Conscripts received one or two months of basic training, followed by three to six months of advanced training.[19] Most advanced training was conducted by the conscripts' brigade.

If a soldier intended to have a military career, he had to become an officer or a contractor. The system encouraged specialization and technical proficiency. A contract soldier remained in his military occupational specialty (MOS) for his career.

Russian military leadership was familiar with the concept of NATO's use of NCOs but had rejected it. Russian contract solders were often incorrectly referred to as NCOs but there was a significant difference, in that they lacked leadership responsibilities and decision-making authority.

Contract soldiers could have become 'Officer Assistants', the equivalent of a NATO Warrant Officer, by attending an academy. With the restrictions noted above they could have performed the duties of a first sergeant, colour sergeant or gunnery sergeant. These soldiers were neither expected nor encouraged to exhibit initiative in the absence of commissioned officers.[20] The result was a very weak Russian NCO corps, the majority of which were just higher-paid soldiers.[21]

With a weak or non-functioning NCO corps, the Russian Army unfortunately inherited the brutal practice of hazing (*dedovshcina*) by senior conscripts of new draftees. Senior soldiers often robbed and brutalized new conscripts, while officers too often ignored the problem. This hazing obviously had a negative impact on unit cohesion and retention. To improve readiness and in part as an attempt to stop this brutality, the Airborne Corps created a thirty-four-month NCO course in 2009, called the Ryazan Higher Airborne School.[22]

In a BTG, 30 per cent of the personnel positions required contract soldiers. They served in combat vehicle crews and technical positions. The dismounted rifle squads and combat service support positions were filled with conscript soldiers.[23] By law, conscripts could not serve outside of Russia, except in the case of declared war. This resulted in an initial shortage of infantry within the Russian motorized and mechanized infantry companies during the invasion.

Motorized (wheeled) and mechanized (tracked) infantry battalions of the BTGs should have numbered about 500 soldiers each. However due to the legal limitation on conscript deployments, motorized and mechanized infantry battalions of the BTGs entered combat with approximately only 345 soldiers manning all their combat vehicles. Fielding a battalion that small obviously reduced the number of soldiers in its nine-person squads to a mere 5 or 6. Each squad consisted of a tracked IFV or wheeled APC containing a 3-man crew, and a dismounted team of 2 or 3 riflemen.[24] Each company had only 18–27 dismounted infantry and 54–81 in a motorized battalion. A BTG based on a tank battalion had 30 tanks, but only 18–27 infantry soldiers.

The VDV airborne battalions were almost fully manned with contract soldiers. Each squad of 7, consisted of a crew of 3 and a dismounted fire team of 4. Each company had a dismounted strength of 36 soldiers and each battalion had a dismounted strength of 108 soldiers.[25] A naval infantry battalion had 400 men, and each of the three infantry companies mustered 103 men, mounted in 10 BTRs with 30 crew and 73 dismounted infantry soldiers.[26]

In comparison, an American balanced combined-arms battalion (2 tank companies and 2 Bradley IFV companies) has 84 infantry soldiers in a company and 168 in a battalion.[27] A Stryker (motorized APC) battalion contains 84 dismounted infantry soldiers in each of its 3 companies, totalling 252 soldiers in the battalion.[28] A British Mechanized Infantry Battalion, armed with Warrior IFVs, contains 54 dismounted infantry per company and the battalion contains 162.[29]

If fully manned, the Russian BMP BTG's dismounted infantry contingent would have been significantly smaller than a two-company American Bradley IFV formation, but similar in size to a British Warrior battalion. However, the comparison ends there since the British and American soldiers were better equipped, trained and were led by professional NCOs.

The Black Sea Naval Infantry, part of the Black Sea Fleet, was under command and control of the 22nd Army Corps, headquartered in Sevastopol, Crimea. Its major units were the 126th Separate Coastal Defence Brigade, 810th Naval Infantry Brigade, 61st Naval Infantry Brigade, 8th Artillery Regiment and the 15th Separate Rocket Brigade.[30] The Naval Infantry had seen action in the Donbas (2014–15) and in Syria (2015–16).[31] A typical motorized naval infantry brigade included a headquarters, a motorized battalion, an air assault battalion, a reconnaissance battalion, a tank battalion, two self-propelled artillery battalions and an anti-aircraft artillery battalion. Its complement of combat service support units was similar to that supporting the Army brigades. Naval infantry brigades mustered about 2,500 men and the infantry battalions contained approximately 500.[32]

The Russian Airborne Force formed their own branch, Desantnye Voyska Rossi (VDV). Like the naval infantry, airborne units were primarily contract soldiers. Unlike American and British paratrooper battalions, VDV battalions were heavily mechanized, with air-droppable infantry fighting vehicles (BMDs and BTR-Ds). Several VDV divisions remained within the VDV structure. However, during the invasion, BTGs of the VDV deployed without their parent division headquarters.

VDV Air Assault and Airborne (parachute landing) units were all jump-qualified and mechanized. Airborne battalions only included a quarter of the mechanized vehicles assigned to an Army unit. A typical air assault brigade contained an airborne battalion, two air assault battalions, a towed artillery battalion, several anti-aircraft and anti-tank missile batteries, a reconnaissance battalion, sniper company, tank company, engineering company and the normal range of combat support and combat service support platoons and companies.[33] Airborne troops were easily identifiable due to their unique light blue berets and BMD infantry fighting vehicles, a shorter and lighter version of the standard BMP.

Spetsnaz operated covertly, providing the Russian government plausible deniability.[34] As Russia's answer to American SEALS and Delta Force, British Special Air Service (SAS), Special Boat Service (SBS) and Canadian Special Operation Forces, they were professional and historically well-trained and equipped with the best modern equipment.[35] They were active in Moldova in 1999, Georgia in 2008, Ukraine 2014 to 2022, and Syria. They were instrumental in organizing and leading armed civilian separatists in the Donbas 2013–2015.[36]

Russia initially preferred the brunt of the fighting to be done by proxy forces. For that purpose, Russia organized Donetsk and Luhansk militias in 2014.[37] Their anti-Ukrainian activities triggered the Donbas War of 2014–2015. By August 2014, there were 3–4,000 Russian 'volunteers' serving in the militias assigned to battalions led by Russian officers.[38] With the creation of the Donetsk and Luhansk People's Republics these militias developed into national armies.

On 24 February 2022, the Donetsk People's Army was organized under the 1st Army Corps, under the 8th CAA. It consisted of nine motorized rifle regiments, one motorized rifle brigade, two separate battalions and a Republican Guard. The Luhansk People's Army was organized as the 2nd Army Corps (under the 8th CAA) with four motorized rifle regiments, an unknown number of Cossack battalions and the Prizrak (territorial defence)

Brigade.[39] The DPR and LPR forces were armed with older Soviet arms and equipment.[40]

Russia's historic attempt to deal with breakaway former Soviet Republics in the twenty-first century, through 'hybrid' asymmetrical and unconventional warfare continued. To ensure deniability for its harsh actions, Russia employed armed civilian proxies, and paramilitary units (eg, the Cossack Vostok Battalion) and mercenaries such as the much-vaunted Wagner Group, in place of, or in advance of regular troops.[41]

The private military company Wagner Group, ironically named after Hitler's favourite composer, developed as a tool of Russian hybrid warfare.[42] The Kremlin developed private military companies as an inexpensive alternative to the Russian Army. These private military organizations such as Wagner, could be deployed with plausible deniability. They had an additional benefit of hiding personnel casualties and KIAs from the public. The Wagner Group was not the only private military company involved in the invasion, but it has received the most press.[43]

The Wagner Group originated from the Slavonic Corps, another mercenary group, that deployed to Syria in 2013. With the disbandment of the Slavonic Corps, the Wagner Group was formed by Dmitry Utkin, a veteran of both Chechen wars, and a former member of the GRU and Spetsnaz. The group continued under the patronage of oligarch Yevgeny Prigozhin, with close links to the Russian government. While it is apparently against the Russian criminal code to serve as a mercenary, private armed security forces are allowed. The main base of the group is in the town of Molkino, in Krasnoda Oblast. The facility was shared with the GRU (Military Intelligence), and the 10th Separate Special Purpose Brigade.[44]

Before Putin's 'Special Operation' the Wagner Group maintained approximately 1,000 contractors in the Central African Republic and Mali and was active in Syria as well as the Middle East.[45] It was estimated that the group had 10,000 well-equipped contractors fighting in Ukraine, equal to the manpower of two Russian brigades.[46]

Since March 2022, the Wagner Group recruitment greatly expanded and two tactical organizations developed, 'contractors' and 'inmates'. Contractors were recruited from various sources and were mostly combat veterans. Contractors from Syria, Africa and South America have been reported in Ukraine. Pre-war contractors were paid $3,000 to $5,000 a month, which was increased to $10,000. Contractors were well-equipped by Russian standards.[47] It has been reported that former members of the Afghan National Army Commando Corps, trained but abandoned by the US, fled to Iran and were probably recruited into the group even though Prigozin denies this claim.[48]

In July 2022, the Wagner Group started recruitment of inmates from Russian prisons. The inmates were promised pardons after serving in combat for six months. They were paid 100,000 roubles ($1,700) per month. These penal Wagnerites received little training and were poorly equipped. Like Stalin's penal battalions, the convicts were used to lead attacks in the first echelon to clear the way for Wagner's second echelon of better-equipped contractors. On 5 January 2023, 24 of the first 300–350 inmates who enlisted in July 2022 received their pardons. In December 2022 the size of the Wagner Group was estimated at 20,000 contractors and 50,000 convicts in Ukraine.[49]

Russian Air Force (VKS)

In 2022 the Russian Air Force (VKS) fielded 3,829 aircraft. This total included 1,364 helicopters, 194 close-air support fighters, 125 strategic bombers, 1,188 jet fighters, 387 transports, 485 trainers, 19 aerial tankers and 67 special-mission aircraft such as airborne command, EW, and reconnaissance aircraft.[50] The VKS was a distant second to the US Air Force but on paper had similar capabilities.

In theory, the VKS underwent a reorganization during the twenty-first century incorporating modern technology and lessons learned in combat in Georgia, Ukraine (2014–2015) and Syria.[51] However, it soon became apparent during the Russian invasion that the VKS lacked the institutional capacity to plan and execute complex air missions against a near-peer adversary.

Despite this massive modern air fleet, VKS had been starved for funds for flight hours and training of its pilots.

The Russian Black Sea Fleet

The Russian Navy had approximately 346 ships and patrol craft manned by 150,000 to 160,000 active-duty personnel.[52] On 1 March 2022, Turkey blocked transit between the Mediterranean Sea and the Black Sea, leaving Russia's Black Sea Fleet isolated.

Sevastopol, on the Crimean Peninsula, was the home port of the Black Sea Fleet. During January and February 2022, the fleet contained a combined total of 49 ships of various classes and 7 kilo-class submarines.[53] At the beginning of the war, the Russian surface fleet consisted of 24 missile corvettes, frigates, and amphibious ships, led by the flagship cruiser *Moskva*.[54] Of the surface ships, 7 were amphibious landing ships (3 Alligator- and 4 Ropucha-class) that provided the lift for 2 naval infantry battalion tactical groups.[55]

Chapter 9

The Effect of Russian Corruption and Deceptive Reporting, and Ukrainian Corruption

O n 24 February 2022, the Russian armed forces appeared, at least on paper, to be a highly motivated, well-trained, fully equipped modern armed force. The world held its breath as the invincible Russian Goliath rushed toward the Ukrainian David, expecting the 'Special Operation' to last only a few days. The worst enemy Putin faced that day was not the feisty Ukrainians, but the inherent corruption within his own government and that of oligarchs and Russian generals who had set his army up for defeat before the gates of Kyiv.

Government corruption is prevalent in all countries. With the notable exception of Russia, corruption is kept in check in sophisticated countries by laws with heavy penalties that include fines and long prison sentences. Special well-paid police units and administrative inspectors audit government expenditures and contractors. In the Russian system of governance these watch dogs are part of the problem.[1] To examine the corrupt system of Russian governance would take a book. Here it is important to examine only how the corruption and false reporting became major factors in the decisive defeat of Putin's invasion force during the first months of the war.

Russian military corruption can be divided into three levels: individual, cultural, and political. For Russian officers the potential for profit and personal gain was high, while the risk of being caught was low. This paradigm increased with rank, as senior officers had access and control over greater funds and material. The culture of corruption protected the individual since peers also skimmed profit from the system.

The Russian officer corps believed it was vastly underpaid, especially considering the obscene fortunes amassed by the political and business elite (oligarchs). The military profession was prestigious in the Soviet period and was relatively well-paid.[2] This was no longer the case in modern Russia and the decline in status produced dissatisfaction in the officer corps. The defenders of 'Mother Russia' lived in relative poverty while the oligarchs conspicuously flaunted their luxurious lifestyle, mostly financed by government assets acquired after the fall of the Soviet Union. This perception was not unfounded. The failure of the political leadership to equitably distribute the failed government's wealth ostensibly justified the officer corps' individual diversion of official funds into private pockets.[3] Former (corrupt) Russian President Dmitry Medvedev, suggested that during his tenure (2008–2012), 20 per cent of the defence budget was stolen or misdirected every year.[4]

The Kremlin's attempt to correct this problem resulted in the 2009 reforms. Over the following decade, it appeared to the world that the worst of the problem had been addressed, and large-scale military exercises were held every four years. In between field exercises, snap inspections tested readiness for BTGs and air squadrons. The 2014–2015 Crimean annexation and Russian-backed insurgency in the Donbas demonstrated that the limited number of BTGs deployed were in fact well-trained and equipped. The Russian armed forces appeared to be a competent twenty-first century force, but behind the curtain it soon became obvious that the reforms had failed to curtail the corruption.[5]

Prior to the invasion, grievous corruption existed at all levels: senior political leaders, generals, brigade and regimental commanders, and supply officers. The corruption and budget skimming extended all the way down to individual 'Ivans' (Russia's GI Joes or Tommies).

The *silovikii* extended political control over the generals by encouraging their graft and corruption. Russia had strict laws against corruption of all forms, but the selective enforcement of these laws and prosecution was a very effective tool. Just the threat of exposure provided Putin with serious leverage that helped him gain control of the military. Historically, senior officers convicted of corruption received light punishments, perhaps restitution and a bar to promotion.[6] Had these crimes been convicted in a NATO country they would have been punished with long prison sentences.

At the highest level, political leaders controlled the defence budgets, appropriations, procurement, and senior military appointments. They awarded contracts for grossly overestimated budget items, providing kickbacks and illegal profits. The power to appoint political allies to important civil and military positions came with tremendous financial and political reward. Literally billions of dollars at the national level were diverted or skimmed from the military budget into private hands. Historic corruption at this level resulted in the appointment of politically connected generals rather than those best qualified to lead a fighting force in combat. The Russian Army had a plethora of 'yes men', lacking the intestinal fortitude to point out false assumptions in the Russian invasion plan.

The national military budget provided funds to purchase precision munitions, weapons, weapon upgrades, other equipment, and supplies, as well as funding for advanced research and development. A significant amount of these funds must have been diverted, as it was clear from battlefield observations that these items had not been realized. For example, experts reported that upon inspection some of the destroyed T-72s were missing the middle layer of frontal armour. The frontal glacis should have three layers of armour, two rolled steel sheets with a thick fibreglass material in the middle. The fibreglass middle layer was missing in some tanks.[7] After action inspections revealed substandard ball bearings in many captured and/or destroyed tanks that had resulted in the turrets being unable to fully traverse. Artillery barrels, made from substandard steel were discovered on many of the captured vehicles. They deteriorated faster than indicated by specifications, especially with constant use in severe weather conditions.

At the next level down of military budgeting and spending were the senior generals. They supervised the contracts awarded by politicians to provide equipment, goods, and services to the Russian armed forces. Fraudulent contracts, overpaying for goods and kickbacks were the norm. Instead of receiving military training, conscripts were often rented out as labour. Field exercises were expensive, and fuel, ammunition and rations were often diverted. Contractors were given funds to purchase top-quality truck tyres, but poor-quality Chinese re-treads were obtained instead, and the difference was pocketed.[8] Standard military vehicle batteries were replaced with substandard short-service batteries. One and a half million uniforms were budgeted but disappeared in the Russian supply system, presumably sold on the black market, or never delivered and never reported undelivered. Rations provided to the invading units in 2022 had expired in 2007 and were inedible, forcing soldiers to forage and loot for food.

Corruption and graft continued at all levels. Regimental and brigade commanders hired their soldiers out as labour, diverted supplies, sold surplus equipment, and pocketed training money. It is unclear when and where the funds to purchase encrypted tactical radios and night vision devices (NVGs) for the BGTs and helicopter pilots were diverted. The resulting shortages left helicopters in support of the initial invasion lacking NVGs, limiting their operation to daylight. The invading tanks lacked secure communication equipment and were forced to coordinate their operation with unencrypted radios and civilian cell phones that were connected to the Ukrainian cellular network.

At all levels, supply officers operated the armouries, warehouses, storage depots and induction centres. They maintained inventory records and were easily in position to divert equipment and supplies, pocketing the profit. Weapons and equipment were often written off as damaged or destroyed during an exercise or stolen or just simply missing.

On 21 September 2022, Putin signed an order for partial mobilization of 300,000 men. On 2 October 2022, Russian General Andrey Gurulev announced that 1,500,000 sets of Russian uniforms and kit to equip these men had suddenly gone missing.[9] Along with the uniforms, body armour was also missing. Many of the newly mobilized troops had to buy their own body armour, uniforms, and kit. There was a good chance that the uniforms and body armour existed only on paper invoices and inventories.[10]

Ivans, conscripts and contract soldiers saw everyone above them getting a piece of the action. A conscript made $30 a month and a contract soldier made $900 a month. Food was bad, equipment substandard and living conditions brutal. Stealing fuel and items that were not nailed down to sell on the black market provided extra income. The two most corrupt branches of the Russian armed forces were reportedly the rear services and the railway forces. Ivan was known to strip wires and parts out of T-72 tanks stored in depots. Plundered copper, gyroscopes, range finders and optics were sold for a few hundred dollars but rendered a $2,000,000 modern tank worthless.

Graff and misappropriation were not the only problems within the Russian supply system. Neglected maintenance on tanks and IFVs in depot rendered them non-operational in short order. It has been estimated that 40 per cent of the equipment in long-term storage was inoperable when called to replace combat losses in April and May 2022.[11]

The railway battalions were reportedly staffed with many substandard officers and conscripts with a high percentage of ex-convicts, alcoholics, and drug abusers.[12] Large quantities of diesel and other commodities were routinely lost in shipment. The simple expedient of altering the temperature of bulk fuel resulted in the appearance of more fuel on hand than was delivered.[13]

Deceptive reporting known as '*vranyo*' is a unique characteristic in Russian culture.[14] Lying to both subordinates and superiors but not expecting to be believed by either is not unknown.[15] It is expected that others will see the lie. Lies deflect blame, enhance intimidation, and cover mistakes.[16]

Military supply accounting needs to accurately reflect the items on hand, those items damaged and in need of repair, those missing and those on order. Combat effectiveness is obviously hindered if supply records are not accurate. Accurate training records should reflect the actual training conducted, the ammunition expended, and fuel and rations consumed. Combat effectiveness is obviously hindered if training records are not accurate. If records are distorted due to theft and profiteering, false reports must be submitted to justify the high readiness rate required by the Minister of Defence. Russian officers generally agree that lying is simpler than dealing with reality and readily ignore uncomfortable truths: *vranyo*. At the time of Putin's 'Special Operation' Russia was probably in worse shape than the Soviet Union when it came to accurately reporting readiness, logistics, administrative and personnel strength.[17]

Internal politics within the Russian armed forces supported dishonesty. It was particularly perverse when the system punished the honest and rewarded the dishonest. A commander filing a false readiness report, indicating his unit was at 97 per cent combat proficiency was promoted, while a commander who reported an accurate readiness level of only 50 per cent was considered less competent.[18]

The corruption and profiteering generally accepted in peace time had disastrous results in war. The Russian armed forces planned the invasion based upon the assumption that the BTGs were fully equipped, at full strength and combat ready, as was reported. These assumptions were patently false, based on inaccurate readiness reports. The elite VDV (Airborne), Naval Infantry and some politically important Army BTGs (i.e., 1st Tank Army and 200th Separate Motorized Rifle Brigade) were fully operational, while most other units lacked key equipment and had not conducted company or battalion combined-arms training during the months prior to the invasion. Due to the poor performance during the first weeks of the invasion, it is speculated that Russian armies based their planning assumptions on falsified reports from the BTGs, resulting in defeat before the gates of Kyiv, Kharkiv, and Sumy.

False contact and battle reports were also problematic. The ebb and flow of battle below battalion level was chaotic, made more so by false reports. As an example, in many instances, an assaulting first echelon company was unable to overcome the resistance of a strong enemy position in a typical village. To look good the captain reported that he had successfully breached the enemy position, so the battalion commander sent in the second echelon to support the frontal assault, instead of flanking the defenders in the village. The BTG commander reported up to the army commander that the village was captured, and the Russian media trumpeted another victory. Yet the village had not been captured and fighting continued for days or weeks. The assaulting BTG was decimated by repeated frontal attacks, but the commander continued to report the unit had high morale. In fact, his troops had not been fed in days and lacked fuel for their vehicles.

To get an accurate picture of the situation the Deputy Army Commander, a general, would often deploy to sector to discover ground truth. Upon assessing the situation at the front, he contacted army headquarters. Lacking an encrypted radio, he used his private unencrypted cell phone supported by the Ukrainian cell towers. Intercepted by Ukrainian intelligence, the general received a return call from a defending artillery battery or sniper's bullet. This scenario explains the battlefield deaths of four Russian major generals and lieutenant generals in March and a total of twenty-nine generals and colonels killed in 2022. There was no other reason for these high-ranking officers to be in the field at the time they were killed.[19]

During the first months of the invasion, this scenario was repeated many times. While Russian communications improved, false reporting of battlefield successes by the Russian armed forces, the Wagner Group, LPR(LNR) and DPR(DNR) plagued Russian operational planning throughout the rest of 2022. The combination of corruption, profiteering, and a culture of rampant false reporting undermined the combat effectiveness of the Russian armed forces at all levels. These serious institutional problems plaguing the facade of a modern military, must have been known and understood by the senior Russian military leadership. Putin presumably assumed the war would be over in a week or two before the weakness within the Russian armed forces materialized.

Ukraine was not without the same problems, but to a much lesser degree. Inheriting Soviet intuitional corruption, Ukraine had struggled for the past three decades to curtail the worst abuse. In the past, corruption within the Ukrainian government had made foreign investors and other countries wary of doing business with Ukraine. Anti-corruption reform since 2014 had progressed at a snail's pace, in part due to pro-Russian Ukrainian oligarchs' political power and influence. As then Vice-President, Biden held up $1 billion in aid money until Ukraine fired its top prosecutor for failure to prosecute corruption cases.[20] The Ukrainian people elected President Zelensky in 2019 on an anti-corruption and anti-establishment platform. Lacking the political support of the pro-Russian Ukrainian oligarchs his initial anti-corruption progress was slow.

The pace of Zelensky's effort to reform increased after Biden was elected President, partly in exchange for assurances of continued military aid. In order to successfully implement his anti-corruption reform programme Zelensky had to overcome the influence of Ukrainian oligarch Medvedchuk, who was very pro-Russia, pro-Putin. Using his control over several Ukrainian news outlets, Medvedchuk opposed Zelensky's anti-corruption efforts.

His 'fifth column activities' had been a thorn in the side of peace efforts between Russia and Ukraine since 2014. Medvedchuk's wife was discovered to have been channelling profits from their Russian-based oil facility to the separatist republics in Eastern Ukraine. As a Putin ally, Medvedchuk actively subverted Kyiv's attempt to find a peaceful solution over the Donbas invasion, while using his news media operations to spread fake news and promote the Kremlin's agenda to Ukrainian audiences.

By 20 February 2021, Zelensky was politically strong enough to sanction Medvedchuk and force his pro-Russian, often-fake news channels off the air. As an aside Medvedchuk was arrested for crimes committed within Ukraine but was later part of a prisoner exchange with Russia. A few days later Russia started moving soldiers along Ukraine's border.[21]

In July 2022, 200 Ukrainian government employees were fired due to engaging in criminal activity that aided the Russians in relation to the fall of Kherson, including providing information on the city's defences. An additional 60 employees remained in Russian-held territory working for the occupation authority. Upon dismissal, 200 employees were informed that legal action would be taken against them.[22]

During the war, safeguards by the US and Ukraine were put in place to ensure the US weapons provided did not disappear into the black market.[23] Despite those safeguards, in the spring of 2022 International Legion soldiers accused their Ukrainian officers of stealing light assault rifles and machine guns. Items reported stolen were fifty-four US M4 carbines, several anti-tank weapons, grenades, pistols and several thousand rounds of ammunition. In June 2022 helmets and other kit disappeared. These reports were taken seriously by the Ukrainian Bureau of Investigations and in late June 2022 they opened a case against the Legion's Commander Kapuscinki for abuse of power. If convicted, he faced twelve years in prison. In August 2022, the case against Kapuscinki was expanded to include theft of arms and humanitarian aid. Polish investigators have built the case for fraud against him and want him extradited. By the end of the year his case had not gone to trial.[24] Kapuscinki's abuses made the headlines. Based upon the principle 'trust but verify', US troops were sent to weapons delivery sites inside Ukraine to ensure the $18,000,000,000 dollars of military aid did not disappear.[25]

On 21 January 2023, Ukrainian news (*Mirror Weekly*) reported allegations of a scam involving several Ministry of Defence officials who used a dummy cooperation to over-price food purchased for the Ukrainian armed forces. The National Anti-Corruption Bureau (NABU) investigated the allegations. Deputy Minister of Infrastructure Vasyl Lozynsk was arrested along with accomplices who attempted to flee the country.[26] The investigation expanded to include Ukrainian oligarch Ihor Kolomoisky, suspected of stealing oil products worth $15,000,000,000 and evading customs payments. His two oil companies were seized and nationalized in November 2022.

Most critical to the war effort, was the corruption involved in obtaining the food contract for the Ukrainian armed forces. Before the war, members of the

Ministry of Defence had set up a shell company to secure food stuffs for the UAF. During the war, through contracts with this company, the Ministry of Defence was paying two to three times the market rate for food supplies. As the profiteering was discovered, Defence Minister Oleksii Reznikov chose to resign and was replaced on 5 February 2023 by law-maker David Arakhamia. His resignation was based on avoiding the appearance of impropriety because, while he was not involved in the scandal, it was his responsibility to provide the oversight and supervision to prevent such profiteering. Reznikov remained in the government as Minister for Strategic Industries. Deputy Defence Minister Vyacheslav and Bodhdan Khmelnysky were both arrested for their participation in the money-making scheme on 2 February 2022 but were freed on bail to await prosecution.[27]

As part of the crackdown on corruption, the Cabinet of Ministers dismissed Vyacheslav Demchenko, head of State Customs Service and deputies Oleksandr Shchutsky and Ruskain Cherassky on the grounds of suspicion of illegal importation of foreign ambulances into Ukraine.[28] On 24 January 2023, thirteen senior officials from national and oblast governments resigned due to corruption scandals and President Zelensky warned of strict enforcement of anti-graft statutes.[29] Nine more were fired for vacationing in Spain and France during the war and taking bribes.[30]

The G7 Ukraine Support Group had been working with Ukraine since 2015 on various issues, including anti-corruption.[31] In January 2023, the G7 ambassadors told Ukraine's National Agency on Corruption Prevention Minister Olekasnadr Novikov that the fight against corruption was of critical importance for the post-war reconstruction of Ukraine. During the meeting Novikov briefed the ambassadors on Ukraine's plan to tackle the problem. The Ukrainian anti-corruption strategy was approved.[32] At the following meeting on 2 February 2023, the group discussed restoration of the Ukrainian economy and reconstruction.[33] US/Ukrainian relationship advocates prioritize anti-corruption efforts in light of future post war reconstruction aid.

Chapter 10

Comparison of Ukrainian and Russian Armed Forces' Combat Capabilities on the Eve of the Invasion

A s the invasion commenced in February 2022, the Russians had an overwhelming combat force, at least on paper, when compared to the UAF. Comparing numbers of personnel, tanks, combat brigades, ships, and aircraft, the Russian armed forces seemed invincible. Before the war, the media reported on the relative strength of the combatants by comparing total manpower and various weapons systems.

The operational plan was to invade Ukraine on four main fronts. On the Northern Front, OSK-Central would push south, along both banks of the Dnipro River from Belarus, with the 29th, 35th, and 36th CAAs assigned the objective of capturing Kyiv. Also on the Northern Front, the OSK-Central would push south, along the eastern bank of the Dnipro, with the 41st CAA having the objective of capturing Chernihiv, Krolevets (road junction), and Konotop (road junction). On the Eastern Front, OSK-West's 2nd Guards CAA's objective was Sumy, while the 1st Guards Tank Army attacked Kharkiv and the northern Donbas. The 20th CAA attacked the northern Donbas from the east. On the Southern Donbas Front and Crimea Front OSK-South with, the 8th CAA, supported by DPR and LPR armies, attacked Ukrainian forces in the Donbas to pin them in place. On the Crimea Front, OSK-South, with the 58th, 49th, 8th CAAs, 22nd Army Corps (Naval Infantry), VDV's 7th Air Assault Division and the 11th Air Assault Brigade, attacked with a main effort toward Mariupol, and supporting efforts north toward Zaporizhzhia, and west toward Kherson and Odesa.[1] Total manpower committed to Putin's 'Special Operation' at the time of invasion was 200,000.

Russia fielded a standing army of 900,000 soldiers backed by 2,000,000 reservists. Ukraine's standing army fielded 209,000 and 900,000 reservists. Russia maintained a fleet of 12,000 main battle tanks, while Ukraine was only able to field 2,600. Russia boasted 1,500 jet fighters, while Ukraine fielded approximately 100. Russia had a clear superiority in numbers of military equipment and in theory could have projected overwhelming force. These bare numbers however failed to take into consideration the critical importance of adequate logistical support.

Each CAA or tank army could probably operate between 36 to 72 hours (3 days) with the supplies issued to its subunits. Due to the limited number of trucks, armies could not operate more than 140km/90 miles from a railhead. Russian logistics planning assumed that as the armies advanced, fuel and water could be pumped to the forward transfer points via pipelines. Tactical pipe battalions from the army material technical support brigades would lay pipes as the armies advanced away from the railheads.[2]

Russian invaders encountered the same problem that its nineteenth century imperial predecessor faced during the Crimean War. Putin was simply unable to adequately supply and/or maintain his invading force. A short and easy campaign was expected based upon faulty planning assumptions. With all its massive military might Russia could only deploy an invasion force of 200,000 troops, with the main manoeuvre force divided into 107 of 170 available BTGs.

Russia's conscript army was only approximately 40 per cent fully trained at the time of invasion. Therefore, each brigade or regiment could only field 1 or 2 fully trained combined-arms battalions to form BTGs. Complicating this problem, since the invasion was a 'Special Operation' and not a declared war, only contract soldiers and volunteer conscripts could be deployed pursuant to Russian law. This legal hurdle reduced the possible invasion force from 510 tank and infantry battalions to only 170 small, undermanned battalions (lacking sufficient dismounted infantry), each with 3 attached artillery batteries. It was estimated that the initial attack echelon into Ukraine consisted of 94 under-manned BTGs with 13 BTGs held in reserve. The remaining 63 BTGs were not deployed in theatre.[3]

Invasion First and Second Echelons
94 Battalion Tactical Groups
Personnel Strength & Key Equipment

- 940 x T-72/80/90 Tanks
- 3,102 x BMPs/BTRs (Armoured Personnel Carriers)
- 376 x ATGM Carriers
- 564 x 152 mm 2S19 P (Field Artillery)
- 564 x BM-21 122mm MLRS (Field Artillery)
- 56,400 troops in the BTG formations.

The rest of the Russian invasion force of over 150,000+ is in the support forces.

Source: https://www.thefivecoatconsultinggroup.com

Of the 200,000-soldier invasion force only 56,400 in the 94 BTGs were combat-arms soldiers (infantry, tank, and tactical artillery crews). The remainder of the invasion force (150,000+ troops) included supporting-arm artillery groups, logistics personnel and possibly partially trained conscripts. Support units that remained in Russia were probably fully staffed by conscripts. Command and control of the invasion was provided by a combined-arms army headquarters. Only a few division and brigade C2 groups were activated. In the case of the 1st Guards Tank Army, it deployed from the Moscow area with two division headquarters and 20 BTGs out of its total 32 tank and infantry battalions.[4]

Ukraine has a long indefensible border with Belarus and Russia. Taking this into consideration, the Ukrainian strategic defensive plan was to take advantage of natural and man-made obstacles, anchored on major cities, to enhance its defence. Urban fighting is the bane of all armies. Cities, like modern fortresses, are costly in lives to attack. Kyiv's northern and eastern flanks were protected by Chernihiv, Sumy and Kharkiv, in addition to hundreds of kilometres of open steppe in both directions. The border in the northern Donbas was screened by border guards. Its defence was established along the Siversky-Donets River, anchored in the north by Izyum and in the southeast by the cities of Lysychank and Severodenets. From that point to the Black Sea, Ukrainians had previously constructed major fortifications during the fighting in 2014. These fortifications were anchored in the south by Mariupol and in the north at Bakhmut.

The Crimean avenue of approach was screened by border police. The western avenue of approach toward Odesa was screened by defenders in Kherson and

---

Ukrainian Regular Army 17 Manoeuver Brigades 134 Manoeuver Battalions

- 630x T-72/80/90 Tanks
- 2,215x BMPs/BTRs (Armoured Personnel Carriers)
- 306x 152 mm 2S19 (Field Artillery)
- 306x BM-21 122mm MLRS (Field Artillery)
- 476x MT-LB ACRV (command and control)
- 150 Territorial Light Infantry Battalions
- 40,800 soldiers in the BTG equivalents and a total of 209,000 soldiers in the Ukrainian Army.
- 900,000 Reserves.

Source: https://www.thefivecoatconsultinggroup.com

along the Dnipro River. Lacking any natural obstacles, the eastern avenue of approach toward Mariupol was defended by the 57th Motorized Brigade.

At the start of the war, the UAF fielded the equivalent of 68 Russian BTGs, plus 46–62 additional CABs.[5] These figures did not include the Territorial brigades. The Russians committed 94 BTGs to the first echelon of the invasion. The general rule for any offensive operation is that a ratio of 3:1 is required for success. Putin needed a 3:1 superiority in combat power. As the lead Russian tanks crossed the Ukrainian border, the invaders had a combat ratio of 1:1 in personnel, 1.5:1 in tanks, 1.5:1 in tactical self-propelled artillery and 1.5:1 in tactical multiple launch rocket systems (MLRS). Russia only had a sufficient combat ratio in fighter jets, 10:1 and in naval assets with a ratio of 4:1.

It is difficult to understand how Russian military and political strategy was apparently based on two simple but false assumptions: (1) the Ukrainian government would within two weeks be replaced with a puppet government or a government in exile in Russia lead by Putin's close friend and ally Medvedchuk, and (2) the Ukrainian Army would not fight for its nation's liberty. With these two flawed strategic assumptions, the normally competent Russian General Staff supported the political assumption that the campaign would be over in less than two weeks.

The strategic plan commenced with massive missile and air strikes against Ukraine air defences, C2, airfields and ammunition storage depots. Russian ground forces would advance to capture and occupy administrative centres on the east bank of the Dnipro in addition to the cities of Kyiv, Kherson, Mykolaiv, and Odesa. The northern group was the main effort, focused on the encirclement and capture of Kyiv, neutralizing the government. The OK-West would encircle the Ukrainian troops in the Donbas from the north. OK-South would establish a land bridge with Crimea, occupy the Black Sea Coast as far as Odesa and encircle the Donbas from the south.

The FSB was tasked with the capture of local officials and dividing Ukrainians into four categories: those to be liquidated, those to be arrested or intimidated, those who would be neutral and those who would collaborate. For those to be murdered, the FSB trained with special VDV paratroopers to conduct the kill or capture missions.[6]

Captured documents indicate that the invasion plan was formulated by a small group of officers and officials directed by Putin personally. Many generals executing elements of the plan were unaware of the wider intent to kill or incarcerate all political opposition. Russian deputies of military branches were unaware of Putin's wider intent until days before the invasion. Tactical units did not receive orders until hours before they crossed the line of departure.[7] Unlike the Soviet staff prior to the German invasion during the Second World

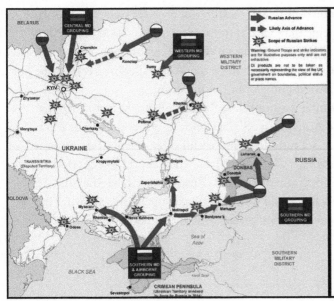

**Russian Invasion Plan
February 2022**

Duration of the Operation 10-14 days.

1. **Shaping Operations**: VKS would conduct a series of air and missile attacks against Ukrainian ADA and cities. VKS would achieve **air superiority** on the first day.

2. **Air Assault** operations to isolate Kyiv.

3. **Ground attack** to capture key Ukrainian cities and Black Sea Coast.

4. **Expected Result**: Ukraine defeated. NATO would not react in time to prevent Ukraine's defeat. Liberal democracy suppressed.
Source:
UK Defense Intelligence: February 2022

War, the 'Special Operation' plan was not wargamed with an honest 'red cell', which would have produced potential alternative courses of action. No one questioned the planning assumptions or seemed to ask what would happen if the planning assumptions were wrong.[8] There was no 'Napoleonic corporal' to whisper in Putin's ear that the king had no clothes.

With the invasion plan set and BTGs massed, the Kremlin informed the world that the Russian Army was simply conducting training exercises throughout December 2021, and until early February 2022. The troops were told they would be deployed from their home bases for nine months.

Despite announcing massive field exercises, troops massed along the border were not conducting combined-arms training. Aerial and satellite photos indicated that the training being conducted utilized only a small percentage of vehicles. Photos revealed massed armoured vehicles and trucks parked in administrative assembly areas, but the undisturbed snow on the ground and atop the vehicles indicated few of the vehicles had been moved.[9] While the Russians may have spent time on the firing range, they were not conducting combined-arms training.

With the projected length of the campaign being less than two weeks, it was perhaps a realistic political assumption that, similar to what had happened during Putin's invasion of Georgia, the West would be unable to effectively intervene before his military objectives were attained. Moscow was aware that economic sanctions would be imposed, but presumably assumed these would be offset by defeating and occupying Ukraine. Putin's assumption that NATO and the West would not intervene in any meaningful way was unrealistic. With that in mind, it was a strategic blunder not to protect the $330,000,000,000 of oligarch and governmental funds invested in Western institutions. Part of his cavalier attitude may have been justified, since the West failed to freeze those assets until 29 June 2022, five months after the invasion.[10]

Based upon faulty planning assumptions, Russian planners of the 'Special Operation' discounted the near-parity of the opposing ground combat force. Russia had the appropriate 3:1 ratio for a successful offensive on the southern routes of advance, but nowhere did Russia have the 10:1 ratio reported by the press and Ukrainian government sources. Russia must have included in their calculations that the VSK would quickly gain air superiority, allowing the ground units to outmanoeuvre Ukrainian forces and compel surrender.

Chapter 11

Putin Invades and Stumbles

Putin's desired end state was Ukraine politically aligned with the Kremlin, militarily neutral and partnered with Russian armed forces, with conditionally transparent borders to facilitate cultural and economic integration into the Eurasian Economic Union (EAEU).[1] Putin's demands at the beginning of the 'Special Operation' were nothing short of the end of Ukrainian democracy and incorporation into his new Russian Empire.

The Battle for Kyiv was the political main effort of Putin's 'Special Operation'. Despite lacking a 3:1 ground combat ratio in the Kyiv assault, the rapid tempo of the operational plan assumed that a 'shock and awe' air strike and air-assault blitz would paralyze Ukrainian command and control. The armoured assault was expected to overwhelm the leaderless defenders, to be followed by a negotiated peace and installation of a puppet government that would order the UAF to surrender.

The 2nd Guards CAA that attacked Sumy, probably did not expect to take Kyiv as a secondary objective. With the 'Special Operation' projected to last two weeks, there was no need for 2nd Guards CAA to cross hundreds of

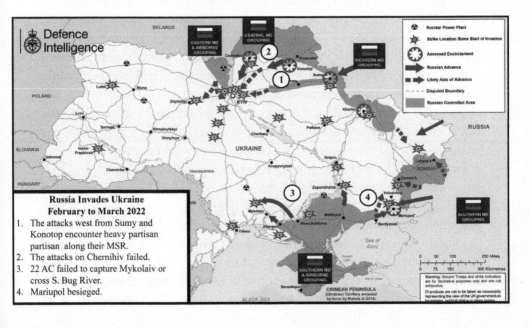

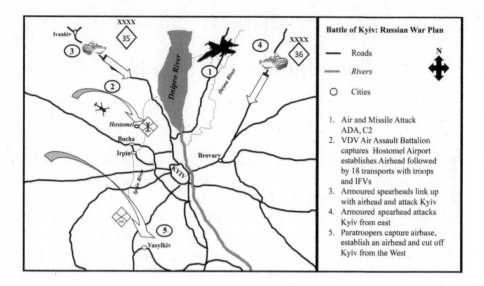

Battle of Kyiv: Russian War Plan

—— Roads

===== Rivers

O Cities

1. Air and Missile Attack
   ADA, C2
2. VDV Air Assault Battalion
   captures Hostomel Airport
   establishes Airhead followed
   by 18 transports with troops
   and IFVs
3. Armoured spearheads link up
   with airhead and attack Kyiv
4. Armoured spearhead attacks
   Kyiv from east
5. Paratroopers capture airbase,
   establish an airhead and cut off
   Kyiv from the West

kilometres of steppe and conduct an assault river crossing of the Dnipro to attack Kyiv from the west.

Based on the expectation of a quick victory, Russia apparently decided to disregard the rule of three that stands for the proposition that a headquarters can effectively control no more than three subordinate manoeuvre commands. By omitting some brigade level headquarters to oversee the battalion tactical groups it soon became evident that overall command and control was degraded. BTGs from different brigades and military districts were thrown together under CAAs and engaged individual battalion battles on all four fronts.[2]

The Russian battle plan for the capture of Kyiv was simple and would have passed muster at any Command and General Staff College. Air, missile, cyber-jamming, and electronic attacks would disrupt Ukrainian command and control and gain air superiority, while air assaults with paratroopers would isolate Kyiv from reinforcements and supply. Special forces teams, which had infiltrated into Kyiv, would kill or capture key government leaders. With the defenders leaderless and communication in disarray, Russian ground attacks along the east and west banks of the Dnipro River would capture Kyiv.

Per Russian doctrine, the ground attack of the 35th CAA and 36th CAA was conducted in two operational elechelons of BTGs. The facts indicated that the lead BTGs crossed the international border in a 'meeting engagement' formation with advance guards. The advance guards and main body travelled in close columns (administrative formations) without flank guards, in order to speed their rate of advance.[3] A supporting attack by the 36th CAA would initially capture the key road junction at Chernihiv then attack 131km/81 miles along the east bank of the Dnipro River to Kyiv.[4] A supporting attack by airborne (paratroopers) and air assault forces (heliborne troops) would capture Antonov Airport and the Vasylkiv military airfield to isolate Kyiv.

In late February 2022, Ukrainian intelligence concluded that Russia's most dangerous course of action would be an offensive in the Donbas. Despite warnings from the US, California, and NATO, that Kyiv would be the Russian main effort, Ukraine still focused its main effort on the Donbas. Their reasoning was based primarily on the fact that Russia had failed to mass sufficient troops to isolate and capture Kyiv along the northern border. Secondly, the terrain north of the city was unfavourable for a major attack. The tactical preparations of the northern invasion force did not reflect CAAs preparing to take the offensive. Finally, interception of Russian military and civilian communications along with human intelligence indicated the soldiers did not believe they were going to war.[5]

Since it appeared to the Ukrainians that the Donbas was the main effort, ten active UAF brigades were assigned to the Donbas. Brigades were deployed to Kharkiv, Sumy and Chernihiv in the north. Kyiv was assigned one manoeuvre brigade, a National Guard brigade and two artillery brigades plus special forces units. The avenue of approach from Crimea was assigned one brigade with a second brigade assigned to defend Odesa.[6]

Ukrainian OC-North prepared an active defence of Kyiv Oblast. The Ukrainian obstacle plan was to destroy key bridges and flood minor river valleys limiting the northern approaches into the Kyiv defensive zone. The Irpin River and its swampy banks blocked key avenues of approach into Kyiv from the north and west and would become the main line of resistance. The defences were held by the Ukrainian Regular 72nd Mechanized Brigade and National Guard 4th Rapid Reaction Brigade, augmented by special forces units, the Georgian Legion, Territorial and hastily raised volunteer militia battalions. The 95th Air Assault Motorized Brigade was deployed at an unidentified location somewhere south and west of Kyiv. The 1st Tank Brigade and the 119th Territorial brigade defended the key road junction at Chernihiv.[7]

The invaders mistakenly believed they were attacking the 72nd Mechanized Brigades' six combat battalions with fifteen BTGs, which would have given them a 3:1 combat ratio. They must have known the six Territorial battalions were in Kyvi Oblast but apparently discounted their effectiveness. Additionally, based on their assumption that they had air superiority on the first day of the invasion, they erroneously concluded that they held a combat power ratio of 10:1. Russian intelligence failed to detect the National Guards' 4th Rapid Reaction Brigade of one tank and three motorized infantry battalions sitting in defensive positions near Antonov Airport.

Despite warnings from Washington and the California National Guard throughout January and early February 2022, Ukrainian political and military leadership remained unconvinced of an imminent Russian invasion. It was not until Putin's speech on 21 February 2022, that UAF Commander in Chief General Zaluzhnnyi and Ukrainian political leadership were finally convinced that Russia would attack.[8]

General Zaluzhnnyi sent a reply to Putin's speech on all websites and social media: '[Y]ou will attack us in 10:1 and 15:1 ratios. We will not meet you with flowers. We will meet you with guns. Welcome to HELL!' The message was rebroadcast to all Ukrainian units and the public. Under cover of darkness on the night of 22 February 2022, Ukrainians deployed from garrisons to battle positions. Expecting Russia to immediately seize air superiority, units were well-supplied with Stingers and other MANPADS.[9] The defenders did not have long to wait.

At 0400 on 24 February 2022, Russia commenced a short but incomplete air campaign targeting Ukrainian air defences, supply depots, airfields and command-and-control nodes across Ukraine. Russian electronic warfare (EW), jamming and cyber-attacks blinded Ukrainian intelligence-collection methods, disrupting targeting and communications between battalions, brigades, and high command. The jamming and resulting repositioning of Ukrainian assets created gaps in the air-defence coverage over Kyiv Oblast.

The invaders' initial strike of 100 missiles and 75 bomber aircraft sorties killed many but failed to destroy the Ukrainian Air Force, or its anti-air defence, nor did it succeed in completely disrupting Ukrainian military and political command and control infrastructure.[10] In comparison to NATO's 15-day 'shock and awe' air campaign against Iraq in 1991, Putin's one day air bombardment was a 'pop and fizzle'. Ukrainian combat units with disrupted communications fell back on their NATO training and executed the defensive plan. When the plan was no longer viable, they used their initiative and improvised.[11]

The Russian Air Force and missile force had more than sufficient aircraft and weapons for a NATO-style 'shock and awe' campaign. However, Russian Air Force planners were limited in target selection by the overriding assumption that the 'Special Operation' would topple the Ukrainian government in a matter of days and the UAF would either not fight or would surrender quickly. Putin apparently wanted to preserve some facilities for Russia's use after conquest and occupation. The targets selected had military value or were civilian locations with political significance. As a result, insufficient ordnance was allocated to initial strikes.

Heeding the US warning, two weeks prior to the attack the commander of Antonov Airport in the suburb of Hostomel established multiple new defensive positions. The airfield was defended by 300 reservists. However, a traitor at the airport reported these new positions to Russian intelligence.[12]

OSK West's main effort against Kyiv was by BTGs (BMDs and tanks) from the VDV's 11th and 31st Guards Air Assault Brigades.[13] As aerial bombardment commenced, the armoured assault units crossed the international boarder and started the 135km/85mile blitz toward Kyiv via Chornobyl and Ivankiv.[14] The 36th CAA's BTGs east of the Dnipro started their 70km/43mile journey to the key road junction of Chernihiv and the alerted 1st Tank Brigade defending the city.

Expecting little resistance, the armoured formations rolled down the highways in massed administrative formations.[15] Assuming the population would be friendly or cowed into submission by Russian armed might, advancing armoured formations failed to secure towns and villages along their routes of advance.[16]

The battle for Antonov Airport commenced at 0800, 24 February 2022. Under the cover of the air and missile assault on Kyiv, 30 Mi-8 assault helicopters, supported by Ka-52 gunships, ferried a battalion of paratroopers from the VDV's 11th and 31st Guards Air Assault Brigades to capture Antonov Airport. The airborne operation was part of Russia's attempt to achieve air superiority by capturing critical Ukrainian airfields to use as airheads. If successful, Russian paratroopers could have flown armoured vehicles and supplies into the Ukrainian rear, outflanking Kyiv's defences.

At morning's twilight, two dozen Mi-8 helicopters carrying over 100 elite air assault troops, supported by Ka-52 gunships, crossed the Ukrainian border to cover the 250km/155 miles from their base in Belarus to their objective, Antonov Airport in Hostomel. Compared to their Western counterparts in NATO the Russian elite paratroopers and aviators were ill-equipped and significantly short of night vision devices. The lack of NVGs forced the assaulting battalion to conduct this risky operation in daylight. Despite this limitation, it was planned that the assault force would land after the Russian missiles, airstrikes, and electronic weaponry (EW) disrupted Ukrainian air defences and C2. The assault force flew fast and low to avoid Ukrainian targeting radars but in broad daylight were observed by the defenders along their flight path. The flight path was poorly chosen and as the Russian formation flew near the Dnipro River it lost the cover of trees and buildings. This error allowed the defenders to engage the formation with heavy machine guns, downing one of the Mi-8s as the Ka-52 gunships tried to suppress the ground fire. A Stinger MANPAD replied, downing a second Mi-8. Flying through the heavy fire, the assault force proceeded toward their objective. As the formation approached the airfield, Russian Ka-52s raced forward to suppress the heavy machine guns and other defensive positions with cannon and rocket fire.[17]

The defenders quickly recovered from the initial attack by the Ka-52s and subjected the gunships to heavy fire. As the one-sided duel continued, the inbound Mi-8s threatened to overwhelm the defenders and they started to withdraw. National Guardsman Serhily Fatatyuk refused to retreat. He shouldered a MANPAD and downed a Ka-52 gunship. The defenders rallied and as the Mi-8s began to land they were subjected to heavy fire, dropping a second Mi-8 as it landed. As the paratroopers disembarked, they realized they were surrounded by defenders. The Russian platoon leaders quickly established a perimeter that included a nearby airport building. As the paratroopers pushed back the defenders, two Russian Su-25 jet fighters destroyed a Ukrainian position. Following the air strike, the paratroopers pushed the defenders out of the airport. After taking light casualties and securing the airport, the Russian commander called in eighteen Il-76 transport aircraft to reinforce their acquisition with infantry and armoured vehicles.

The Russian paratroopers' hold on the airport was weak. Almost immediately, Ukrainian militia ringed the airport and subjected the paratroopers to sniper fire.[18] They were soon reinforced by the Ukrainian Special Forces' 3rd Special Purpose Regiment. Realizing the threat, General Zaluzhny changed the priority of fire for his artillery and ordered bombardment of the airfield. A battalion from the 72nd Mechanized Brigade was committed to recapture the airport. The first major counterattack was repelled by the paratroopers with anti-tank weapons and automatic grenade launchers, but the Russians were forced to reduce their perimeter. The paratroopers realized they needed to hold the airstrip so that the inbound transport aircraft could land. The defenders were equally aware of the importance of keeping the airstrip closed to prevent reinforcements from reaching the embattled paratroopers. Ukrainian artillery observers were having difficulty locating the paratrooper positions and could not successfully mass artillery.

Understanding the critical situation, General Zaluzhny ordered a combined-arms battalion from the National Guard 4th Rapid Reaction Brigade to attack. By late morning Ukrainian defenders were joined by a Ukrainian National Guard combined-arms battalion (10 T-64 tanks, 40 APCS and 200+ infantry) supported by Su-24 and MiG-29 jets. The paratroopers had relied on the Ka-52s for anti-armour support but the gunships had expended most of their ATGMs. In the desperate fight the Guardsmen lost tanks and APCs to Russian air while several more Russian helicopters were destroyed, and short on fuel and out of missiles the Ka-52s were forced to leave. As the Russian helicopters started to withdraw, a Ukrainian MiG-29 appeared in support of the counterattack. As the battle raged, a battalion of the Georgian National Legion entered the fight. During the heavy fighting that ensued the Russian paratroopers ran out of ATGMs and, low on ammunition, retreated into the woods north of the airfield. It was rumoured that Mamuka Mamulashvill, Commander of the Legion, jumped into a car and literally ran down retreating paratroopers.[19] The Russian commander on the ground realized he could not protect the inbound transports. He contacted his headquarters via satellite and told them to turn the transports around. By late afternoon the invading paratroopers were pushed off the airfield.[20] As night fell on 24 February, the fighting around the airport calmed down.

Antonov Airport is located 30km/18 miles from Kyiv's city limits. Prior to the invasion, Russian troops were given a series of conflicting briefings. Dependable troops such as the paratroopers, naval infantry, pilots, and missile operators were informed that they were going into combat in Ukraine. Less dependable troops, eg most of the rank and file in the BTGs, were instructed that they were either going on a training exercise 'in Russia' or they were liberating Ukrainian people from a neo-Nazi government.[21] The majority of ground armoured assault troops crossed the border expecting little to no opposition. As they rolled through 'liberated towns and villages' they were surprised by attacks on their supply trucks by partisan groups.[22]

As Russian invaders approached Kyiv, they unexpectedly encountered stiff resistance from Ukrainian regulars and militia forces. Advancing without ground reconnaissance, entire battalions rolled into ambushes as if on parade. As an example, the advance guard of the lead BTG reached the towns of Irpin and Bucha as desperate fighting raged at Antonov Airport. They were met with the message; '[W]elcome to Hell' painted on walls and on cement mixers and bulldozers blocking the roads. Town council member Volodymyr Korotya had organized a militia of psychotherapists, bus drivers and citizens from many occupations dressed in civilian clothing, armed with shotguns, hunting rifles, assault rifles and a few rocket-propelled grenades.

As the ten-vehicle vanguard (BMDs) started crossing the Irpin River Bridge, the Irpin militia opened fired. A three-hour fire fight ensued, destroying several vehicles and forcing the Russians to retreat.[23] The small Irpin River became the key defensive line for the survival of Kyiv.

Ukrainian ground forces failed to implement in timely fashion the Obstacle Plan to protect Kyiv from an attack from the north. With communications in disarray, Colonel Vdovychenko Oleksander, Commander of the 72nd Mechanized Brigade, executed the Obstacle Plan. Between 24 and 25 February, the bridges over the Teteriv River and in the city of Irpin and suburb of Hostomel were destroyed.[24]

With the Irpin River running 4.5m/15ft higher than normal, Colonel Oleksander ordered the dam flood gates opened and intentionally flooded 13,000 hectares (32,000 acres) of wetlands, establishing an anti-tank obstacle that reduced the length of the defensive line.[25] With the bridges destroyed and river in flood, the Russian advance was halted. Cut off from command and supply, Russian soldiers looted stores for food and vodka.[26]

On 24 February 2022, President Zelensky signed a decree for general mobilization.[27] When the American embassy offered to evacuate Zelensky he rebuffed the offer and replied: 'The fight is here; I need ammunition not a ride.'[28] Between 24 and 25 February, 18,000 assault rifles were issued to civilians in the capital. Ukrainian civilians answered the call and, following the example of their president, volunteered in combat, combat support and combat service support roles. When the Territorial battalions could take no more volunteers, citizens formed militias. Bank tellers trained with teachers on assault rifles, others erected roadblocks, dug trenches, weaved camouflage, or made Molotov cocktails in their homes. Civilian drone operators volunteered their services and their drones, expanding UAF capabilities, and expert cyber hackers targeted Russian communications.[29]

While millions fled the Russian invasion, many military-age men escorted their wives, children and elderly relatives to the Polish border, returning to defend Kyiv. Local citizens familiar with the countryside volunteered as scouts for the UAF.[30] The UAF mobilized cadets and teaching staff from its military academies to provide trained leadership to newly created militia battalions. Within a week of the invasion, militia battalions reinforced the regular, National Guard and Territorial battalions.

The combat effectiveness of hastily raised militia can be determined by their uploaded footage of 'hunter-killer patrols'. The militia was effective in destroying Russian armoured vehicles with RPGs, NLAW anti-tank missiles, and converting civilian drones to drop grenades. More-disciplined regular army patrols did not broadcast their success because of the GPS trackers in most cell phone cameras. The militia was also effective in patrolling the streets of Kyiv, freeing trained soldiers, and police for frontline service.

On 25 February 2022, 5th Guards Tank Brigade (possibly two BTGs) attacking south from Belarus, after breaking through the defences near Chernobyl nuclear power plant, met heavy resistance in the town of Ivankiv. The 5th Guards mission was to relieve the paratroopers and recapture Antonov Airport. Ivankiv (72km/44 miles NW of Kyiv) is located at a key crossing of the Teteriv River. The defending militia and Ukrainian paratroopers were outnumbered and outgunned. After losing several tanks and IFVs, part of the invading armoured column was able to force a crossing before the Ukrainians could blow up the bridge. The 5th Guards Tank Brigade fought its way through several Special Forces and partisan ambushes. The reduced armoured column approached the airport and linked up with the paratroopers. With the help of air support, the 5th Guards finally succeeded in capturing the airport but Ukrainian artillery had destroyed the runways. The Russian capture of the airfield was a 'Pyrrhic victory', as the runways were cratered to such an extent as to make them useless. Fighting continued around the airport until the Russian withdrawal in late March 2022.

On 25–26 February 2022, a second airborne assault was launched in an attempt to capture the Vasylkiv airfield, 35km/21 miles southwest of Kyiv. Capture of this airfield would have isolated Kyiv and placed an armoured enemy airhead deep in the Ukrainian rear. However, as the Russian attack materialized on the early morning of 26 February, Ukrainians were alert on the ground and a combat air patrol was aloft. The first wave of paratroopers made it to the airfield. At 01:30 a follow-on wave of paratroopers was killed when their Il-76 transport was shot down by a Ukrainian jet fighter.[31] At 03:20 a second loaded transport was downed. Air Force security personnel and maintenance crews at Vasylkiv pushed the Russian paratroopers off the airfield.

Communications between Russian units was poor. On 25 February, a special Russian police unit trailing a BTG from the 5th Separate Guards Tank Brigade reached Chernobyl nuclear facility. Following the tanks, the police unit in their twelve to fifteen vehicles, drove down Highway Po2 toward Kyiv. The tanks turned to attack the city of Ivankiv (80km/50 miles NW of Kyiv), but for some reason the trailing police vehicles continued on toward Kyiv. The Russians failed to station military police to control traffic on the battlefield and failed to direct entering support units to secure areas.

Lacking situational awareness, the police unit drove ahead of the attacking Russian tanks. Passing the ongoing battle for Antonov Airport the police finally realized they were ahead of the tanks. Lacking communication with command, they discussed the situation amongst themselves. They could have turned around and re-joined a combat unit but decided to press forward. Like all Russian vehicles in the Kyiv assault, their KamZ armoured trucks and BTRs were clearly marked with a white 'V' painted on the sides. As the lead truck crossed a small bridge over the Irpin River it was destroyed by an anti-tank missile, as was the last vehicle in the convoy, trapping the entire unit in a kill zone. Anti-tank missiles and machineguns completed the destruction. Of the eighty police officers who entered the kill zone only three survived.[32]

One of the key engagements of this period was between the 72nd Mechanized Brigade versus the Russian first echelon BTGs from the 76th Guards Air Assault Division, 98th Guards Airborne Division and 155th

Separate Naval Infantry Brigade. A local farmer reported a large concentration of tanks in the forest north of Moschun. Drones were dispatched to verify the sighting. The thick forest prevented the drones from identifying the target. An artillery mission was fired based on the farmer's information, resulting in massive secondary explosions. Having been discovered, the Russian armour units immediately attacked the 72nd Mechanized Brigade. Russian EW and jamming effectively disabled the Ukrainian drones and interdicted communications. After heavy fighting the assault was halted.[33]

As the Russian tanks left the cover of the forest, defending Ukrainians successfully stopped the formation by shooting the lead armoured vehicle with NLAWs, Javelins and other anti-tank missiles. This halted the enemy's advance, allowing Ukrainian artillery to mass fire on the formation. Unless fired en masse, standard artillery rounds are not effective against tanks. Massed artillery fired against lighter-armoured and unarmoured vehicles, and unprotected soldiers, easily destroyed the vehicles and killed the enemy. The infantry on both sides rode on top of their APCs and IFVs for fear of mines and improvised explosive devices. As a result, they were unprotected from surprise artillery fire. The stiff fighting of 24–28 February stopped the Russian operational first echelon along the Iprin River.

Chapter 12

Defending Kyiv's Eastern Flank

There were three defensive battles protecting the eastern flank of Kyiv. The defence of the Sumy, Kharkiv and Chernihiv Oblasts were anchored in several non-contiguous strongpoints within these urban centres and along the roads heading toward Kyiv. Territorial infantry covered the gaps in the strong points, first delaying then disrupting and finally ambushing or calling artillery and drone strikes on Russian supply routes. The invaders were soon required to divert combat troops to protect their main supply routes.[1]

On 24 February 2022 at 0300, security patrols of the 1st Tank Brigade captured the reconnaissance platoon from a BTG of the Russian 74th Motorized Rifle Brigade on the outskirts of Chernihiv.[2] The simple fact that the reconnaissance platoon was in the area indicated that the Russians had crossed the border and the invasion had begun.

The 1st Tank Brigade defended Chernihiv with three tank battalions, a BMP-mounted mechanized battalion and three artillery battalions, supported by Territorial, militia, partisan and nearby artillery brigades. The invading 74th Motorized Rifle Brigade attacked later in the day and was repulsed.

On 25 February, Chernihiv was surrounded and was assaulted on the 26th. Uncoordinated attacks by several BTGs, with at least one from the 35th Guards Rifle Brigade, were thrown back with heavy casualties. The 35th was based in Aleysk, Russia.[3] This attack was possibly the one reported by a babushka in Aleysk. In late February 2022, she informed a friend on a WhatsApp group that 'just 18 out of 150 guys survived and 40 coffins had returned to town'.[4]

Despite repeated attacks, Chernihiv remained in Ukrainian hands. By 6 March 2022, the 36th CAA's BTGs littered the ground as they piled up around the defended road intersection. Russian senior officers attempting to get the stalled BTGs moving, repeatedly exposed themselves to Ukrainian fire. Both generals Vitaliyy Gerasimov and Andrei Sukhovesky, deputy commanders of the 41st CAA, were killed in the effort to push the assault forward toward Kyiv.[5]

Throughout March, the city was bombarded daily with artillery, missiles and aircraft. Civilian infrastructure was deliberately targeted. Ukrainian artillery and partisan attacks destroyed fifty-four supply and fuel trucks. The defenders slowed the 36th CAA, preventing its timely participation in the battle for Kyiv. By 7 March, the 36th CAA was able to start moving a few BGTs toward Kyiv but were halted near Velyka Dymerka, 29km/18 miles northeast of Kyiv.

On 18 March, the 36th CAA finally launched a full-scale attack down the Chernihiv Highway but was stopped 13km/8 miles south of Velyka Dymerka.[6] On 31 March 2022, Ukrainian forces from Kyiv lifted the siege of Chernihiv. The 36th CAA retreated all the way back to Russia without achieving any of its objectives.[7]

The small town of Nizhyn is 130km/80 miles northeast of Kyiv and 80km/49 miles south of Chernihiv. The town sits near Highway M02 that could easily be used to bypass Chernihiv. There is an important rail line running though Nizhyn toward Kyiv. The town could have become an important logistics link on a Russian supply line.[8] Initially the town was defended by a Territorial battalion and militia. Having surprisingly obtained anti-tank mines, the untrained militia laid the mines on the Russian axis of advance. Unfortunately, the mine field was not well marked and on 3 March a regular Ukrainian infantry battalion reinforcing the region entered the area. Luckily no one was injured.[9]

The defenders of Nizhyn and the 1st Tank Brigade at Chernihiv eventually linked up and turned the heavily forested region into a partisan stronghold. Raiding from the forest they interdicted Russian supply lines between Chernihiv and Kyiv. Bypassing Chernihiv and continuing to the south toward Kyiv, the 41st CAA was forced to defend its supply line by siphoning off troops from its main attack. To avoid the partisan raiders, the advancing 2nd Tank Army was forced to screen Nizhyn and bypass the region.[10]

On 24 February 2022, Russians nearly captured Sumy. Having been warned by Russian friends, the 150th Sumy Territorial Defence Battalion was alerted, but the word was slow to spread, and many defenders were caught by surprise.[11] At 03:00 the first Russian tanks entered the city. The Ukrainians quickly recovered and took up position, resulting in heavy urban combat.[12] By 22:30 the Russians had reached the positions of the 27th Artillery Brigade near the Sumy State University. By 01:39 on 25 February, the Russians fell back, out of the city to regroup. Heavy fighting resumed on 26–27 February, causing the Russians to run short of supplies. Their troops looted local markets for food. With the Russian failure to establish air dominance, Bayraktar TB2 drones began to attack Russian vehicles. By 28 February, Ukrainians had reportedly destroyed ninety-six tanks, twenty BM-21 multiple launch rocket systems (MLRS) and eight fuel trucks.[13]

Heavy fighting continued for a week while the city was heavily bombarded. Volunteers of both sexes, from teenagers to pensioners, stepped forward to fight. People that could not fight made Molotov cocktails, prepared food and cared for the wounded. Russian armoured assaults were repulsed and stalled before the gates of the city.

By 4 April 2022, the Governor of Sumy, Dmytro Zhyvytskyi announced that the Russians had withdrawn from the oblast. The stubborn defence of the oblast prevented the assault on Kyiv from the west. The defenders of Sumy oblast included militia, partisans and soldiers striking Russian supply convoys travelling across the open steppe just west of the city. Russia's inability to move its railhead supply operations beyond Sumy doomed the attack on this axis to fail due to lack of supplies.

On 24 February 2022, the Russians crossed the border, heading toward Kharkiv. At 0400 Colonel Pavlo Fedosenka, commander of the Ukrainian 92nd Mechanized Brigade, heard explosions near his headquarters. He received a call from his commander-in-chief and received orders to hold the invading Russians. He ordered his battalions to occupy their firing positions.

On 24 February the Russian 200th Motor Rifle Brigade crossed the border in a 100-vehicle convoy and headed toward Kharkiv. The 200th Brigade, under the command of Colonel Denis Kurilo was at its full strength of 1,400 men and organized into two BTGs. The brigade had been stationed on the Kola Peninsula along the Arctic Ocean coast near the nuclear submarine base in Murmansk Oblast. By Russian standards it was highly trained and well-equipped, with its tank companies operating T-80 tanks. The 200th Brigade had the advantage over other formations attacking in this sector in that it fought as a brigade, not as independent BTGs.[14]

Between 24–26 February, the Ukrainian 92nd Mechanized Brigade fought a delaying action near the borders of Kharkiv, Sumy and Luhansk Oblasts. After fighting through several ambushes, the 200th Brigade's convoy reached the outskirts of Kharkiv. The Russians established roadblocks with their tanks. Patrols attempting to establish order within the city were ambushed by Territorial, National Guard, police, and citizen militia units. By the end of the day, the 200th Brigade had suffered dozens of casualties, with several tanks and artillery vehicles destroyed or abandoned on the roadsides near Kharkiv. On 26 February, heavy fighting resumed and the 200th Brigade was forced out of the city. Short of food, ammunition and fuel, the brigade dug in north of the city.[15]

By 26 February, Russian pressure forced the Ukrainian 92nd Mechanized Brigade to fall back to the city limits of Kharkiv. Units like the 200th Brigade that had by-passed the 92nd Mechanized were fighting inside the city. With added reinforcements from the Territorial, National Guard, police, and citizen militias, the 92nd Mechanized defended the city and by sunset on 26 February had once again pushed the Russians out. As they retreated, the Russians left their wounded and looted the city. They were observed loading consumer goods such as washing machines onto their combat vehicles.[16]

Having neglected to establish traffic control points on roads leading into the city, a Russian supply convoy of fifty vehicles unknowingly rolled into a Territorial ambush.[17] Attempting to bypass the city on their advance west to Kyiv, the invaders floundered on the ancient ramparts in the town of Zmiev, 16km/10 miles south of Kharkiv.

The defenders of Zmiev and Kharkiv successfully interdicted the Russian line of supply and communication. The defenders of Zmiev's earthen medieval fort held despite heavy artillery bombardment. The invaders were forced to bypass this fortified position, extending their supply lines from the Kharkiv Oblast to the Dnipro River.

By 1 March it was clear that the first operational echelon of the 35th, 36th and 41st CAAs would not take Kyiv by blitz and a battle of attrition ensued. The failure at the gates of Kyiv in February was compounded by failure of the 2nd CAA and 1st Guards Tank Armies to capture Sumy and Kharkiv with their hasty attack. The Russians failed to gain air superiority and were experiencing severe logistical shortages on all axes of advance. Reassessing the situation, the Kremlin decided that Sumy and Kharkov would be isolated and bypassed. The 2nd CAA and 1st Guards Tank Army turned their spearheads west and commenced crossing the 500km/310 miles of steppe to the Dnipro River and Kyiv. Leaving an undefeated enemy in a fortified position, capable of striking supply lines, is a blunder as old as warfare.

The UAF mounted a non-contiguous strongpoint defence in depth of the Chernihiv, Sumy, and Kharkiv Oblasts. While static defence forces held strongpoints centred on urban and other key terrain, light infantry roamed the gaps between these strongpoints. The UAF infantry was familiar with the terrain and easily disrupted Russian logistics efforts along critical ground lines of communication. This defence in depth of Chernihiv, Sumy and Khakriv Oblasts denied the invaders resupply for their armoured thrusts toward Kyiv's eastern flank. Russia's inability to secure its 500km/310-mile lines of communication, through eastern Ukraine to its armoured spearheads marching toward Kyiv, forced Russian commanders to divert infantry to defend vulnerable road-based logistics. The failure of the CAAs attacking via Kharkiv and Sumy to enter the battle led to defeat.[18]

Chapter 13

Battle for Kyiv March 2022

Western aid to Ukraine went from a trickle in February 2022 to a flood in March 2022. Shoulder-fired anti-tank missiles such as Javelins, NLAWs and similar 'fire-and-forget' missiles were rapidly transferred to Ukraine en masse. With effective ranges of 2,500–4,000m/1.5–2.4 miles, they had similar ranges as Russian tanks and transformed every Ukrainian squad or section into a tank hunter-killer team. Anti-aircraft weapons were also supplied and helped prevent Russia from gaining air superiority. The Stinger and similar MANPADs, of NATO and Soviet design, are fire-and-forget, heat-seeking, ground-to-air missiles with a range of 8km/5 miles and able to reach altitudes of 3,000m/10,000ft into the air. The advantage of all these man-packable systems was that they were simple to operate and required very little training. Bayraktar TB2 drones from Turkey provided Ukraine with an offensive aerial capability. This relatively inexpensive, slow, lightweight drone has a 12-metre wingspan and can loiter over the battlefield for up to thirty hours. Russia's failure to integrate its air defence weapons during the first two weeks allowed the Bayraktar TB2 drones to successfully destroy Russian fuel and supply trucks. Spectacularly, these

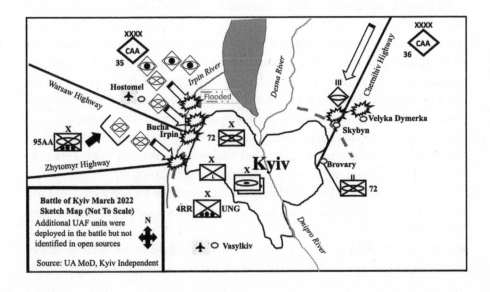

drones were used to target and destroy combat vehicles, including anti-aircraft systems, in a stalled 63km/40 mile-long convoy north of Kyiv.[1]

In March 2022, Russian attacks on Kyiv from the east, north and west had paused. Ukrainians observed that the water previously released from the Irpin dam had been mostly absorbed by the marshland and the Russians were preparing an assault river crossing. On 8 March 2022, a Ukrainian militia demolition team destroyed the dam, flooding the marshland.[2]

The 35th CAA became the main effort, focused on attacking Ukrainian defenders from the west and north. The attacking 36th CAA was held at the defences northeast and east of the city and was partly stalled due to logistical challenges. Since the invaders had been forced to bypass the fortress city of Chernihiv their supply train had detoured off all-weather roads into the countryside and was greatly hampered by muddy conditions and partisan attacks.

Lieutenant Colonel Roman Darmohrai, 29, commanding a battalion from the 72nd Mechanized Brigade was assigned to defend Kyiv's eastern flank at the town of Brovary, 24km/15 miles northeast of Kyiv. Ms Tetyana Chornovol, 42, an investigative journalist, joined the battalion as they dug ambush positions. Locals assisted the soldiers with backhoes and shovels. Chornovol joined an ambush team near the village of Skybyn a few kilometres north of Brovary.

On 9 March 2022, the 6th Guards Tank Regiment under command of Colonel Andrei Zakharov was detected rolling south toward Brovary though the village of Zalissya, 6km/3.7 miles north of Skybyn. Ukrainian drones shadowed the column and as the lead tank emerged from a tree line, an NLAW missile slammed into its side destroying it. The following tanks drove off the road into the mud, while others returned fire. Stunned by the attack, most of the column halted and fell back to regroup. Instead of deploying into battle formation, the Russians continued their advance in road column, probably due to the muddy ground. As they approached the village of Skybyn, Ms Chornovol picked up and fired an NLAW. Missing with her first shot, she hit a tank with her second. Artillery soon joined the battle and bombarded the Russian tanks. Tanks deploying from the road slipped on the muddy roadside as they attempted to turn around, providing flank shots for Ukrainian gunners. When the Russians finally retreated, they left seventeen tanks and three armoured vehicles burning and dozens of bodies littering the battlefield.

Colonel Andrei Zakharov had been severely wounded when his vehicle was hit. As the 6th Guards retreated to Bohdanivka, they carried Zakharov from his vehicle into Mrs Bobko's barn where he died. Mrs Bobko heard one of the soldiers say, '[W]e lost our commander. We don't know what to do, go forward or back.' With their Colonel dead, the Russian regiment stayed in the village, looting beer, wine, brandy, cigarettes and stealing sneakers and jeans. Junior officers were present and eventually ordered the tank crews to prepare defensive fighting positions. On 19 March 2022, the regiment made one last half-hearted attack toward Brovary. The tanks fired on Ukrainian positions but as they advanced Ms Chornovol again reportedly returned fire with an NLAW, hitting and destroying the first tank. The remainder retreated.[3]

The 35th CAA's attack focused on the Moschun and Irpin sector of the line. Russian paratroopers attempted three unsuccessful river crossings of the Irpin River. On or about 16 March, a company of 80 soldiers from the 72nd Mechanized Brigade defeated a Russian assault river crossing over the Irpin.[4] A Russian assault force of over 500 men attempted to set up a pontoon bridge near the town of Moshchun. A heavy firefight ensued. Russian infantry and tanks secured the north side of the river, establishing a 'support-by-fire position' as combat engineers attempted to set up the bridge. NLAW missiles and artillery engaged the Russians, preventing the engineers from bridging the river. A local civilian teenager managed to steal a radio from a BMD paratrooper crew while they slept. Passing though several Russian check points he arrived at the Ukrainian command post with the radio. Using the purloined radio, the defenders were able to monitor Russian communications. After suffering heavy losses, the paratroopers broke contact and retreated.[5]

According to Russian doctrine, an opposed hasty river crossing is one of the most difficult combat operations. It requires detailed planning and coordination with a regiment or brigade headquarters to command and control the operation.[6] While the assault force probably included two or more understrength BTGs, they were supported by artillery and combat engineers. Despite the courage of the BTG commander and individual Russian soldiers, the operation required the expertise and coordination of a brigade commander and trained staff. The attempted river crossing lacked the required staff coordination, expertise, and training in combined-arms tactics. In the face of heavy defensive fire from the opposing river bank the operation failed.

While the paratroopers were attempting to cross the river, a Ukrainian blogger in his hometown of Moschun uploaded a live feed on the internet of a Ukrainian artillery battery firing in support of the defenders. Monitoring the feed, the Russians reverse triangulated the location and hit the battery with a hypersonic missile. The battery suffered heavy casualties. Justice was swift and the Ukrainian court sentenced the unfortunate blogger to fifteen years in prison.

Major Dmytro Zaretsky's battalion was deployed to reinforce the 72nd Mechanized Brigade. He was ordered to recapture Bucha and then Irpin. Not knowing where the town was located, he logged into 'Google Maps' to locate the town. As a Russian force advanced toward his position, Zaretsky's staff used Google Maps to formulate a battle plan. Being unfamiliar with his recently acquired weapons, Zaretsky called up 'YouTube' videos for instruction on the use of Stinger, NLAWs and Javelin missiles. Passing Moschun on his way to recapture Bucha a Stinger gunner destroyed a Russian helicopter. Zaretsky's unit successfully fired their newly acquired and now-familiar Javelins, destroying a total of six Russian tanks and APCs.

As Zaretsky's battalion approached Irpin it ambushed a Russian airborne battalion. His NLAWs destroyed the first and last vehicle, trapping the column in the town. Well-placed machineguns raked the column while NLAWs destroyed the BMDs. Communications within his battalion were jammed but, taking advantage of the available internet connection, the battalion resorted to 'WhatsApp' to send messages and call artillery missions on the trapped Russians. Availability of the internet obviously played a vital part in this battle. A local teenager was able to hack into circling Russian drones, providing Zaretsky with the Russians' view of the battle. Based on this data Zaretsky was able to counter the Russian attempt to break out and the Russian battalion was destroyed. Zaretsky credits Elon Musk for providing StarLink satellites and portable dishes which allowed him to defeat the Russians.

By the middle of March 2022, Colonel General Chaiko, Eastern Group, finally established situational awareness and coordinated the efforts of the 35th and 36th CAAs. Ukrainian reinforcements were attacking his western flank. Chaiko was left with two options: (1) break through Ukrainian lines and cut Kyiv's line of communication to the west, or (2) withdraw.

On 21 March 2022, the Russians were positioned to overrun the 72nd Mechanized Brigade. Ukrainian Colonel Olesksandr requested permission to fall back, but General Zaluzhnny denied the request. Lacking available reserves, the general feared that Russia would break into Kyiv if the 72nd retreated. Fighting desperately, firing Javelins, NLAWs and Stingers, with supporting artillery fire, Ukrainian defenders checked the Russian advance. The Russians were unable to bring up sufficient ammunition for their artillery to achieve a breakthrough. Threatened with encirclement from the west, and suffering heavy casualties, Chaiko ordered a retreat.[7] Olesksandr gave credit for the victory in part to the challenge caused by Russians having to cross the Iprin River and to the bravery of the Ukrainian people.[8]

Suffering heavy losses, the Russians transitioned to the defensive. Ukrainians gained the initiative and transitioned to the offensive and began to liberate territory. Russian morale dropped. It was rumoured that the soldiers in the 37th Guards Motorized Rifle Brigade were so demoralized after suffering 50 per cent casualties that a crew ran over their colonel with their tank.[9]

Between 22–25 March 2022, the Russians were pushed back onto their overextended supply lines. Irpin was liberated on 28 March 2022, and Bucha was liberated on 1 April 2022.

Discoveries after the liberation of Bucha shocked the world. Withdrawing Russians had left 400 dead. Bodies of men, women and children were discovered in mass graves and laying out in the open. There was clear evidence that many had been raped and tortured. Many of the men had been bound and executed.[10] It was alleged that the 64th Separate Motor Rifle Brigade of the 35th CAA committed the war crimes. Amazingly Putin awarded the honorary 'Guards' status to the Brigade on 18 April 2022, after emergence of evidence that it had committed such horrific war crimes hit the press. The heavily attritted BTG was then transferred to the Izyum sector where it may have been destroyed.[11] The war crimes discovered in Bucha were only the beginning. As more towns and villages were liberated more war crimes against civilians were discovered. [12]

As Sun Tzu taught thousands of years ago: 'If you know the enemy and yourself, you need not fear the result of a hundred battles. If you know yourself but not the enemy, for every victory you gain you will suffer a defeat. If you know neither yourself nor your enemy, you will succumb in every battle.'[13] The Russian defeat at the Battle of Kyiv was due in part to their grandiose self-delusion of invincibility and their underestimation of the Ukrainian will to resist.

Despite outnumbering the Ukrainian Air Force, Russia failed to gain air supremacy over the battlefield. Flying over 200 sorties per day they failed to defeat the Ukrainian Air Force flying fewer than 10 sorties a day. The Ukrainian air defence denied Russia air superiority. The air defenders continually relocated their anti-aircraft missile batteries, successfully downing Russian aircraft with minimal use of radar. Ukrainian defenders successfully employed a volunteer network of spotters to watch and listen for Russian aircraft, calling in coordinates and estimated speed, altitude, and direction.[14] Mobile tracked or wheeled launchers and MANPADs then ambushed attacking jets and helicopters.

Ukrainian defenders denied Russia control of cities, complicating Russian communication and logistics. Attacking Kyiv from the east was further complicated by the robust defence of major road junctions by Ukrainian forces and partisans. Due to muddy conditions, Russian BTGs racing forward outran their supply columns. Supply columns racing to catch up were ambushed by Territorial units and partisan action. Poor discipline, lack of training, plus intense pressure from Moscow combined to drive the BTGs forward, racing into ambushes while still in administrative formation.[15] The cities of Chernihiv,

Kharkiv and Sumy, located astride the main roads and railways through these muddy regions, were key to the Russian campaign. Defending these cities successfully disrupted the Russian supply lines for the eastern flanking attack on Kyiv.

The invasion force did not have a 3:1 combat ratio against the Ukrainian defenders. Russian planners erroneously assumed little or no opposition. This invalid assumption resulted in thousands of Russian casualties during the first weeks of the invasion.

Russians used encrypted communications to coordinate the manoeuvres of BTGs, but only a few vehicles in each BTG had encrypted radios, resulting in the use of unencrypted radios to communicate between companies and firing batteries. As Russian radio communications failed, leaders reverted to using the local civilian cell phone net, which was monitored by the defenders. This lack of communication security enabled Ukrainian intelligence to target Russian senior officers. During the first six months of the 'Special Operation' forty Russian commanders were killed due to operational security violations.

With communications jammed, Ukraine quickly adapted. Elon Musk had supplied Ukraine with large numbers of Starlink satellites and base stations providing the defenders with alternative communications. The internet provided everyone from the Ukrainian President to his company commanders the ability to communicate and coordinate combat operations. Ukrainians shifted from standard military communications to Starlink internet command and control in a matter of days. Starlink satellite ground stations were an obvious major combat multiplier for the defenders.

The Russian invasion force failed to field sufficiently trained infantry to secure lines of communication and supply. This was a direct result of Putin designating the invasion as a 'Special Operation' instead of a declared war. Russian law prohibited the use of conscripts outside of Mother Russia, denying the invaders hundreds of thousands of troops. An additional 100,000 even partially trained conscripts could have guarded checkpoints along lines of communications and patrolled the main supply routes. Of course, the downside of such a potential augmentation was Russia's inability to feed and supply the 200,000 troops already in Ukraine.

Finally, the Russian defeat comes down to 'Putin's Big Lie'. Russian propaganda to the effect that the Ukrainian military would not fight, and the government would surrender was repeated so many times, that the *souvlaki* and oligarchs apparently believed it to be true. Consequently, they based their logistical support plan on invalid assumptions. As a result, the Russian bear showed up at Kyiv's gate and Ukrainian sheep dogs mauled it and chased it back into the forest.

Chapter 14

Battle for the Donbas
24 February–1 April 2022

The capture of the Ukrainian Donetsk and Luhansk Oblasts was one of the main military objectives of the war. Capture of the Donbas would give Russia control of the rich natural resources of the region and the undeveloped Ukrainian oil/gas fields around the town of Kramatorsk in the Donetsk Oblast. Kramatorsk sits upon the second largest undeveloped gas reserve in Europe, estimated at 1.09 trillion cubic metres of natural gas. While this gas field remained undeveloped, Ukraine had recently entered agreements with Western oil companies to tap this resource. Unlocking this field would undercut Russia's ability to render Europe dependent on its gas surplus.[1] Capturing Kramatorsk would have resulted in the proclaimed 'liberation of the Ukrainian occupied Donetsk Oblast'. An even more important objective was securing a land bridge to Crimea. Capturing the port city of Mariupol, the second-largest city in the Donbas, was critical to establishing a land bridge from Russia to Crimea.

Ukrainians had been fighting the Russians and their allied separatists in the Donbas since 2014. The 2022 Donbas offensive can be divided into two battles, one along the Siversky-Donets River line, linking the cities of Izyum, Lysychank, and Severodenetsk, and the second battle along the fortified zone, linking the cities of Bakhmut, Volnovakha, and Mariupol. Ukrainian positions had been fortified on higher ground with interlocking fields of direct and indirect fire. To attack these positions an invading force had to cross open fields.

At the beginning of March 2022, the 6th CAA and LPR militia captured Svatova. On 4–6 March the invaders continued their advance attacking Izyum.

BTGs from the 20th CAA and 1st Guards Tank Army attacked Izyum. Izyum was the northern anchor of the base of the Donbas salient where four UAF brigades were holding the front. It was also a railhead and, if captured, Russia could have quickly massed supplies and ammunition. With Izyum in Russian hands, the Donbas salient could be cut, trapping the defenders in a pocket.

Shaping operations by the Russians began on 28 February 2022, with an artillery bombardment of Izyum and surrounding towns, in preparation for a ground assault. On 3 March, lead BTGs of 1st Tank Army and 20th CAA attacked the town but met stiff resistance. With the bends and marshes of the Siversky-Donets River region the Ukrainians linked their defensive line into natural obstacles.[2] Between 3–7 March, the battle raged. The Russians gained a toehold in the town, only to be pushed out by a counterattack. Between 9–10 March 2,000 civilians were evacuated out of Izyum under heavy shelling. The seesaw battle for the town continued until 20 March. The Russians eventually were able to get two pontoon bridges across the Siversky-Donets River and tanks were able to enter the town centre. In the heavy fighting 19 Russian engineers were killed, along with their commander, Colonel Nikolay Ovcharenko.[3] Heavy fighting continued throughout March with parts of the city exchanging hands several times. By 1 April, the UAF confirmed that Izyum and surrounding villages were in Russian hands.[4]

Between February and April 2022, the 8th and 49th CAAs conducted frontal attacks against the Popasna, Volnovakha, and Mariupol fortified zones to fix Ukrainians in their defensive positions. The main effort of this offensive was directed at Mariupol.

The Battle for Popasna began on 3 March, when LPR units supported by Russian troops shelled the city, while directing their main attack toward Kreminna farther north. With the fall of Kreminna, Popasna was subjected to heavy shelling by the invaders. The Ukrainian 24th Mechanized Brigade, defending the region, repelled several ground assaults that included mercenaries from Libya, Syria and the Wagner Group.[5] By the beginning of April, the invaders failed to breach the Ukrainian defences.

Battle for Donbas
February– April 2022

1. 49th CAA broke through Ukrainian lines and attacked Mariupol from the east as the 58th CAA attacked from the west. The 58th CAA captured Volnovkha.

2. 8th CAA with 1 & 2 AC attacked Ukrainian entrenched defenders holding the line in Donets and Luhansk Oblast. These attacks made little progress.

3. 1st Tank Army slowly attacked down the Siversky-Donets River toward the Donbas.

4. 6th and 20th CAA slowly attack into Ukrainian Luhansk Oblast toward Siversky-Donets River .

Map Source: UK Defence Intelligence

The Battle for Volnovakha (24 February-11 March 2022) is an operational example of a series of frontal attacks by separatists, supported by the Russian Army. The town of Volnovakha (population 21,000) was a strongpoint near the centre of the Ukrainian defensive zone. The Russian battle plan was to pin the defenders in Volnovakha, in order to cut the lines of communication to Mariupol.

The town and the area around the city were defended by the 53rd Mechanized Brigade, supported by the Ukrainian National Guards' Aidar Assault Infantry Battalion and elements of the Azov and Donbas Battalions. The Ukrainians were initially opposed by DPR's 100th Brigade and the 3rd Separate Guards Brigade. The Ukrainian 53rd Tank Battalion formed a defensive perimeter in the centre of town around the bus station.[6]

Vasyl, a Ukrainian tank driver remembers that on 24 February 2022 his battalion was attacked by tanks and BMPs from two sides. As he was backing up, his tank was hit but remained fully operational. As the battle raged his tank's camo net caught fire and he jumped out to extinguish it. As he fought the fire, a Russian tank appeared 50m in front of him. His gunner fired and blew off its turret. Smoke from the battle obscured their ability to see any other targets, so his tank changed positions and engaged a second enemy tank at 200m. He disabled it and the Russian crew dismounted and fled. The enemy retreated after losing several vehicles, while the 53rd Tank Battalion lost only one tank, from which the crew survived. The DPR brigades assaulted Volnovakha daily until 28 February 2022, when the Ukrainian 53rd was reinforced with the Georgian Legion, 15th Mountain Assault Battalion, 503rd Naval Infantry Battalion and elements of the 54th Mechanized, 56th Motorized (mounted in Gazelle vans) and 109th Territorial Brigades. The DPR was reinforced with Russian units.[7] While the main effort of the 49th CAA was to capture Mariupol, the assaults on Volnovakha resulted in heavy losses of men and equipment in exchange for little territorial gain.[8] On 11 March, the invaders captured Volnovakha, but the town had been reduced to rubble. During the battle, Ukrainian Senior Lieutenant Pavlo Sbytov, commander of the 503rd Naval Infantry Battalion, was killed.[9]

The first phase of the Battle for the Donbas raged from 24 February to early April 2022. It received less news coverage than the Battle of Kyiv, but its outcome was equally as important as the fight for the Ukrainian capital. At first glance, the Russian frontal attacks appeared pointless at the tactical level. However, at the operational level they pinned Ukrainian brigades in place, preventing them from reinforcing Mariupol. This type of operational reasoning was used by the Soviets against the Germans during the Second World War. With top-down decision-making, the failed frontal assaults executed by battalions were justified by operational results. Separatist and Russian soldiers were considered expendable in exchange for the operational and political strategical objective of capturing Mariupol.

Chapter 15

The Naval Battle for the Black Sea Coast

Ukraine, along with the US and Canada, was a major supplier of the world's grains. Ukrainian grain, grown in its rich soil, is particularly critical to the Middle East, North Africa, and the Third World. It was critical to Moscow's war plan to cut Ukraine off from the Black Sea to prevent military supplies from being imported. As a secondary objective Putin wanted to cripple the Ukrainian economy by preventing the commercial export of agricultural products and raw material from the Donbas and steppes to world markets. Of equal importance to Putin was protecting the multi-billion-dollar Kerch Strait Bridge linking the eastern Crimean Peninsula with the Russian mainland.

After the illegal annexation and occupation of Crimea, Russia found itself in a strategic economic crisis. Russia lacked land access to the peninsula and access by sea was problematic. All land routes were controlled by Ukraine. The only solution was to build a 19 km/11mile-long road/rail bridge from the Russian mainland across the Kerch Strait.

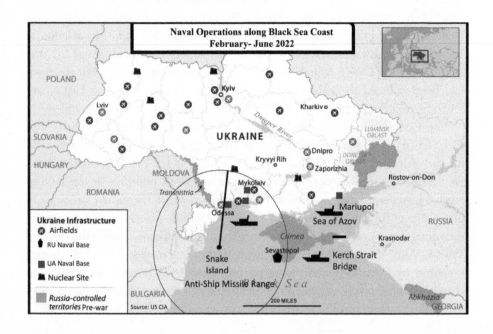

Beginning construction in May 2015, the $3.7 billion bridge was completed in December 2019.[1] The bridge had a separate rail line in addition to several paved lanes for vehicular traffic. If Ukraine could destroy or damage this huge target it would severely damage the local Russian economy and cut the supply line to Russian forces in Crimea, severely embarrassing Putin, and the Russian navy.[2]

The Kremlin believed the bridge was unassailable, being well beyond the range of Ukrainian artillery and missiles. That illusion of safety was dashed on 8 October 2022, when a truck bomb on the highway part of the bridge exploded. The explosion damaged the paved road section and, more significantly, caused the collapse of a section of the rail bridge. In retaliation, the Russians responded with massive missile strikes at civilian targets across Ukraine.[3]

The Crimean Peninsula divides the Ukrainian Black Sea coast in half. Russia had previously illegally annexed the peninsula and the seaport of Sebastopol, leaving Ukraine with its remaining three large deep-water strategic ports on the Black Sea (Mariupol, Mykolaiv, and Odesa[4]) serving as both commercial seaports and naval bases. Tiny Snake Island, off the Romanian coast, controlled the approaches to Mykolaiv and Odesa and commanded a strategic value far larger than its diminutive size.

Snake Island, also known as Zmiinyi Island lies in the midst of the Black Sea. It is 45km/28 miles from Romania and 48km/30 miles from Ukraine. The Greeks called it 'White Island' after a rock formation or the colour of the snakes found there. It was associated with Achilles of Trojan War fame. After his death before the walls of Troy, Achilles' spirit flew to the island. In the legend Achilles' spirit was joined by Helen of Troy.[5]

It was a spooky place and ancient sailors were advised not to sleep over night on the island so as not to anger the gods. A temple to Achilles was built there, the remains of which were in the island museum. In the nineteenth and early twentieth centuries, Snake Island was contested by the Ottomans, Imperial Russia, and Imperial Germany.[6]

The island sits atop significant hydrocarbon deposits. Romania controlled the tiny island until 1948, when it was transferred to the Soviet Union by treaty. Romania disputed the treaty, and the island was eventually returned to Romania upon the dissolution of the Soviet Union.

Ownership of the island was subsequently claimed by Ukraine as it fell within the maritime border dispute between Romania and Ukraine. If the tiny island was so small that it was considered a rock, then under international law the maritime boundary would give ownership to Romania. But if it was considered an island, then the continental shelf around it would be within Ukrainian water. Both countries agreed to submit the dispute to the Hague

International Court of Justice, which split the baby. The 2009 Hague Court ruling determined that the island was within the continental shelf of Ukraine and was therefore owned by Ukraine but divided ownership of the oil and gas resources between Ukraine and Romania.[7]

The placement of a Russian S-400 anti-air missile battery (with a range of 400km/248 miles) or anti-ship missiles (with a range of 305km/190 miles) on the island would not only threaten Odesa, but also NATO's southern flank.[8]

Since the beginning of the war, Putin's Black Sea Fleet followed a classic naval strategy; blockade, bombardment, and amphibious landings.[9] Ukraine's 'mosquito fleet' of patrol boats was rapidly neutralized by the Russians and a blockade of the Ukrainian Black Sea coast was quickly established.

The Russian fleet quickly closed the Kerch Strait and all access into and out the Sea of Azov. This action was intended to protect the Kerch Strait Bridge from Ukrainian attack. Russian ships assumed station off Odesa and other Ukrainian ports. The resulting commercial blockade cut Ukraine's economic supply lines and denied defending combat troops resupply by sea. The illegal blockade also prevented the Middle East from importing the grain it depended upon to feed its population. On 24 February 2022, the fleet launched over a hundred Kaliber land-attack cruise missiles into Ukraine.

Mariupol (pop. 450,000) represented a major maritime target for the Russian fleet. Capturing the city would anchor a land bridge from Crimea into Russia.[10] Russian ships positioned themselves to provide anti-aircraft missile support to tank and infantry units attacking toward the city. By gaining control of the Sea of Azov and the north Black Sea coast, Russia effectively blocked Ukraine from receiving humanitarian aid and military support by sea. Russian ships concentrated on the brutal, indiscriminate bombardment and destruction of civilian targets in Mariupol. Despite some major setbacks, unlike the northern Russian armies, the Black Sea Fleet accomplished its primary mission, with Mariupol falling on 16 May 2022.

With the Port of Odesa successfully blockaded, container ships bound for Odesa were diverted to the Romanian seaport of Constanta, near the mouth of the Danube River.

At the beginning of the Kremlin's naval operations, a company of Ukrainian defenders on Snake Island grabbed headlines with their defiance of the Russian navy's demand for surrender. Despite its tiny size, Snake Island was key to controlling Ukraine's Black Sea coast from the Dnipro River Delta to the Moldovan border. If Russian troops had established long-range anti-aircraft and anti-ship missile systems on the island, they would have been able to dominate Ukraine's western Black Sea coast.

Captain Bohdan Hotsky, 29 years old, of the Ukrainian Border Guards, was assigned to control the island. His unit included thirty Border Guards. The tiny island included living accommodations for the Guards and their families, a radio station, a pier, a lighthouse, and a museum containing Greek artefacts from the temple. There was no fresh water on the island and as a result supplies were flown in weekly for the garrison.

Before the war started, President Zelensky visited the island twice with members of his military intelligence service. A platoon of fifty infantry joined the Guards, increasing the total number of defenders to eighty. The population of the island included two handymen, some sheep, dogs, and more than several feral cats.[11] Civilians and family members were evacuated before the invasion.

Russia's Black Sea Fleet flagship, the cruiser *Moskva*, transmitted this message to the Ukrainian defenders:

'I suggest you lay down your weapons and surrender to avoid bloodshed and needless casualties. Otherwise, you will be bombed.'[12]

The Ukrainian response, 'Russian warship FUCK You,' is now a legendary act of defiance, commemorated by a Ukrainian postage stamp.

Shortly after their defiance the defenders were captured. It was initially believed that they had been killed; however, Russia subsequently released videos of the Ukrainians, and they were released in the early weeks of the war during a prisoner exchange.[13]

The Russian Navy accomplished its strategic objective quickly, but maintaining the blockade became costly and embarrassing as the 'curse of Snake Island' soon took its toll. On 13 April 2022 *Moskva* was patrolling off Snake Island while providing anti-aircraft missile support to the ground attack toward Kherson, when two Neptune anti-ship missiles slammed into her. Losing power, the pride of Russia's Black Sea Fleet sank two days later while being towed to port for repairs. Russia officially acknowledged only that there had been a fire on board causing munitions to explode and that the ship was being towed to port for repairs, later confirming that the *Moskva* had sunk while being towed.

Turkey closed passage of the Bosporus to Russian military ships, prohibiting two reinforcing cruisers from entering the Black Sea. The loss of the cruiser *Moskva* resulted in a gap in the Russian anti-air missile coverage along the western Ukrainian coast. On 2 March 2022, two Russian Raptor assault boats near Snake Island were damaged or destroyed by Ukrainian-operated, Turkish-supplied TB2 armed drones. Ukraine was able to deploy drones over Snake Island only because the *Moskva* had been sunk.

There was no place to conceal Russian naval infantry anti-aircraft and anti-ship batteries on tiny Snake Island. They were at the mercy of various surveillance platforms in the air and in space. Lacking reinforcing ships from the Mediterranean, it became difficult for Russia to maintain its regional anti-aircraft missile umbrella.

Russia suffered other embarrassing naval losses. On 22 March 2022, Ukrainian commandos heavily damaged a Raptor assault boat off Mariupol, using an anti-tank missile to set off ammunition on the ship's deck. On 24 March, a landing ship at a pier in Berdyask was spotted by Ukrainian intelligence. It was destroyed by a Ukrainian OTR-21 Tochka ballistic missile.

Another amphibious landing occurred on an undefended beach 48km/30 miles southwest of Mariupol. Russian doctrine sought to avoid contested amphibious landings due to the vulnerability of the attacking force during an assault landing. As the Russian naval infantry discovered, even the illusion of a secure pier landing can result in devastating casualties. On 21 March 2022, Russian state media aired a report of the tank landing ship, RFS *Orsk*, unloading BTR-82A APCs along the pier at Berdyansk. The empty *Orsk* sailed and was replaced by its fully loaded sister ship, RFS *Saratov*. On 24 March, *Saratov* surprisingly exploded. It was not known whether the ship blew up due to an ammunition handling accident, a Ukrainian cruise missile or a Bayraktar TB2 UAV with smart laser-guided munitions.[14]

The primary defence employed against the Russian navy was coastal defence anti-ship cruise-missile batteries.[15] Rather than fixed defences like old coastal defence artillery, the missile launchers were mobile and tied into a series of targeting radars, and various manned and unmanned intelligence-collection systems. These weapon systems prevented the Russian navy and its naval infantry from closely blockading the Ukrainian coastline.[16]

On 27 June 2022, Ukrainian troops conducted more than ten high precision missile strikes at Snake Island.[17] On or about 30 June 2022, Russian forces abandoned Snake Island. Putin's official position was that the withdrawal was intended to demonstrate that Moscow would not obstruct UN efforts to open a humanitarian corridor, to allow grain to be shipped from Ukraine.[18] This face-saving statement distracts from the fact that tiny Snake Island was a death trap for Russian soldiers. With the resupply of longer ranged missiles from the West, the Russian position on the island became untenable.[19]

Despite Putin's claim, Russia's retreat from Snake Island did not open a humanitarian corridor for grain shipments. The Russian fleet continued in control of the Black Sea. Ukraine rejected Russia's illusionary offer to escort grain shipments.[20] Within hours of a UN-negotiated agreement with Russia to allow grain shipments to commence, Russia bombed the port of Odesa on 23 July 2022 with four Kaliber cruise missiles.

Chapter 16

Ground Conquest of the Black Sea Coast

T he campaign by 58th and 49th CAAs and 22nd Army (Naval Infantry) Corps to capture the Black Sea coast was professional and well-executed. Their military expertise and professionalism were what the world expected of the Russian Army and why the media expected Ukraine to be defeated within a week.

The Ukrainian Black Sea coast was divided into three operational sectors.[1] The Kherson-Odesa Sector ran along the lower Dnipro River from the dam and hydropower plant on the Kakhovka Reservoir (24km/15 miles wide and 240km/149 miles long) at Novo Kakhovka, past Kherson to the Dnipro River Delta. The unfordable Dnipro River, between the dam and the delta is a major strategic obstacle to any attack from the Crimean Peninsula. Three bridges cross the Dnipro, two at Kherson and one at Novo Kakhovka. Failure to capture the bridges would halt a Russian blitz in its tracks and require a major river crossing operation.

The port city of Mykolaiv and its strategic swing bridge across the Southern Bug River are 90km/55 miles along highway M14 to the northwest of Kherson. The Southern Bug River is a strategic military obstacle on the route to Odesa. The terrain between the two rivers is rolling farmland and steppes. The distance

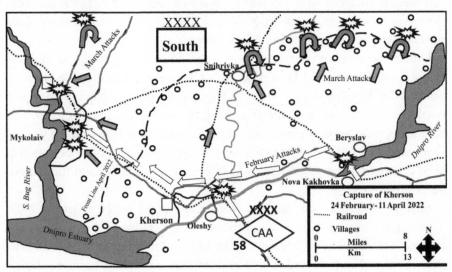

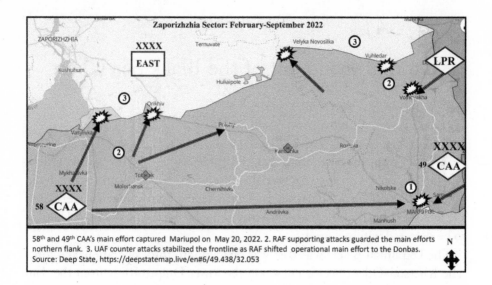

58th and 49th CAA's main effort captured Mariupol on May 20, 2022. 2. RAF supporting attacks guarded the main efforts northern flank. 3. UAF counter attacks stabilized the frontline as RAF shifted operational main effort to the Donbas. Source: Deep State, https://deepstatemap.live/en#6/49.438/32.053

from Novo Kakhovka to Mykolaiv is 190km/118 miles along secondary and unimproved farm roads, through fields and steppe. In February and early March 2022, the steppe and farmland were muddy and off-road movement was difficult for tracked vehicles and impossible for wheeled convoys.

The Kakhovka Reservoir (24km/15 miles wide and 240km/149 miles long) divided the Zaporizhzhya-Dnipro Sector from the Kherson-Odesa Sector. A high-speed approach from the Crimean Peninsula followed highway E105, 367km/228 miles northeast to Melitopol, then north along E105, skirting the reservoir to Zaporizhzhya. There were no strategic obstacles on this axis.

The Melitopol-Mariupol Sector did not have any strategic obstacles for east-west traffic. The strategic port of Mariupol was 192km/119 miles from the traffic transportation hub of Melitopol. The primary and secondary roads traversed steppes, farmland, and minor streams.

Unlike the shaping operations performed during the first day of the war in the Kyiv, Kharkiv, and Donbas sectors, Ukrainian defenders failed to fully protect the Kherson-Odesa Sector. The most obvious shaping operation would have been to destroy the three bridges crossing the Dnipro River. The Kherson-Odesa Sector defence was of secondary importance to the Kyiv and Donbas sectors and was allotted few regular army defenders. If the bridges had been destroyed, the one UAF motorized brigade could have held the Dnipro River line.

Shaping operations on the Kyiv front only started on 24 February 2022. The major bridges at Kherson and the secondary bridge at the dam had not been set for demolition, clearly a case of treason for which 200 local officials were dismissed and charged. These bridges were ultimately destroyed during the Kherson counteroffensive in September. While cutting the supply lines of advancing Russians, destroying the bridges also limited future Ukrainian military options.

Within the Melitopol-Mariupol and the Zaporizhzhya-Dnipro sectors there appeared not to have been any strategic shaping operations by Ukrainian defenders. The Kakhovka Reservoir protected the defenders of the Zaporizhzhya-Dnipro Sector from being outflanked from the west. Once the mud dried in May and June 2022, both sectors became suitable for large-scale manoeuvres of mechanized and motorized formations. The rolling terrain and numerous intervisibility lines rendered the terrain suitable for a mobile defence.

OSK-South's major formations initially included the 58th, 49th and 8th CAA and 22nd (Naval Infantry) Corps, reinforced with VDV Airborne forces serving as ground manoeuvre units. Unlike the Kyiv Sector, the Russians of the 58th CAA and 22nd Army Corps charged forth from Crimea ready to fight. The main effort of this blitz quickly captured its intermediate objective, the road junction at Melitopol, then quickly advanced east to the port of Mariupol. The initial objective of the supporting attack by the 22nd Corps was to capture the bridges over the Dnipro, followed by an intermediate objective of capturing the swing bridge over the Southern Bug River at the port city of Mykolaiv.

During the early evening hours of 24 February 2022, a Russian BTG's forward reconnaissance element (3 APCs) reached the city of Kherson and attempted to capture the critical Antonivka Bridge over the Dnipro. However, when they crossed the bridge, they rolled into an ambush on the west side and were destroyed. The following advance guard successfully crossed and captured the west side of the bridge. During the early hours of 25 February, a Ukrainian counterattack recaptured the bridge, only to lose it again by the end of the day. The Russians probably committed three BTGs to the fight for control of the bridge.

Simultaneously with the battle for the Antonivka Bridge, a second group of three BTGs captured the bridge/dam at Nova Kakhovka. After establishing a bridgehead on the west bank of the Dnipro River, on 25 February, the group turned downriver, unhinging the defence of the Antonivka Bridge. Advancing along the ring road they captured the airport at Kherson.[2]

A Russian forward detachment was despatched on 26 February from the Kherson airport and arrived at the outskirts of Mykolaiv, at 18:52 hours. Twelve Russian tanks attacked Mykolaiv resulting in a three-hour battle with Ukrainian Navy personnel, National Guard, Territorial and militia troops. The Russians fell back from the city and awaited reinforcements. The attack was renewed on 28 February and the battle for Mykolaiv raged for a week.

On 27 February, a second supporting attack by the 58th CAA advanced toward Zaporizhzhya, covering the flank of the 58th CAA main body, as it moved toward Mariupol. This group captured the Zaporizhzhya nuclear power plant. Captured Ukrainian technicians continued working under extremely stressful conditions.[3] The Russian Zaporizhzhya group was too weak to take the city, but successfully protected the flank of the 58th CAA.

As the 22nd Army Corps main force attacked Mykolaiv on 1 March, a BTG attempted to outflank the defenders by attacking through the town of Bashtanka (pop. 12,000). The 50 Territorial soldiers and 16 armed town councillors set up an ambush. The UAF was contacted, and attack helicopters were put on strip alert. A Russian BTG divided into 3 march elements and entered the town. The first element consisting of tanks and APCs was allowed to roll through the town. Armed with only Kalashnikovs (assault rifles), hunting rifles and Molotov cocktails, the defenders could do very little damage to armoured vehicles.

As the second element, consisting of supply trucks and anti-aircraft vehicles advanced, it was ambushed and trapped in the town. The armoured vehicles that had just passed through, turned, and fired back into the town, destroying some buildings and several of their own trapped vehicles. As the Russians retreated, Ukrainian attack helicopters struck, destroying several armoured vehicles.[4]

The Russians had committed a classic mistake, failing to clear an enemy town on the route of advance; in other words, rushing to failure. The textbook procedure would have been to dismount infantry to secure a town or choke point. The BTG had probably rolled through small towns without opposition. With their guard down, their luck ran out at the small, tactically insignificant town of Bashtanka. The cost was the loss of up to several hundred vehicles, including BTR-80 APCs, towed D-301 Howitzers, Pantsir ADA missile vehicles and supply trucks. They also suffered several hundred casualties.[5]

On 3 March, heavy fighting within Mykolaiv forced the Ukrainian Navy to scuttle its frigate *Hetman Sahaidachy* on the South Bug River to prevent it from being captured. Heavy fighting continued for several days, but ultimately the Russians failed to capture the swing bridge spanning the southern Bug River and were forced out of the city.

On 4 March 2022, the Russian attack on a Mykolaiv airbase was repulsed.[6] On 7 March, as the battle for Mykolaiv raged, the Ukrainian Naval Infantry conducted a raid on the Russian occupied Kherson Airbase destroying eighteen helicopters.[7]

By 10 March, it was clear that the two BTGs committed to the battle for Mykolaiv required reinforcements. This task force was reinforced that night and on the morning of 11 March Mykolaiv was attacked from three sides.[8] Only the invader's inability to conduct an assault river crossing of the Southern Bug River prevented the city from being encircled. Russian ground reconnaissance troops, supported by drones, entered the city, only to be defeated by defenders armed with Molotov cocktails.[9] By 13 March it was clear that the Russian main attack to capture Mykolaiv had failed.

Bogged down in Mykolaiv, the Russians attempted to outflank the defenders by capturing the bridge over the Southern Bug River at Voznesensk. On 2 March, a BTG of 400 naval infantry and forty-three vehicles (tanks, APCs, MLRs, and trucks) from the 126th Coastal Defence Brigade (22nd Army Corps), supported by attack helicopters, advanced on Voznesensk.

Voznesensk is 80km/49 miles upriver of Mykolaiv.[10] The citizen militia of Voznesensk had established roadblocks within the city, along the approaches to the bridge. Backed by regulars, the Territorials and militia were armed with assault rifles, hunting rifles, RPGs, Javelins, and artillery.[11] Mi-24 Hind attack helicopters supported the defenders. After heavy fighting, resulting in 100 Russian casualties and the loss of 30 vehicles, the Russians retreated 64km/40 miles to the southeast. Ukrainians were able to capture and salvage 15 tanks.[12]

On 9 March 2022, Russians attacked the town again, this time capturing the bridge. However, during the subsequent counterattack Ukrainian defenders destroyed the bridge and pushed the Russians out of the town. The battle raged in the vicinity of Voznesensk for another week, but the Russian advance toward Odesa was stopped.

Russians had successfully captured their tactical objective, Kherson, and had established a lodgement or beachhead over the Dnipro River. While Russian naval infantry had failed to capture their operational objectives, the bridges over the Southern Bug River, they had established a bridgehead line to protect the bridges over the Dnipro River from Ukrainian artillery fire. They had established a conventional defensive zone between 45–55km/28–34 miles. Soviet-era artillery and American M777 towed 155mm howitzers could not range the bridges over the Dnipro.[13] To protect their control of the Dnipro bridges and the city of Kherson the Russians should have seized the opportunity to gain control of the bridgehead line on the west bank of the Southern Bug River, but they failed to do so, instead concentrating their efforts on taking the Donbas.

Russian failure to capture Mykolaiv and Odesa can be directly attributed to insufficient forces assigned to the 22nd Corps, considering the objectives assigned. BMD, BMP and BTR armoured vehicles are capable of swimming, and could have crossed the Southern Bug River if they had been properly equipped with effective water seals. Knowing that their vehicles were not properly equipped with effective water seals, the Russians did not attempt to cross the river. For want of water seals, the battle was lost.[14]

As the battle for Kherson Oblast raged, the 58th CAA blitzed toward the port city of Mariupol.[15] On 26 February 2022, Mariupol was surrounded by units from the 58th CAA attacking from the west, and units from the 49th CAA attacking from the Donetsk People's Republic (DPR). This successful manoeuvre resulted in the Russians establishing a land bridge between the Donbas and Crimea.[16]

Chapter 17

The Battling Bastards of Mariupol

The siege of Mariupol (pop. 100,000) officially commenced with a Russian artillery bombardment of the city on 24 February 2022, and ended on 20 May 2022, when the last organized resistance surrendered. Between 24–27 February, vastly outnumbered Ukrainian defenders defeated some, but not all, of the 49th CAA units advancing from the DPR.[1]

During the heavy fighting, Russian artillery destroyed large sections of the city. On 14 March Russians allowed an initial evacuation of civilians in over 160 cars. The following day 4,000 vehicles and 20,000 civilians were allowed to leave.[2] However, thousands of the refugees were illegally vectored into Russian territory, literally kidnapped, and dispersed throughout Russia.[3]

Heavy fighting continued, pushing the defenders into the Azovstal and Illich industrial complexes. During the night of 11–12 April, the Ukrainian 36th Naval Infantry Brigade attempted a breakout but failed. Brigade Commander Colonel Baranyuk and his chief of staff, Colonel Kormiankov, were captured along with 160 men. Some of the naval infantry infiltrated and joined the Azov Regiment at the Azovstal plant, while over 1,000 reached the Illich steel plant. Lacking ammunition and medical supplies, they surrendered on 12 April 2022.[4]

The defenders at the Azov industrial complex continued to fight on until 20 May 2022. Like the 'Battling Bastards of Bataan' in the Second World War, the Azov Regiment and Naval Infantry made the Russians pay in blood, beating back repeated Russian assaults between heavy artillery bombardment.[5] There was no hope of Ukrainian forces breaking the siege, yet the heroic 'Battling Bastards' fought on. The Ukrainian government ultimately ordered the defenders to stand down and according to Russian authorities the last defenders surrendered on 20 May 2022.[6]

The 58th and 49th CAA captured their primary objectives. But in hindsight, the 58th CAA should have assigned more BTGs to the 22nd Corps. Additional troops may have resulted in the capture of Mykolaiv and succeeded in creating a viable threat to Odesa. That window of opportunity was closed as more Ukrainian Regular and Territorial forces entered the battle zone.

The deliberate bombardment of civilian targets and infrastructure (such as maternity and children's hospitals) and kidnapping of refugees was well-documented by the media and was investigated by international organizations. Terrorising civilians is justified by Russian military doctrine.[7]

The capture of Mariupol on 20 May 2022 and the opening of the freshwater canal to Crimea was the high point of the Russian ground offensive to capture the Black Sea Coast during the first phase of the war. Putin propagandized the capture of Kherson on 2 March 2022, to divert attention from his defeats at the Battles of Kyiv, Sumy, Kharkiv and Mykolaiv.

Chapter 18

Russian Reorganization After Decisive Defeat

As Russia invaded, its original objectives were to capture Kyiv, replace the Ukrainian government, establish a land bridge to Crimea and liberate the Donetsk and Luhansk Oblasts. On 25 March 2022, without acknowledging their defeat at the Battle of Kyiv, the Russian General Staff announced that the objectives of the war were to liberate the Donetsk and Luhansk Oblasts. With its failure to topple the Ukrainian government, the Kremlin revised its political objectives to align with its diminished military capability. Having accomplished acquisition of the land bridge through occupation of Mariupol, they touted their success to gloss over their defeat before the gates of Kyiv.

Russia withdrew approximately half of the BTGs from the northern CAAs and redeployed them to OSK South to reinforce the Donbas operation.[1] The northern armies remained a viable threat to Kyiv and Kharhiv, forcing Ukraine to leave a counter force in the Kyiv region.

Faced with a humiliating defeat and the poor performance of his first-line combat units, and the incompetence of his OSK generals and their staffs, Putin appointed General Alexander Dvornikov to command the battle for

---

Russian Losses According to Ukrainian Ministry of Defense: 7 April 2022

- 17,300 KIA
- 131 Aircraft
- 130 Helicopters
- 605 Tanks
- 75 Fuel Trucks
- 81 UAVs

- 1723 APC/IFV
- 305 Artillery Pieces
- 96 MLRS
- 1184 Trucks
- 7 Ships
- 54 AAA Systems
- 4 Mobile Tactical Ballistic Missile System

Total Casualties: 86,500 KIA, WIA, MIA and POW. (KIA x 5= Total Casualties)

the Donbas. Dvornikov, age 60, was the first commander of Russia's military operations in Syria. During his tenure (September 2015 to June 2016) Russia provided air support to Assad's regime. Dvornikov's aircraft bombarded densely populated neighbourhoods, causing major civilian casualties. From 2000 to 2003 Dvonikov participated in the lengthy pacification campaign in the Caucasus, including the second Chechen War, that left Chechnya and Grozny in rubble.[2]

Dvonikov faced the same challenge as People's Commissar (later Field Marshal) Semyon Timoshenko before him. During the First Soviet-Finnish War (30 November 1939–13 March 1940) Stalin's invasion force was decisively defeated by the small Finnish Army. Stalin gave overall command to Timoshenko, who then successfully reorganized a demoralized and decimated Soviet Army, leading it to victory. Dvonikov faced the same problems as Timoshenko, but with a shorter timeline. He was given less than four weeks to reorganize and redeploy his demoralized army before the next battle.

Putin's 'Big Lie' led to the death of approximately 17,500 Russian soldiers as of 7 April 2022. Ignored by the press were the estimated 86,000 total number of Russian casualties (5 x KIA = total casualties). Many of the wounded returned to their unit within a few weeks or months, however thousands were permanently disabled.

NATO has published a formula for estimating casualties based on historical record. The formula is used to forecast numbers of required replacements and the level of medical supplies required to support an operation. The formula assumes that 80 per cent of all reported casualties are within the ranks of combat arms, e.g. infantry, tanks, helicopter, and artillery, so of the estimated 86,000 total Russian casualties, it is assumed that up to 68,000 (i.e., 80 per cent) were from Russia's combat arms. This high number of total casualties was supported by the number of BTGs claimed to have been rendered combat ineffective by Ukraine.

Significant problems with the BTG formations surfaced from the first day of the 'Special Operation'. Being ad hoc units, the soldiers and staffs had not trained together, and their composition was not uniform. They were armed with whatever weapons, vehicles, and other equipment were available to their parent brigade or regiment. As an example, a BTG from the 228th Motor Rifle Regiment of the 9th Tank Division mustered 400 personnel, and 40 vehicles, including only 23 APCs, 6 tanks, 6 122mm self-propelled howitzers and 3 MLRS BM-21s. Whereas a BTG from the 57th Motor Rifle Brigade mustered 800 soldiers, and included 60 vehicles, including 30 IFVs, 14 tanks, 6 122mm self-propelled howitzers, 6 152mm self-propelled howitzers, and 6 MLRS

BM-21s. Despite the differences in BTG composition, the CAA staffs treated all BTGs as comparable, without considering their respective capabilities.[3]

During April 2022, Russia massed its BTGs for a major offensive in the Donbas. The BTGs shifted from the Kyiv axis had suffered heavy losses in men and equipment. Some BTGs were merged, intermingling surviving soldiers and officers with strangers. While creating the appearance of combat capable units, the merger caused problems in chain of command, communications, and supply, making the simplest combined-arms operation challenging. BTG and company commanders lead from the front. Intense fighting and heavy causalities had greatly depleted their ranks. Junior officers stepped up to fill senior command and staff positions, denuding companies of leadership as there were no NCOs to fill the void.[4] Command and control issues were somewhat eased when their 152mm howitzer batteries were detached and assigned to artillery tactical groups.[5] Hampering the rebuilding of combat units was the low morale of surviving initial invaders.[6]

On 9 April 2022, Ukraine claimed that it had destroyed 20 BTGs and rendered 40 more combat ineffective, or approximately 30 per cent of Russia's 170 BTGs.[7,8]

The Royal United Services Institute for Defence and Security Studies reported the Russian strength in the war zone, as of April 2022, at 146 BTGs, with only 93 at effective strength, 13 being rebuilt (after being destroyed) and 40 BTGs in reserve.[9] However, many of the reportedly effective 93 were BTGs in name only, being critically short of men and material.

Dvonikov's refitting and reorganization of the 200th Motor Rifle Brigade is an example of Russian 'rushing to failure'. The 200th Brigade had entered battle on 24 February 2022, with its full complement of 1,400 contract soldiers and trained company-grade officers. It had engaged in heavy fighting in the Kharkiv Oblast through June 2022. The Brigade Commander, Colonel Denis Kurilo had been severely wounded on 22 April. His command vehicle took a direct hit, and he was initially reported killed by Ukrainian sources. The 200th Brigade was pulled out of the line to rest and refit near Belgorod with less than 900 effective soldiers. A request to Murmansk for replacements resulted in a mixed volunteer battalion of sailors and logistic specialists filling the Brigade's ranks. Some of the hospitalized soldiers simply disappeared, while others refused to return to their units. Most of their modern T-80 tanks and artillery had been destroyed or captured. When the brigade was ordered to re-enter the fighting in June 2022, it was demoralized and its ranks were filled by inexperienced and badly trained personnel, armed with obsolete equipment.

The 127th Territorial Defence Brigade encountered the 200th Brigade in a village north of Kharkiv. After a series of artillery duels, Ukrainian Brigade

Commander Shevchenko convinced the area artillery command to hold fire, creating the illusion that the defenders were low on ammunition. Amid the lull, drones were deployed to observe the 200th Brigade. Their video feed depicted Russian troops sunbathing, washing, and walking around without body armour. The Ukrainians fired a surprise 40-minute barrage and launched a ground attack the next day. The 200th Brigade was routed, leaving their wounded.[10] In mid-July 2022 an intercepted transmission from a tank company commander within the 200th Brigade, to his platoon leaders shouted: 'Should I show you how to kill Ukrainians? I'll get into a tank myself.' The commander led his 12 tanks into a 92nd Mechanized Brigade kill zone. ATGMs destroyed all 12 tanks, killing the commander and most of the crews.[11] Dvonikov's rush to reorganize was ultimately unsuccessful and resulted in significant casualties.

It became painfully obvious by April 2022, that Russia could not replace the 600 tanks and 1,700 IFVs/APCs lost during the first two months of fighting. The 10,000 tanks reported to be standing by in immediate reserve were a myth. A civilian analyst, using Google Earth, tracked down and posted photos on the internet of many Russian tank storage depots. Thousands of Russian tanks and armoured vehicles were seen rusting away, due to lack of maintenance, while others had obviously been stripped for major parts. It was estimated that only 2,000 tanks could have been made operational within a few weeks, and that an additional 4,000 tanks could have become operational, but only after months of refit.[12] In one case, the commander of the 13th Tank Regiment (4th Tank Division) tank storage depot near Ukraine shot himself when it was discovered that 90 per cent of his tanks were inoperable, as their parts had been stripped and sold on the black market.[13]

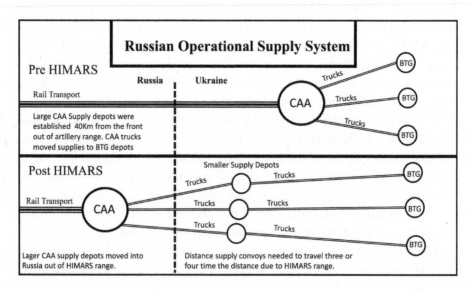

With the failure of the BTGs to achieve decisive results on the northern and northeastern fronts, Dvonikov reverted to Soviet artillery attrition tactics. He stripped artillery from the BTGs and created artillery tactical groups to augment his CAA artillery brigades. The reliance on artillery placed a heavy burden on the supply system, which was already unreliable.

During the first phase, the CAAs and BTGs relied on a limited number of supply vehicles. Russian Military Railroad Brigades (MTS) repaired the captured Ukrainian railroad lines from the border to the frontlines. Re-establishment of the rails corrected the chaotic logistics system and allowed Dvonikov to mass troops and supplies for his Donbas offensive.

Railhead supply dumps in the Donbas Sector were established 30–50km/18–31 miles from the frontlines. CAA trucks moved supplies from the railhead dumps to field depots and ammunition transfer points, located at predictable distances between the frontlines and railheads. Trucks from combat units moved supplies from the forward CAA depots to the front lines. Since the CAA forward depots were beyond Ukraine's Soviet-era artillery range, they became massive and easily detected by drones and satellites.[14] With his troops and supplies massed, Dvonikov opened his offensive on 18 April 2022, with a massive artillery bombardment along the front lines in the Donbas.

Chapter 19

Battle for the Donbas, Summer 2022

With the appointment of General Dvonikov, the Battle for the Donbas entered a second phase. Phase Two commenced on 19 April 2022, as massive artillery and air bombardments prepared the Ukrainian- held Donbas region for a huge ground assault.[1] Putin had given Dovnikov a deadline to achieve at least the illusion of victory by Putin's 9 May 2022 May Day Victory Parade.

General Dvonikov's offensive was expected to unfold like a scaled-down Cold War Soviet front (army group) offensive. Like its Cold War and Great Patriotic War predecessors, Putin's conscript army was led by generals trained in the Soviet art of war. The Russian armed forces had acquired tools of modern warfare: drones, EW, laser-guided and smart munitions, all benefiting from satellite reconnaissance. Significantly however, Putin's stock of precision munitions was limited, (due to profiteering), while Russian magazines and warehouses were bursting with unguided 'dumb' Cold War-era ammunition. Russian armies historically fired massed artillery with devastating results. With modern precision ammunition its artillery should have been even more successful, while using fewer rounds. However, graft and corruption had depleted the stocks of precision ammunition, forcing the Russian armed forces to revert to the imprecise, massed-fire tactics of the First and Second World Wars. As a result, massive ammunition dumps were required behind the front lines.

During the Battle of Kyiv, Russian doctrine was ignored and, in its place, the bureaucratic Russian General Staff placed faith in the effectiveness of employing a swarm of BTGs within each CAA to accomplish the mission, without providing a brigade headquarters to coordinate tactical manoeuvres. In 2008, the Russian Army had reorganized from a division-centric tactical force to a brigade tactical organization. In 2014–2015, it shifted to the new BTG-focused organization, without a corresponding shift in doctrine. The result was uncoordinated battalion attacks, badly supported by CAA. General Dvonikov reverted to brigade-centric doctrinal tactics.

In Russian doctrine, an attack was a rapid non-stop forward movement of tanks BMP and BTRs, supported by intense integrated fire support, to close with an enemy and break his defensive line. In theory the CAAs attacked with its brigades deployed into two echelons, with a tank brigade normally the main effort. Each brigade was assigned an attack zone of 6km/3.7 miles wide, with a strike zone that may be only 2km/1.2 miles wide. The brigades' combat support and service support area extended 10–15km/6–9 miles behind the tanks and infantry. This would mass 120 IFVs or APCs and 30 tanks on a 2km/1.2mile front.

In the offensive, Russian brigades were organized into three combined-arms battalions (infantry and tanks) often with a small armoured reserve. The brigade would focus its efforts on an immediate objective 5km/3 miles behind the enemy frontline and a final objective 15km/9 miles deep in the enemy rear. The first-echelon battalions would defeat the enemy front line. The second echelon would exploit the breach and drive to the immediate objective. The reserve addressed unexpected events or became a forward detachment to pursue a retreating enemy.[2]

Doctrinally, the brigade artillery group (BrAG) was to be deployed 2–4km/1.2–2.4 miles behind the second echelon, in an area 1–2km/0.6–1.2 miles deep by 3–5km/1.8–3 miles wide. An ADA missile battery and MANPADs would protect the infantry and tank battalions, while a second battery protected the BrAG. The BrAG would contain the brigade's organic artillery consisting of one 152mm howitzer battalion and one 122mm MLRS battalion, plus any additional artillery battalions assigned by the CAA. An anti-tank reserve and mobile obstacle detachment (mines) protected the flanks of the brigade. Depending on the operation, additional engineer units could be attached to clear obstacles and deploy tactical bridges for assault river crossings. The brigade HQ provided the combined-arms integration required for a successful attack.[3] The battalions would then form into two echelons for a breakthrough attack, a first-echelon battalion attacking on a frontage of 2km/1.2 miles and 1km/0.6 miles deep.

The Russians were in contact with the Ukrainians. Doctrine provided that the first, fresh echelon battalion would conduct a relief in place of the tired, battalion holding the front line. Stormy weather, smoke fired by artillery or deployed by a chemical company, or bombardment of the enemy position could also be used to conceal the relief in place.

When the attack was launched with heavy bombardment on a 2km/1.2mile frontage, the defenders would have been faced with forty IFV supported by ten tanks. The original defending battalion would then become the second echelon, with an additional forty IFVs and ten tanks (minus previous losses).[4]Executed with his fifty-four BTGs, and adhering to doctrine, General Dvonikov expected these brigade tactics to break the Ukrainian lines at Izyum.

During the Second World War, many of the major battles in western Ukraine involved an attack striking from a salient or attempting to cut off a salient. The Germans attempted to cut off a salient in the famous Battle of Kursk (1943), that ended in its decisive defeat and loss of the strategic initiative for the remainder of the war.

A salient is a bulge in the battle line, often protruding a significant distance into the rear of an opposing combatant. It is formed when an attacker penetrates an opponent's rear, but is then contained by the defender, or when a defender holds key terrain at all costs during a fighting withdrawal. A salient can be a springboard for attack into an opponent's rear and it hampers lateral movement of the defender's reserves. However, since a salient extends the frontline, it is defended by more troops than are required to hold a straight defensive line. There is a real danger that a salient will become a death trap if the opponent cuts the base, trapping the defenders in the pocket or cauldron.

To trap enemy units in a salient, an inner and outer cordon must be established. The inner cordon keeps the trapped units from breaking out, while the outer cordon prevents relief forces from breaking in. To be successful, the attacker needs a ratio of 3:1 at the breakthrough strike zone and almost 5:1 to establish the inner and outer cordon to maintain sufficient manoeuvre forces to block a relief force.

At the Battle for the Donbas, seventy-four BTGs were massed, twelve of which had not been previously committed to combat. Of these seventy-four BTGs, fifty-eight had been committed along the Iyzum axis and had just fought at the frontlines for almost fifty straight days without an operational pause. Many were shifted into the Donbas with little or no time to rest or refit.[5]

On paper, this concentration of force massed the equivalent of 56,000 combat troops with their 700–1,000 tanks and 1,260 artillery systems. While the actual field strength was not officially reported, it was known that these BTGs had recently and continually been in combat and had suffered significant losses of men and equipment.

A salient had been formed in the Donbas as a result of the fighting in 2015. The salient was delineated by the border of the unrecognized Luhansk People's Republic to the south and east and the Russian border on the north and northeast. The six Ukrainian brigades holding the Donbas salient, and its shoulders (6 tank and 12 mechanized/motorized battalions) theoretically fielded 15,000 combat soldiers, manning 180 tanks, and 12 battalions of infantry in APCs and IFVs. These combat formations were supported by artillery, anti-aircraft, combat support and combat service support units. On paper, there were 44,000 defenders in the Ukrainian Donbas Battle Group, however like the Russians they had suffered significant losses.[6]

Initially, the Ukrainians appeared to be over-matched. Combat ratios are not computed by simply counting the number of tanks and soldiers on each side. It should be remembered that the NLAWs and Javelin Anti-Tank Missiles had an effective range similar to the T-72 tanks, used by both sides.[7] In the defence, a Javelin- or NLAW-armed Ukrainian infantry squad, transported in a light APC, was the equivalent of a T-72 tank under most situations.

The Ukrainians were well-armed and greatly motivated to defend their homeland. Russian atrocities against civilians and horrific documented war crimes added to their motivation, whereas most Russian units had previously faced defeat with heavy casualties. As a famous maxim of Napoleon points out: 'in war the moral is to the physical as three is to one'.[8]

On 18 April 2022, Russia began an intense bombardment along the front lines in the Luhansk, Donetsk, and Kharkiv Oblasts.[9] The massive bombardment had three functions. First it covered the redeployment of Russian forces into the Donbas, specifically into the area of the Izyum-Slovyansk Sector. Secondly, it disrupted the Ukrainian defenders and created weaknesses to be exploited by massing armour and mechanized BTGs. Finally, the indiscriminate bombardment terrorized the Ukrainian civilian population. The frontal assaults in the Donetsk and Luhansk Oblasts continued to pin down Ukrainian combat units, preventing them from being redeployed.

In support of preparing for the second phase of the Battle for the Donbas, fixing attacks from Kherson, north along the Dnipro River toward the cities of Zaporizhzhia and Dnipro, continued to pin down defenders. Fixing attacks on the defenders of Kharkiv Oblast protected the northern flank of the main assault on the Izyum-Slovyansk axis.[10] A final supporting effort was deployed to threaten Kyiv. Approximately twenty-two heavily attritted BTGs remained north of Ukraine, in Belarus and Russia, to maintain a viable threat to Kyiv, requiring Ukrainians to maintain a substantial defensive force in the region.[11]

Dvonikov's tactics followed the new Russian doctrine and tactics. Russian brigades and CAAs would have attacked in at least two echelons. CAAs had a third echelon that functioned as an operational manoeuvre group. Reconnaissance or troops in contact would locate a weak spot in the enemy lines that would become a strike zone. Massed artillery fire would then target defenders and the first echelon would assault, breaking through the weak spot. The second echelon would pass through the breach and strike shallow into the enemy rear, surrounding the strong point. The third-echelon operational manoeuvre group would pass through the breach and drive deep into the enemy rear to create a cordon or attack enemy logistics.[12]

Dvonikov's operational plan included two such attacks. The main effort and northern arm of the Russian main attack massed northeast of Izyum, while the southern supporting attack massed behind the front lines, west of Donetsk City, assigned to capture the fortified city of Posasna, and then drive north to link with the force from Izyum.

Dvonikov's shaping operations utilized heavy firepower to cover the probing attacks and to weaken Ukrainian defenders. As the BTGs redeployed from Kyiv and other sectors, the Russians continued their tactical pattern of committing small collections of units to attack on a widely dispersed multiple axis. Russian generals decided to delay an operational pause until after the Battle of the Donbas in order to maintain pressure on the defenders and set conditions for a decisive battle. As a result, the BTGs newly redeployed from combat in the Kyiv Sector, arrived for the main offensive in the Donbas tired and demoralized.[13]

Operationally, the second battle for the Donbas raged from 18 April to 16 July 2022. The objective of the operation was to surround four to six brigades within a pocket or cauldron. During the fighting General Dvonikov's campaign plan was repeatedly modified as his forces suffered tactical defeats. After each defeat his operational goals became less ambitious.

During the initial fighting (7 April-1 May), Dvonikov attempted a pincer movement with attacks from Izyum and Posasna in order to cut the Donbas salient and trap six Ukrainian brigades in a large pocket.[14] The attack by the 1st Guards Tank Army failed to achieve decisive results. Between 19 and 30 April 2022, the attack from Izyum south advanced only 19km/12 miles on two very narrow axes. After two weeks of heavy combat, the attack from Svatove

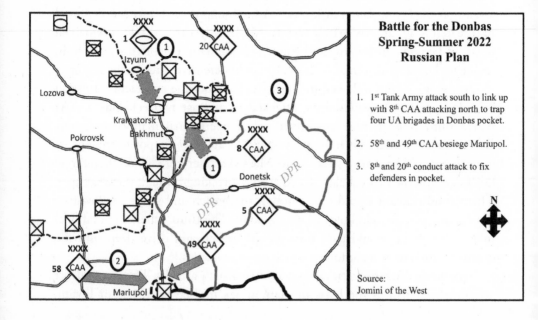

Battle for the Donbas
Spring-Summer 2022
Russian Plan

1. 1st Tank Army attack south to link up with 8th CAA attacking north to trap four UA brigades in Donbas pocket.

2. 58th and 49th CAA besiege Mariupol.

3. 8th and 20th conduct attack to fix defenders in pocket.

Source:
Jomini of the West

to Lyman had advanced 56km/35 miles. No breakthrough into the Ukrainian rear happened on either axis. Local Ukrainian counterattacks hampered the flanks of the assault from Izyum. After advancing only 28km/17 miles from Izyum, the 1st Guard Army attack had culminated.

When the northern arm of the pincer failed, Dvonikov shifted east, and during 1–10 May attempted a shallower envelopment by assault river crossings of the Siversky-Donets River. When these attempts failed, Dvonikov shifted his main effort to the southern pincer.

Posasna was captured by 24 May. The loss of this city threatened the Ukrainian main supply route to Lysychansk and Severodonetsk. Between 24 May and 25 June, Dvonikov shifted the main effort to the south, and pushed into the rear of Lysychansk and Severodonetsk, while conducting supporting frontal assaults to pin the defenders in the ruins. As the jaws of the shallow pincer started to close on 25 June, the Ukrainians withdrew from the ruined cities.

The offensive commenced on 18 April 2022. The battle would last until 15 July. Between 18 April and 19 May, the main effort, by the 1st Tank Army and 6th CAA (54 BTGs) attacked the salient at its northern base from Izyum. As the supporting effort, the 8th CAA attacked the southern base at Posasna. Fixing attacks by the 20th CAA hammered Severodonetsk and Lysychansk from the east.

In late April, the Russian 1st Guards Tank Army attacked south from Izyum. Heavy resistance slowed the advance and the attack only covered 23km/14 miles by 4 May. On that same date the 2nd CAA reached the gates of Lyman near the Siversky-Donets River.[15]

In the south, the Russians were successful against the southern Ukrainian anchor, at the fortified city of Posasna. Fighting as projected in three echelons, the 8th CAA successfully employed Soviet breakthrough tactics. The terrain was very flat and initially all attempts of the first echelon to directly assault the city failed. Territorial battalions from Dnpiro and Zaporizhzhia were sent as reinforcements to defend Posasna and were deployed in the gaps between the fortified city and surrounding towns. Detecting this deployment, the Russians employed their first-echelon units to fix the defenders of Posasna and the second echelon to punch through the gap defended by the Territorials. Their third echelon then passed through the gap and manoeuvred into the Ukrainian rear, cutting off Posasna. On 7 May, Posasna was captured with the assistance of the far-right Wagner Group mercenaries spearheading the frontal attack. After breaking though, the Russians then attacked north, west and south, expanding their penetration. They made slow advances from Posasna but by 24 May the invaders were threatening highway T1302, the main supply route (MSR) to Lysychansk and Severodonetsk. On 29 May, the Russians cut T1302, leaving the defenders one supply road that was in range of Russian artillery.

After two weeks of heavy fighting, the northern arm of the pincer failed to break through the defences south of Izyum. By the beginning of May, Dvonikov realized that while he had succeeded in the south, his attempt to form a cordon anchored at Izyum and Posasna had failed. He shifted his main effort east, from the 1st Guards Tank Army to the 2nd CAA and attempted a less-ambitious plan to isolate Severodonetsk and Lysychansk.

On 2 May, the first Russian attempt to cross the Siversky-Donets River failed. The second attempt, on 4 May, also failed. On 9 May, a brigade with at least two BGTs attempted a crossing at Bilohorivka, with the objective of cutting the northern supply route to Lysychansk and Severodonetsk. The attempt was discovered by Ukrainian scouts and drones as a pontoon bridge was being deployed. On 10 May 2022, one tightly massed BTG finally crossed the bridge, while a second BTG massed north of the river preparing to cross. The Ukrainian 17th Tank Brigade's artillery fired a surprise massive barrage, knocking out the pontoon bridge, causing heavy casualties and stranding a BTG on the Ukrainian side of the river.

Over the next three days the Russians attempted to get a second pontoon bridge operational but heavy Ukrainian artillery fire disrupted the effort and hammered the Russians who had crossed the river. Desperate to escape the trap, a Russian tank company (8 tanks) drove into the river, with its guns positioned to fire over their back deck. All eight tanks bogged down in the river. While the fate of their crews is unknown, they may have attempted to swim toward the illusion of safety on the Russian occupied bank. The Russians lost 30 vehicles and an additional 40 were damaged. At least 485 Russians were killed in the failed river crossing. One BTG was destroyed and a second BTG was rendered combat ineffective.[16]

With the failure to cross the Siversky-Donets River, Dvonikov shifted his main effort to the southern flank of the salient. The 2nd CAA continued south to capture the northern bank of the Siversky-Donets River and the city of Lyman. Dvonikov changed tactics from attempting a Second World War-style armoured breakthrough to a more methodical, limited-objective attack to grind down the defenders. Instead of seeking to create one large pocket, Dvonikov shifted tactics to create a series of small pockets by small, limited ground attacks, supported by massive artillery bombardment.

Russian doctrine approached fighting in urban terrain differently than in the open. The battalions still fought in echelons, but the lead wave consisted of squads and platoons seeking to capture key buildings and locate and isolate strong points. The follow-on echelon, supported by tanks and IFVs, were to neutralize enemy strong points.[17] These tactics eventually ground down the Severodonetsk defenders.

To take pressure off the Donbas, the Ukrainians attacked on 16 May and established a bridgehead over the Siversky-Donets River, 26km/16 miles upriver from Iyzum. They continued to advance toward Rudneve and Ivanivka, only to be stopped by the 38th and 64th Separate Motor Rifle Brigades. This attack threatened the 1st Guards Tank Army's supply lines.

Between 16 and 18 May, another bridgehead over the Siversky-Donets River was created by the 92nd Mechanized Brigade at Staryl Saltiv, 120km/74 miles upriver from Iyzum, and just east of Kharkiv. A counterattack by the 27th Separate Guards Motor Rifle Brigade and LPR militia stabilized the situation.

During the week of 26 May, the Russian 90th Guards Tank Division finally captured Lyman. The Ukrainian 3rd Tank, 57th Motorized, 79th Air Assault and 128th Mountain brigades and 15th Slavic National Guard Regiment were pushed south of the Siversky-Donets River.

By 28 May, 80 per cent of Severodonetsk fell to the Wagner Group, Chechen Battalion and supporting army units. As the 2nd Army Corps pushed into the city, the 111th and 115th Territorial Defence Brigades withdrew over the river into Lysychansk. The Ukrainian 17th Tank Brigade held the Russian 127th Motor Rifle, 57th Separate Guards Motor and 336th Separate Naval brigades at bay, south and southeast of Lysychansk. The situation became untenable and Ukrainian senior leaders ordered a withdrawal before the defenders were cut off.

On the south side of the shrinking salient, Russian naval infantry along with the Wagner Group forced the 24th Mechanized Brigade and Donbas Battalion to retreat to Soledar, Vrubivka, and Vasylivka, along the MSR (T1304 highway). On 27 May, Lyman was finally captured by the Russians and on 30 May Lysychansk was captured. The Ukrainians established a new defensive line 20km/12 miles to the east.[18]

The result of the second phase of the Battle for the Donbas was a Russian tactical victory, despite an operational failure. The Russians had captured the ruins of Siverodonetsk and Lysychansk, successfully eliminating the Donbas salient and pushing the front line back 20km/12 miles, but they failed to trap any Ukrainian brigades in the pocket. The fortress cities of Bakhmut, Solviansk-Karatorsk, Avdiivka, Kurakhove and Mariinka blocked their path west. Their army was exhausted.[19]

After an operational pause between 4 and 16 July, fighting continued in the Donbas. Despite claims of villages being captured and lost, the Russians made no significant gains between 16 July and 31 August.

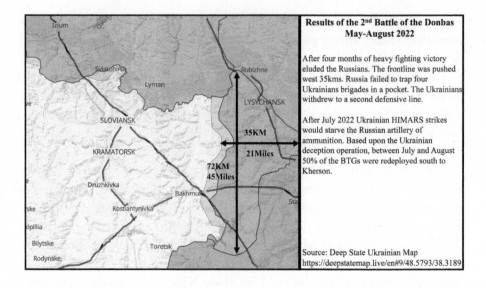

Results of the 2nd Battle of the Donbas May-August 2022

After four months of heavy fighting victory eluded the Russians. The frontline was pushed west 35kms. Russia failed to trap four Ukrainians brigades in a pocket. The Ukrainians withdrew to a second defensive line.

After July 2022 Ukrainian HIMARS strikes would starve the Russian artillery of ammunition. Based upon the Ukrainian deception operation, between July and August 50% of the BTGs were redeployed south to Kherson.

Source: Deep State Ukrainian Map
https://deepstatemap.live/en#9/48.5793/38.3189

Starting in June 2022, the threat to Russian held Kherson became a serious problem. With the threat of a Ukrainian counteroffensive materializing in the south, Russians reduced their force in the Donbas, shifting south into Kherson Oblast. As an example, forty-two BTGs from the 1st Guards Tank Army were transferred south, leaving the 1st Guards Tank Army with only twelve BTGs in Izyum fighting to capture the Donbas. Distracted by the obvious threat in the south, the Russians were oblivious to the hidden Ukrainian build up behind the lines in Kharkiv Oblast.

US Army Major General David Baldwin, Adjutant General of the California National Guard, Ukrainian President Volodymyr Zelensky and California Lieutenant Governor Eleni Kounalakis visit 129th Rescue Wing at Moffett Air National Guard Base, California, 2 September 2021 as part of SPfP. (*CNG PAO*)

Ukrainian soldiers conduct training with Javelin in Donbas, 23 December 2021. (*https://mil.in.ua/en/news/the-ukrainian-military-conducted-training-with-javelin-in-donbas/*)

Ukrainian Naval Infantry (Marine) training with the NLAW. (*https://mil.in.ua/en/news/ukrainian -marines-master-nlaw-anti-tank-missiles-and-m141-grenade-launchers/*)

TOS-1 220mm Thermobaric Rocket Launcher (MLRS). Range 0.6 to 6km. (*US Army Vehicle Recognition Card*)

T-64M tanks of the Azov Battalion defend Mariupol, March 2022. (*https://mil.in.ua/en/news/the-t-64b1m-tanks-engaged-in-combat-with-the-russians-on-the-streets-of-mariupol/*)

Ruins of a Ukrainian residential area in Mariupol, May 2022. (*Azov Regiment. https://mil.in.ua/en/news/defenders-of-mariupol-at-the-azovstal-plant-keep-fighting-against-russian-invaders/*)

On 15 March 2022, Ukrainian infantry capture a BMP-4 from Russian paratroopers near Kyiv. (*https://mil.in.ua/en/news/the-ukrainian-military-has-captured-the-russian-bmd-4/*)

Black Sea Fleet flagship RFS *Moskva*. On or around 14 April 2022 she was hit by two Neptune anti-ship missiles and sank two days later. (*https://mil.in.ua/en/news/the-first-photos-of-the-russian-moskva-cruiser-before-flooding-have-appeared/*)

T-64BV tanks of the Ukrainian 57th Brigade, Luhansk Oblast, 30 March 2022. (*https://mil.in.ua/en/news/kost-gordienko-brigade-uses-lined-t-64-russian-invaders-for-spare-parts*)

A destroyed Russian T-64, Luhansk Oblast, March 2022. (*UA MoD and 57th BDE, https://mil.in.ua/en/news/kost-gordienko-brigade-uses-lined-t-64-russian-invaders-for-spare-parts/ mil.gov.ua*)

At the beginning of the invasion Turkish Bayraktar TB2 drones provided Ukraine with the capability to strike Russian supply convoys without risking pilots. Throughout 2022 drones of all sizes have revolutionized intelligence collection and strike capabilities from the tactical squad/section level to strategic deep strikes into the combatants' rear. (*https://mil.in.ua/en/news/romania-wants-to-purchase-18-bayraktar-tb2-drones/*)

Drones of the UA 71st Brigade located Russian tanks, BMP-3s and troops seeking cover in a forest, August 2022. (*https://mil.in.ua/en/news/71st-brigade-s-drones-assisted-the-artillery-in-accurately-hitting-the-russian-armored-vehicles/*)

Damage to the Antonivka Bridge in Kherson caused by a HIMARS rocket launcher, 27 August 2022. (*https://mil.in.ua/en/news/a-satellite-photo-of-the-antonivskyi-bridge-in-occupied-kherson-appeared-after-the-strikes-of-the-armed-forces-of-ukraine/*)

Germany provided a battalion of Panzer Howitzer 2000 armoured self-propelled artillery. (*Germany Ministry of Defense*)

The UK broke the stalemate on shipping modern tanks to Ukraine by offering Challenger 2 tanks. (*Public Domain*)

The US agreed to send a battalion set of M1A1 Abrams tanks to Ukraine in 2023. (*US Army*)

Chapter 20

Twenty-first Century Lend Lease and the Arsenals of Democracy

On 24 February 2022, NATO countries, the EU, and other allies thought themselves to be neutral, as the US sought to be in 1940. In the twenty-first century however it was Russia, rather than the Nazis, presenting a clear and present danger to world order and European security. Fully aware that direct confrontation with Russia could lead to nuclear Armageddon, NATO and others hesitated to enter the conflict. The solution was a programme much like the 'Lend Lease' of the Second World War, fashioned to provide weapons, humanitarian aid and economic support to Ukraine despite Putin's nuclear sword-rattling.[1] It should be noted that various weapons, from various allies, had been provided to Ukraine prior to, and in anticipation of, the invasion. As an example, in January 2022 the UK had shipped 2,000 anti-armour missiles to Ukraine.[2]

The US, UK and Poland took the lead in organizing military and humanitarian assistance to Ukraine. In 2022, forty countries sent financial, humanitarian and military aid, with the US, UK, Poland, and Germany providing the lion's share.[3] Smaller countries such as Latvia, Estonia and

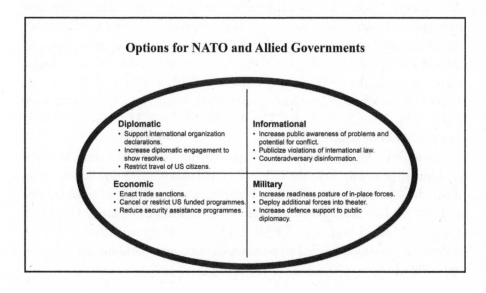

Options for NATO and Allied Governments

Diplomatic
- Support international organization declarations.
- Increase diplomatic engagement to show resolve.
- Restrict travel of US citizens.

Informational
- Increase public awareness of problems and potential for conflict.
- Publicize violations of international law.
- Counteradversary disinformation.

Economic
- Enact trade sanctions.
- Cancel or restrict US funded programmes.
- Reduce security assistance programmes.

Military
- Increase readiness posture of in-place forces.
- Deploy additional forces into theater.
- Increase defence support to public diplomacy.

Lithuania provided less assistance but proportionally their contributions represented a larger percentage of their military budget than the aid sent by any other country.[4]

President Zelensky contacted NATO on 28 February 2022 requesting a 'no-fly zone' be established over Ukraine.[5] A debate in the media over the pros and cons of establishing such a no-fly zone lasted into the middle of March 2022.[6] President Biden and NATO leaders quickly acknowledged that taking such action against a peer adversary would potentially put NATO pilots at risk from Russian aircraft. The risk of escalation into an expanding, potential Third World War was foreseeable.[7] Despite international pressure, NATO rejected the request to establish a no-fly zone.

Each country had laws governing the transfer of military and economic aid to foreign allies. Generally, the chief executive, president, or prime minister had the authority to provide military equipment up to a certain value, without seeking legislative approval. In the US for example, President Biden had approved providing material to Ukraine before the war started, based upon prior congressional authorization.

Total US aid as of 18 November 2022 was $68 billion (FY 2023 Budget) with an additional $37.7 billion projected to be added in spring 2023.[8] The US committed $1.3 billion in security assistance to Ukraine between 1 January 2021 and 23 Febuary 2022. Between 24 February and 10 November 2022 the US provided an additional $18.6 billion. The aid was divided between 'Short-Term Military Support, Long-Term Military Support, US Military Operations, Humanitarian and Financial'.

'Short-Term Military Support' included the transfer of weapons (both American and those purchased from allies), training of Ukrainian soldiers, and intelligence sharing. This Congressional appropriation covered the backfill of equipment and ammunition to replace US stores. The equipment itself had already been paid for and came from American stockpiles. As an example, night vision goggles (NVGs), body armour, individual equipment, small arms, HIMARS rocket launchers and ammunition of all types transferred were replaced by American industry. The 200 M113 series APCs were outdated and would not be replaced within the American inventory.

'Long-Term Military Support' consisted of funds for Ukraine to buy new equipment, primarily from the US, as Ukraine was not in a position to equip themselves with modern armament. Equipment ordered in 2022 would not be available till late 2023. As an example, Ukraine ordered eighteen HIMARS and six NASAMS Surface to Air Missile Systems, along with drone-jamming systems, all of which needed to be manufactured and could not be delivered until 2023.[9]

The funds for US Military Operations covered the deployment of 18,000 troops to Europe as a deterrence to further Russian aggression. The cost of the deployment exceeded the DoD base budget for FY 2022. The aid package added funds required for all US military operations within NATO and covered the cost of a wide range of activities to support Ukraine.

The remaining $37,000,000,000 was humanitarian and financial aid to help Ukraine rebuild its damaged economy and civil infrastructure. Like the 'Marshall Plan', this type of aid helped rebuild Europe after the Second World War. The first $5,000,000,000 was to be spent in FY 2022 and 2023. The remaining $11,000,000,000 was scheduled to be spent during FY 2024 and FY 2031.[10]

Officially, over fifty countries provided more than $41,400,000,000 in aid to Ukraine.[11] Unofficially, the sum was probably closer to $50,000,000,000. The burden of assistance to Ukrainian refugees is not reflected in either number.

The UK and Germany provided substantial military support. The EU and Canada provided significant financial and humanitarian aid. Poland and the Baltic countries provided the highest level of support in proportion to their economies, understandably as they see the Russian bear sitting on their border.[12]

The aid was tailored by NATO's perception of the situation on the ground and Ukraine's requests. During Phase 1 (February-April 2022), weapons and equipment provided were of the type Ukrainian soldiers and militia could use with little or no training. By 15 March 2022, major items sent by the US included 800 Stinger MANPADs, 2,000 Javelins, 6,000 AT-4s and 1,000 other man-portable anti-armour systems. Previous shipments included 600 Stingers and 2,600 Javelins, 4 counter-mortar and 4 counter-artillery radar systems, satellite imagery computers along with EW, C2 equipment, light tactical vehicles, small arms, ammunition, and body armour.[13] The UK shipped individual equipment, small arms, anti-tank missiles, MANPADs and ammunition. The Poles, and other former Soviet Republics and former Warsaw Pact members transferred Soviet-era tanks, self-propelled howitzers, and mobile rocket launchers to Ukraine. The equipment provided was all simple to operate, or at least basic enough that a soldier or militiaman could learn to operate it with a few hours of instruction.

Germany faced initial political divisions within its government. Since the Second World War Germany had a policy of never sending weapons to a combat zone. Germany's initial response to Ukraine's urgent plea was to announce that it would send 5,000 helmets and a field hospital to Ukraine. This announcement was met by outrage from Ukraine and other EU countries, as well as the German public. On 26 February 2022, Germany reversed its policy and announced it would send 1,000 anti-tank weapons and 500 Stinger

MANPADs. It also authorized Netherlands to ship 500 rocket-propelled grenades and Estonia to send nine Soviet-era howitzers despite both weapons containing components made in Germany.[14] Once this political hurdle was removed, Germany began to provide substantial military aid in all categories except tanks.[15]

President Zelensky's requests for heavy equipment included T-72 tanks, S-300 SAM/Buk air defence systems or Western equivalents, Multiple Launch Rocket Systems (MLRS) or American High Mobility Artillery Rocket Systems (HIMARS), military aircraft and NATO 155mm howitzers.[16] Both MRLS and HIMARS fired multiple guided rockets, with a range of 80km/50 miles. A request for the Army Tactical Missile System (ATACMS) with a range of 300km/190 miles was denied because it would have provided Ukraine with the ability to strike within 'Mother Russia'.[17]

After the victory at the Battle of Kyiv, Ukraine's requirements changed. The Battle for the Donbas was fought on the steppes of eastern Ukraine and had become an artillery duel. Ukraine required modern artillery and counter-battery radars. Original NATO members did not have the Soviet-made 152mm howitzer ammunition requested by Ukraine, and instead provided NATO artillery, that fired standard and precision 155mm artillery munitions.[18] These NATO howitzers did not give Ukraine the ability to outgun Russia but did allow precision strikes against ammunition dumps, fuel depots and command posts. Successful firing of these weapons starved Russian guns of ammunition, rendering coordinated fire more difficult.[19]

In response to President Zelensky's request, original NATO members (US, France, Germany, the UK, Canada, and Netherlands) quickly dispatched eight-plus battalions of modern 155mm towed and self-propelled howitzers, along with counter-battery and counter-mortar radar systems and tons of ammunition.[20] While authorizing HIMARS and MRLS to be transferred to Ukraine, President Biden limited the ammunition to smaller rockets, with a range of 80km/50 miles. He feared that the long range ATACMS would escalate the war if Ukrainians fired into Russia.

Due to effective strikes by HIMARS and MRLS, Russia moved its railhead supply depots back into pre-war recognized Russian territory. To destroy these ammunition dumps Ukraine requested ATACM rockets for their HIMARS and MRLS systems. The US had repeatedly denied this request. President Biden's position on this issue was that, to prevent the war from escalating and spreading, ATACMs would not be provided. Escalating the war was a primary concern for some of the smaller former Warsaw Pact and Soviet Republic members of NATO.

NATO sent a total of almost 500 light armoured vehicles, consisting of IFVs (BMPs), APCs (M-113s), and more-modern vehicles such as the German PbV-501s.[21]NATO members in possession of old Soviet equipment (Poland, Czech Republic, Germany, Slovakia etc.) opened their Cold War storage depots and sent replacement weapons to Ukraine with 152mm and 122mm ammunition. Cold War stocks of operational T-72 Tanks were shipped to Ukraine on 24 February 2022 by the Czech Republic. Other countries quickly followed the Czech example.[22]

In April 2022, members of the German government planned to provide 2 battalion sets of older Leopard IA5 tanks (a total of 88) with their 105mm guns and 100 old Marder IFVs.[23] The defence contractor Rheinmetall was ready to refurbish these vehicles for combat and to include an additional 20 new Leopard II tanks to the shipment. If the deal had gone through Germany would have been the first NATO country to provide Ukraine with both obsolete and modern tanks. However, in April 2022 German Chancellor Olaf Scholz blocked the transfer.[24]

There was much internal criticism of Chancellor Scholz's action. Germany had evoked a contract clause that precluded other countries from transferring German-made tanks to Ukraine. While blocking the transfer of main battle tanks, Chancellor Scholz did send other heavy armoured vehicles, such as the Flakpanzer Gepard and Panzer Howitzer 2000. Germany became the third-largest supplier of weapons to Ukraine, excluding modern tanks.[25]

Chancellor Scholz's government offered several logistical and political explanations for refusing to provide tanks. Modern battle tanks such as the M1A1 Abrams or the German Leopard II had not been provided to Ukraine.[26] Modern tanks are complex weapons systems, requiring 22 weeks to train a crewman, 24 weeks for a tank mechanic and longer for depot-level maintenance personnel. In addition, a heavy maintenance infrastructure and readily available spare parts were required.[27] As an example of this problem, after months of constantly firing 300 rounds a day, the 18 Panzer Howitzer 2000s (on Leopard II hulls) had to be removed to a NATO county for depot-level repairs and maintenance.[28] The logistical problems obviously could have been addressed, leaving the real stumbling block a political one.

Chancellor Scholz's government took the position that since no other country had delivered modern tanks, Germany would not be the first to do so.[29] Economically, Germany had business interests tied to Russian natural gas and each new weapon supplied to Ukraine constituted a threat to its continuance. The final issue was a realistic fear that providing such deadly armaments would escalate the conflict.[30] Scholz' government also took the position that NATO and allied countries armed with Leopard II tanks were contractually prohibited from transferring these weapons to Ukraine.

In response to German reluctance, a coalition of countries formed to pressure Scholz into changing the policy. The campaign was aimed at embarrassing Germany for not readily providing the badly needed Leopard II tanks to Ukraine. The campaign was launched by two Finnish politicians and lead to a coalition of countries armed with Leopard IIs to furnish Ukraine a tank brigade of 90–100 tanks. Pro Ukrainian civil demonstrations erupted throughout Germany and across Europe. The call to action was 'free the Leopards'.[31]

The impasse between Biden and Scholz lasted into January 2022.[32] To mount a successful counterattack in the spring and summer of 2023, Ukraine requested 300 modern tanks, 600–700 IFVs and 500 self-propelled howitzers. This equipment would be sufficient to equip 8–10 tank battalions, 18 mechanized infantry battalions and 27 artillery battalions, that could be organized into one armoured, eight mechanized infantry and three artillery brigades.[33] A mechanized force the size of three NATO divisions would be a decisive force during the fighting in 2023.

Scholz's administration hesitated to supply German made modern weapons until other members of the alliance were willing to supply similar weapons. Germany was specifically reluctant to provide the 80 obsolete Leopard I tanks sitting in a Rheinmetall factory warehouse since April 2022. Within the alliance, only Germany, France, the UK and US produce modern tanks that fire NATO-standard 120mm main guns.

On 4 January 2023, France broke the impasse and announced it would provide Ukraine with forty AMX-10 RC wheeled armoured reconnaissance vehicles. Billed as a 'light tank', the AMX-10 was a lightly armoured, wheeled reconnaissance fighting vehicle. It was armed with the 105mm main gun similar to the gun on the German Leopard I tank. It was designed to support lighter armoured scout cars.[34] Literally hours after France's announcement, the Biden and Scholz administrations announced they would provide IFVs. Germany agreed to provide 100 Marder IFVs, while the US announced that it would provide 109 Bradley IFVs and eventually included 100 Stryker APCs.[35]

Rheinmetall was authorized to refurbish the Marders sitting in its warehouse since spring 2022. The first Marder came off the assembly line in 1971. The IFV had been heavily modified over the decades. Its primary armament was a 20mm auto-cannon and a 7.62mm machine gun but it could be equipped with a MILAN ATGM. In addition to its three-man crew, the Marder could carry six or seven soldiers. It weighed 30 tons combat loaded and had a speed of 65kmh/40mph. It had been combat tested in Kosovo and Afghanistan.

The American Bradley M2/3 IFV first entered service in 1981. Over the decades it had undergone numerous upgrades and modifications. Its primary armaments were a 25mm chain gun with a coaxial 7.62mm MG, and a TOW II ATGM. It weighed 30 tons combat loaded and had a speed of 56kmh/35mph. The Bradley IFV served in the Gulf War (1990–1991), the Iraqi War (2003 to 2011) and peacekeeping operations in Kosovo. The Bradley IFVs destroyed more Iraqi tanks in the Gulf War than the M1A1 Abrams.[36] The American Strykers were eight-wheeled APCs and could travel at 95kmp/60mph. They had a crew of three and could carry a squad of nine soldiers. They were armed with a heavy machine gun or automatic grenade launcher.

When employed properly, these IFVs and APCs provided Ukraine with a tactical advantage in the offensive. Bradleys and Marders offered more reconnaissance capabilities with their enhanced optics and other sensors. Significantly better-armoured than the Soviet BTRs and BMPs they conceivably encouraged Ukrainian soldiers to ride inside, protected from artillery, rather than atop in case of IED mines. Due to the threat of mines both Ukrainian and Russian infantry developed the habit of riding on the outside of their armoured vehicles to avoid being trapped inside.

On 14 January 2023, British Prime Minister Rishi Sunak announced that Great Britain would provide 14 Challenger 2 modern tanks and 30 AS-90 155mm self-propelled howitzers. Britain only fielded 250 Challenger 2 tanks. The announcement greatly escalated the type of military aid, providing an offensive weapon that would assist the UAF to regain its occupied territory.[37]

Britain's announcement increased pressure on Washington and Berlin to follow its lead. With the political pressure mounting from all sides on 25 January 2023, President Biden announced the US would send 31 M1A1 Abrams tanks to Ukraine. On the same day Germany announced it would send 14 Leopard II 2A6 tanks to Ukraine and most importantly authorized other countries to send their tanks, even though they contained parts manufactured in Germany, ending months of debate.[38] Other allies quickly followed suit and twelve countries agreed to supply Ukraine with a total of 100 Leopard II tanks, the equivalent of three battalions or one brigade.

The Challenger 2, M1A1 Abrams, and Leopard II A4 and 2A6 tanks had similar advanced optics, thermal sights and had the same NATO 120mm main gun. They accurately fired out to 4,000m and had protected ammunition compartments within their hulls and turrets. All three tanks were far superior in every category to the T-62, T-64, T-72, T-80, and T-90 tanks in use by the combatants. The Challenger 2 tank was a heavily armoured and highly mobile vehicle, powered by a diesel engine. Armed with a 120mm main gun and two 7.62mm machine guns, it entered service in 1994 and had a series of upgrades over the years. It had seen combat service in Bosnia, Kosovo, and Iraq. Only one Challenger 2 tank had ever been destroyed in combat operations, when fragments from the enemy tank's HEAT (high explosive anti-tank) round entered the open turret hatch, killing two crew members. Combat loaded it weighed 62 tons and had a top speed of 56kph/35mph. Only Great Britain and Oman operated Challenger 2s, fielding 386 and 32 respectively.

The Leopard II first rolled off the assembly line in 1979. It had been upgraded several times and in 2023 earned the reputation of being the best main battle tank in the world. Even the older models had superior optics and thermal sights than any tank serving on the Ukrainian battlefield at the time. Combat loaded it weighted 55 tons and powered by a diesel engine it had a maximum speed of 70kph/44mph. Its protected ammunition storage compartment was designed to prevent the catastrophic explosions common in the T-72 series tanks.

Perhaps most significantly, the tank was armed with a standard 120mm NATO cannon and a coaxial 7.62 machine gun. The 120mm gun was particularly important as it allowed Ukraine to fire the large stocks of NATO ammunition. This was critical as their stocks of Soviet 125mm ammunitions were dwindling.

Another reason Ukraine focused on this tank over the American Abrams was that over 2,290 tanks were already in operation in 15 countries throughout Europe and Canada. Finland had 100 Leopard IIA4s in storage, Germany had 200+ and Norway had 16.[39] The Czech Republic and Poland had depot-level maintenance operations within their borders. Adopting the Leopard II required trained crews and maintenance personnel. Training required 3–6 weeks. However well-received, the Leopard II had not yet been tested in heavy combat.

The M1 Abrams entered service in 1980. It had gone through several major modifications. The M1A1+ versions had armour comprising layers of depleted uranium, steel, and a classified material. Its main armament was the 120mm NATO gun and coaxial machine gun with a .50 calibre machine mounted on the turret, controlled from the commander's station. Ammunition was stored in an armoured compartment with blast panels. If the ammunition exploded, the blast doors would protect the crew. During the Gulf War, twenty-one M1A1 Abrams were damaged or destroyed, most by friendly fire. In five cases the ammunition blew up resulting in five wounded. By March 2005, eighty Abrams had been disabled by enemy attacks in the Iraqi War. Of these, sixty-three were put back into service and seventeen were damaged beyond repair.

The M1A1 Abrams had several disadvantages. First its combat weight was 75 tons, making it much too heavy for small rural Ukrainian bridges. Earlier, lighter versions had multi-fuel turbine engines, but the more modern M1A1 used jet fuel. The M1A1 had complicated maintenance requirements that required extensive specialized training.

Supplying Ukraine with three different heavy battle tanks would have been problematic even though the Challenger 2, Leopard II, and the M1A1 all fired NATO ammunition. The tanks did not have interchangeable parts. Three separate logistics chains would have been required to support these heavy armoured vehicles. Three different depot-level maintenance facilities would have been required, probably to be created in neighbouring NATO countries.

While Ukraine did not receive all the heavy weapons in the quantity requested, it did receive sufficient armoured manoeuvre force required for its 2023 counteroffensive. When modern tanks, IFVs and APCs supplemented Ukraine's inventory of Cold War-era NATO APCs and Soviet IFVs and APCs it was much better armed than its Russian opponent. In addition, thousands of light armoured vehicles (American HMMWVs, Australian Bushmasters etc.) were provided. Of equal importance were the large number of drones, guidance and tracking radars, anti-radar missiles and precision-guided munitions of all types, and combat and service support equipment that were provided for the Ukrainian logistics system.[40]

Australia contributed significant amounts of both military and humanitarian aid. The 'Land Down Under' sent $50 million worth of military vehicles to Ukraine. The first shipment of twenty Bushmaster Combat Vehicles was shipped out by aircraft on 8 April 2022. In addition to the combat vehicles, Australia provided $120 million in military and humanitarian aid.[41] Other countries, such as Japan and South Korea, shipped helmets, body armour and humanitarian gear.[42]

As of November 2022, the UK committed £2,300,000,000 in military assistance and £3,800,000,000 in economic and humanitarian aid. The aid included over 10,000 anti-tank missiles, 6 air defence systems, 200 armoured fighting vehicles, 2,600 anti-structure munitions, anti-radar AMRAAM (advanced medium range air to air) missiles, 4.5 tons of plastic explosives and 3,000,000 rounds of small arms ammunition. In addition, the UK established a long-term training programme for Ukrainian soldiers with the potential of training up to 10,000 Ukrainian soldiers every 120 days.[43]Ultimately, 8 countries participated in this programme, with Australia joining the programme in January 2023.[44]

The next phase of support for the war began with the onset of winter's harsh conditions. Russia had launched its missile bombardment campaign inflicting extensive damage to the Ukrainian national electric grid. Canada, Germany, Latvia, Estonia, Lithuania, Norway, Finland, and Sweden all provided winter uniforms as well as equipment to supplement Ukraine's local production and inventory of goods. [45]

Russia's aggression stimulated Poland to re-arm. Poland replaced the T-72s sent to Ukraine with 980 Korean K2 Black Panther tanks, 645 K-9 Krab self-propelled howitzers and 48 FA-50 light fighter aircraft. Under licence, Poland agreed to manufacture 800 tanks in country under the name 'Wilk' (Wolf). Armed with the same 120mm gun as the Abrams but having an autoloader, the K2 tank required a reduced crew of only three. The K2 is equipped with a Korean active protective system designed to intercept rockets and anti-tank missiles. Poland also purchased 250 American M1A2 Abrams tanks. With their Cold War T-72 replacement programme, Poland committed to fielding 1,280 modern tanks. By 2030, Poland will have fielded the most modern tank fleet in NATO. [46]

Much like the 'Lend Lease' programme of the Second World War, the twenty-first century NATO programme provided the weapons and equipment Ukraine required to fight Russia to a standstill. Throughout 2022, NATO and Ukraine's other allies committed to the survival of a democratic Western-orientated Ukraine by providing most of Ukraine's battlefield requirements.

Chapter 21

The Ukrainian Strategic Counteroffensive Shaping Operation

A s the Battle for the Donbas raged, the Ukrainian General Staff was mindful that in order to maintain international support they would need to execute a successful counteroffensive. It became imperative to demonstrate to the world that Ukraine could win this war so that allies would continue to provide arms and equipment. If the world believed that defeat was inevitable support would dwindle.

Offensive operations aim at destroying or defeating an enemy. Offensive (and counteroffensive) operations deprive an enemy of resources, seize decisive terrain, divert enemy attention, develop intelligence, or hold an enemy in position.[1] Effective offensive operations capitalize on accurate intelligence regarding enemy forces, weather, terrain and normally include a deception plan to mislead the opponent and obfuscate the plan. The Ukrainians had been trained in NATO doctrine in developing and conducting high-tempo offensive operations. They developed a battle plan in accordance with NATO doctrine to dislocate, isolate, disrupt, and destroy enemy forces while seizing

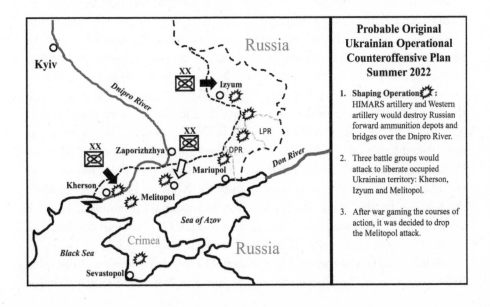

Probable Original Ukrainian Operational Counteroffensive Plan Summer 2022

1. **Shaping Operations**: HIMARS artillery and Western artillery would destroy Russian forward ammunition depots and bridges over the Dnipro River.

2. Three battle groups would attack to liberate occupied Ukrainian territory: Kherson, Izyum and Melitopol.

3. After war gaming the courses of action, it was decided to drop the Melitopol attack.

key terrain. Part of the plan included a supporting attack to deceive and divert the enemy away from the axis of the main counterattack.

While the initial plan for the counteroffensive was primarily a Ukrainian General Staff action, it was in accordance with NATO doctrine. Planning was under the direction of Colonel General Oleksandr Syrsky. The counteroffensive to liberate Kherson was initially the main effort while the Kharkiv operation was a diversionary attack.[2] During the initial planning phase, when their ground manoeuvre plan was in its infancy, the Ukrainian Generals realized they had to neutralize Russian superiority in artillery. With the arrival of HIMARS and ten battalions of various western 155mm howitzers entering the fight, Ukrainians commenced shaping operations by destroying the Russian forward ammunition depots with precision strikes.

Between 14 June and 7 July 2022, HIMARS and other long-range artillery destroyed forty major ammunition depots between the Kherson and Luhansk Oblasts.[3] Toward the middle of July, the Russians had a superiority of artillery, but they were desperately lacking in shells. The impact of this operation denied Russians much-needed ammunition.

Toward the end of July, the Ukrainians took their counteroffensive plan to Germany and sat down with British and American battle staffs to refine it. Initially, the Ukrainian, British, and American planners ran separate wargames using different software and analysis. None of the proposed operations wargamed successfully. While the details of the games were secret, the battlefield map clearly indicated only three viable avenues of attack for the counteroffensive. The initial plan envisioned three separate division-sized counterattacks, each operation to be conducted simultaneously in the Kherson, Kharkiv, and Zaporizhzhia Sectors.[4]

The objective of the counterattack coming from Zaporizhzhia was to advance all the way to the Black Sea in order to cut the Crimean land bridge. However, this plan of attack would have left the Zaporizhzhia Battle Group unsupported in a salient between two Russian CAAs. In order to reach the Black Sea, the Ukrainians would have had to first capture the key road junction at Melitopol, which was securely in Russian hands. They then would have risked being cut off by the division-sized 58th CAA from the Kherson Oblast, and the division-sized 49th CAA from Mariupol. The Dnipro River would have prevented support coming from the Kherson Battle Group, while the Kharkiv Battle Group was too far away to render aid if required. The risk of trapping the Zaporizhzhia Battle Group in a pocket was unacceptable. The result of wargaming this alternative clearly indicated that the Ukrainian armed forces had insufficient forces to be successful in three division-size (nine-plus battalions) attacks. After reviewing the results, US National Security Advisor

Jake Sullivan and the Ukrainian President's Chief of Staff Andriy Yernmak realized the counteroffensive needed to be scaled down.

In truth, the Ukrainians lacked sufficient forces to conduct even two division-size attacks unless the Russians cooperated. The Russian 1st Tank Army alone had massed fifty-four BTGs in the vicinity of Izyum, while at the other end of the line, the 58th CAA had about twenty BTGs defending the west side of the Dnipro in Kherson Oblast.

Faced with unfavourable force ratios to succeed in the counteroffensive, the ultimate plan provided that the battle groups would attack in sequence, with the Kharkiv Battle Group assigned the main effort. The Kherson Battle Group comprised the secondary supporting attack. On 29 August 2022, after speeches announcing the operation, the Kherson Battle Group crossed their line of departure with great fanfare. A week later, the Kharkiv Battle Group, which had secretly massed, crossed their line of departure on 6 September.

The massing of Russian strength in the Donbas in April to July had resulted in weakening their defence of the Kherson Sector, at the extreme end of their supply lines. Russia's failure to establish a bridgehead line 32km/20 miles west of the Dnipro River placed them in a precarious position once the Ukrainian shaping operation began.

In the early months of the war, Russia had captured the bridges over the Dnipro River but failed to capture those over the Southern Bug River. The Ukrainian defenders had earlier forced the Russians back from the Southern Bug River. The BTGs thereafter established their defence in open farmland

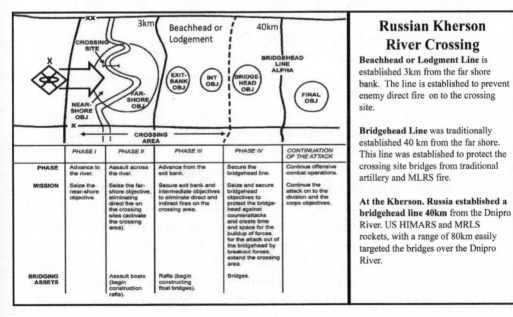

Russian Kherson River Crossing

Beachhead or Lodgment Line is established 3km from the far shore bank. The line is established to prevent enemy direct fire on to the crossing site.

Bridgehead Line was traditionally established 40 km from the far shore. This line was established to protect the crossing site bridges from traditional artillery and MLRS fire.

At the Kherson. Russia established a bridgehead line 40km from the Dnipro River. US HIMARS and MRLS rockets, with a range of 80km easily targeted the bridges over the Dnipro River.

	PHASE I	PHASE II	PHASE III	PHASE IV	CONTINUATION OF THE ATTACK
PHASE	Advance to the river.	Assault across the river.	Advance from the exit bank.	Secure the bridgehead line.	Continue offensive combat operations.
MISSION	Seize the near-shore objective.	Seize the far-shore objective, eliminating direct fire on the crossing sites (activate the crossing area).	Secure exit bank and intermediate objectives to eliminate direct and indirect fires on the crossing area.	Seize and secure bridgehead objectives to protect the bridgehead against counterattacks and create time and space for the buildup of forces for the attack out of the bridgehead by breakout forces; extend the crossing area.	Continue the attack on to the division and the corps objectives.
BRIDGING ASSETS		Assault boats (begin construction rafts).	Rafts (begin constructing float bridges).	Bridges.	

and the steppes west of Kherson. The eastern bank of the Southern Bug River was 30–40km/18–24 miles from the Dnipro River and formed a natural bridgehead line. If the Russians had defended along the Southern Bug River, Ukrainian artillery, especially western supplied HIMARS rockets, could not have easily targeted the bridges over the Dnipro River.

The route between Mykolaiv on the Southern Bug River, and Kherson on the Dnipro River was 32km/20 miles (at the shortest point) of open rolling steppe. In theory this would have been perfect defensive terrain for the Russians, with the villages and road junctions already developed into strong points with interlocking fields of fire from defending ATGMs, tanks and artillery. Approximately twenty BTGs occupied the defences west of the Dnipro River. To support their Donbas offensive, Russia had weakened the Kherson defenders by replacing losses with obsolete T-62 tanks. Their main supply route (MSR) traversed three bridges crossing the Dnipro River.

This Russian defensive deployment contained several obvious operational errors that provided Ukraine with the opportunity for a limited summer counteroffensive in the Kherson Sector. Shaping operations for this counteroffensive began in June 2022, when modern Western artillery became available in quantity. Ukraine successfully targeted Russian artillery ammunition depots in the region. While the HIMARS rocket artillery received credit for these successful attacks, various missile systems were also utilized. The ammunition provided to Ukraine allowed HIMARS to strike targets from a range of 80km/50 miles. Ukrainian missiles, drones, commandos, and partisans were credited for striking deeper targets in the Crimean Peninsula.[5] Ukrainian commandos, partisans and/or missiles successfully destroyed or heavily damaged Saki Airbase and a massive military depot at Mayskoye in Russian-occupied Crimea.[6] On 17 August, Ukrainian artillery destroyed an ammunition dump and five Legenda-2 satellite base stations in Blahodatine. With the destruction of these drone base stations, it became difficult for the Russians to coordinate artillery, missile, and air strikes.[7] Ukrainian attacks eventually destroyed fifty ammunition dumps along with command-and-control infrastructure.[8]

For weeks, Ukraine's shaping operations telegraphed to the world that it was preparing to launch a counteroffensive to liberate the Kherson Oblast and push the Russians back to the east bank of the Dnipro River, threatening their supply lines from Crimea. On 9 July 2022, the Ukrainian government urged residents of the Kherson and Zaporizhzhia Oblasts to evacuate due to an impending counteroffensive. Throughout July, Ukrainians conducted probing attacks against Russian defences. The threatened counteroffensive had the strategic objective of forcing Russia to weaken its Donbas assault force.

In response to Ukrainian shaping operations, the Russians redeployed thirty-six BTGs from the 1st Tank Army and 2nd, 5th, 29th, 35th and 36th CAAs south from the Donbas. Of the thirty-six BTGs, twenty-seven were sent to reinforce Kherson Sector. The problem caused by the relocation of twenty-seven BTGs into the Kherson beachhead was that it exasperated the already existing supply challenges for the 58th CAA, without increasing its ability to attack and push the Ukrainians back to the Southern Bug bridgehead line. In the defence, an additional twenty-seven BTGs in the pocket west of the river would have slowed a Ukrainian attack, but would not have significantly changed the combat ratio. The Ukrainian counterattack was proceeded by a series of artillery bombardments and assaults by tanks with follow-on infantry battalions taking advantage of the effects of fire. Russian defenders fought with limited ammunition as the Ukrainians had successfully interdicted their supply lines over the Dnipro River.

In early August, as Ukrainian fires continued to shape the battlefield, Ukraine launched limited ground attacks to secure key terrain. Ukrainian ground operational objectives included Kherson City, the Antonivka bridges and the Kakovska power plant, dam, and bridge. Fixing attacks within Kherson Sector were conducted along the line to pin Russian defenders, denying them the ability to shift local reserves. With the bridges over the Dnipro River damaged or destroyed, tank and infantry reinforcements from the Donbas were helpless to intervene. Local ammunition dumps were destroyed, and Russian reinforcing artillery fire was greatly reduced.

During this period, General Kovalchuk commanded the Kherson Battle Group. He considered flooding the Dnipro River Valley to trap the Russians west of the river. To test the viability this option, a HIMARS strike targeted the flood gate on the Nova Kakhovka Dam. Three holes were blown through the metal floodgate, demonstrating the feasibility of this option.[9] However, in the course of events he did not blow the dam.

On 29 August 2023, the Kherson diversion ground attack commenced, while the shaping operations continued. Ukrainian ground attacks secured forward firing positions for its artillery batteries. The low-speed ground attacks slowly advanced on five axes. Yurii, a 32-year-old company commander from the 35th Ukrainian Naval Infantry Brigade, fought his way across a small river, under heavy fire from the village of Bruskynske, 80km/50 miles northeast of Kherson. The Russians called in an airstrike and his company was bombed, making little progress. The attacks along that axis met heavy resistance and made slow progress.

Meanwhile the Russian defenders northwest of Nova Kakhovka Dam were in danger of becoming fixed and isolated in a pocket, as their retreat was blocked by the Kakhovka Reservoir. Logistical problems prevented the Russians from reinforcing their beachhead. The BTGs that had shifted south from the Donbas sat idle on the east side of the Dnipro River, consuming rations, unable to influence the battle for Kherson and out of position for the defence of the Donbas. The attack along the Kherson bridgehead focused Russia's attention away from the main event further north and justified the decision to move the BTGs from the Donbas to Kherson Oblast.

Chapter 22

Ukrainian Counteroffensive: Strategic Deception and Shaping Operation, Donbas and Kharkiv Sectors

During the operational pause of mid-July 2022, the Russian General Staff addressed the problem of the Ukrainian armed forces openly massing along the Kherson Sector, obviously concerned that 20,000 soldiers were in danger of being cut off and isolated on the west bank of the Dnipro River. The UAF had dropped leaflets near Kherson warning the population of the pending offensive, encouraging civilians to vacate the city. Russian intelligence missed the indicators that the Kherson posturing was a diversion.

Throughout July and August, the UAF's shaping operations began to isolate the Kherson Sector. At the same time shaping operations from UAF artillery, missiles, drones, commandos, partisans, and aircraft destroyed or damaged over 400 targets, including bridges, air bases, command posts and command and control faculties, and over forty major ammunition dumps across the entire Ukrainian theatre of operations. Some of these targets were destroyed deep in the Russian rear, thanks to the US-supplied HIMARS rockets.[1]

Russian intelligence assumed that the UAF was only capable of conducting one division-size counteroffensive. The Russian generals continued to underestimate their Ukrainian opponents, and apparently believed the deception that the counteroffensive would be launched in the Kherson Sector. In reliance upon this false premise, they shifted thirty to forty BTGs from the Donbas Sector to the Kherson and Zaporizhzhia Sectors.[2] The BTGs that had deployed south were stripped from the 2nd, 5th, 29th, 35th, and 36th CAAs. Among the BTGs sent south was the 64th Guards Motor Rifle Brigade. This brigade was notorious for the atrocities committed against civilians in Bucha during March 2022.[3] Included in this transfer were BTGs from the elite 76th, 106th and 98th Airborne Divisions, technically the best infantry in the Russian Army.[4]

Basically, Putin's generals sent half of the Donbas assault force to the extreme end of the Russian over-extended supply line. These reinforcements took up positions on the east bank of the Dnipro River. However, since the bridges over the Dnipro River had been destroyed, or in the case of the Kakhovka dam bridge rendered unusable, the reinforcing tank and motorized rifle battalions could not reinforce the Russian beachhead on the west bank of the river.

Conversely, because the bridges were damaged or destroyed, the limit of advance of the UAF tank and mechanized infantry battalions was the Dnipro River. In short, this should have been an intelligence indicator that the UAF Kherson counteroffensive was a ruse, or at best a secondary operation. For all intents and purposes thirty to forty BTGs were redeployed to a position where they could not effectively influence events in the Donbas or Kherson Oblasts.

With the redeployment and transition to the defence in the Kharkiv Sector, the Russian General Staff created a situation similar to the situation in the Kherson Sector.

Approximately 20,000–25,000 men were deployed in the Kharkiv Oblast between the Russian border and Iyzum. The Oskil River and reservoir was 60km/37 miles behind the Russian frontlines. This major military obstacle only had three bridges over which the Russians could supply their forces, or in the alternative use to bring reinforcements into the sector. The 1st Guards Tank Army was concentrated along the western, southwestern, and southern approaches to Izyum. The 1st Guards Tank Army originally commanded 24 BTGs to defend the Izyum area. Of these, 12 BTGs had been redeployed south to Kherson. Only 12 BTGs remained near Izyum to defend the forward army-level supply depot along with several thousand combat service support troops.

The 104km/64mile long northern flank of the 1st Guards Tank Army was protected by the 3rd Motorized Rifle Division Headquarters, with a single echelon of second-rate battalions.[5] Second-rate, because they were manned with separatists, volunteers (BARs) and national police rather than regular Army troops. The key fortified cities and towns on the northern flank, south to north, were Savyntsi, Balakliya and Chkalovska (occupied by two BTGs) and Shevchenkove (occupied by one BTG). The distance between Balakliya and Chkalovska was 28km/17 miles. The distance between Balakliya and Savyntsi was 15km/9 miles, but the gap was protected by the Siversky-Donets River and the lakes and marshes on both sides of the river.[6] To properly defend the 104km/64 mile-long front, three Soviet-style divisions (with twelve manoeuvre battalions and eight artillery battalions) each defended a front of approximately 30km/18 miles long and employed a two-echelon defence with four modern Russian brigades (eight BTGs and four additional battalions).

After shifting thirty to forty BTGs south, the Russian generals appeared to have allotted fewer than five BTGs in the first and only echelon defending the 1st Guards Army's northern flank. It was reported that the Russian 144th

Motorized Rifle Division commanded this weak sector.[7] The shortfall in overall strength was compensated for with a few low-quality DPR and/or LPR militia battalions and trained Russian Rosgvardia (National Guard/internal security forces). The Rosgvardia were lightly armed, not combat trained and normally did not operate in conjunction with the Russian Army.[8]

According to a Soviet doctrinal template, the 144th Motorized Rifle Division should have controlled sixteen infantry and tank battalions and should have defended the gap with two battlelines. Pursuant to doctrine, the first defending echelon should have consisted of six motorized rifle battalions and two tank battalions. The second echelon should have consisted of three motorized rifle battalions and four tank battalions. The five second-rate BTGs, with the under-equipped, poorly led DPR and LPR battalions, soon proved incapable of holding the Ukrainian armoured spearhead.

The 106th Guards Airborne Division Headquarters was located 64km/39 miles in the rear at Kupiansk, on the Oskil River, just north of the reservoir. The 106th guarded the few bridges across the Oskil River and protected the co-located supply depot and communication hub. This headquarters probably commanded two BTGs from the 423rd Guards Motorized Rifle Regiment and one BTG from the 13th Guards Tank Regiment.[9]

Throughout August 2022, the UAF slowly assembled an operational manoeuvre group of five manoeuvre brigades between Zmilv and Andrikvka in the Kharkiv Oblast. As the combat battalions massed, the cover story and deception plan focused Russian attention on the Kherson Oblast.[10] On 4 September, the UAF attacked Russian defenders all along the Kherson Sector. Probing attacks in the Donbas were launched along the front at Andrivka, Pryshyb, and Balakliya. These attacks pinned Russian defenders and froze Russian local reserves in place.

On 5 September, the Ukrainians launched their main operational counteroffensive, a blitzkrieg attack in the Kharkiv Oblast. Russian intelligence failed to detect the UAF's massing of four mechanized brigades, five artillery brigades, support units and massive amounts of supplies against a weak spot in their defensive lines.[11]

Between 5 and 8 September, five mechanized and armoured brigades, comprising the UAF main effort, struck the Russian defensive lines, quickly routing the Russian defenders, and blitzed into the Russian rear. A battle group of the 103rd and 112th Territorial Defence Brigades conducted a supporting attack down Highway P07 toward Chkalovske. The attack successfully pinned the Russian 36th Seperate Guards Motorized Brigade's two BTGs, the 59th Guards Tank Regiment's one BTG, and the 254th

Soviet Style Motorized Rifle Division Template

In September 2022, 1st Tank Army's northern flank should have been defended by 9+BTGs.

The template illustrates how such a defense should been organized. The positions of units would be modified by terrain.

Source USA FM-100 Soviet Operations.

Guards Motorized Rifle Regiment's single BTG and prevented them from plugging the breach.

A second supporting attack conducted by the Ukrainian 10th Tank Battalion, 3rd Tank Brigade and 71st Jager Motorized Brigade fought a three-day battle for control of the city of Husarivsak on the southern edge of the penetration. Ukrainian commando groups Dyke, Pole, and Krahen cut Highway T2110 running northeast from Balakliya to Shevchenkove, forcing the defenders of Husarivsak to retreat. Pinning attacks south and southwest of Izyum prevented the twelve BTGs of the 1st Tank Army from defending against the penetration by the UAF main effort.[12]

Forward detachments in light, unarmoured, fast attack vehicles infiltrated Russian lines ahead of the armoured spearhead.[13] Forward detachments are elements of an offensive operation that use surprise and speed to strike deep into the enemy defensive area before its defences can be fully organized and solidified. Traditionally, according to Soviet doctrine, forward detachments were tank-heavy combined-arms task forces that attacked at top speed to seize and hold key terrain.[14]

The Ukrainians employed light armoured vehicles, such as HUMVEES and Bushmasters, to quickly penetrate the Russian rear. Instead of holding ground, these light forward detachments rushed into occupied villages, raised the Ukrainian flag, and rushed on. This rapid advance created confusion and resulted in the surrender of Russian artillery and support units and the capture

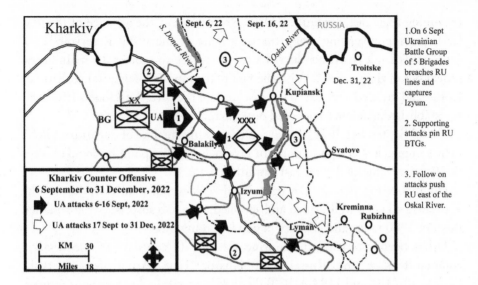

of 3,000 PoWs, as once they saw the Ukrainian flag, they believed the town had been liberated.[15]

At 03:30 on 6 September 2022, Commander Oleh's company of 100 soldiers and 10 APCs from the 25th Airborne Assault Brigade crossed the line of departure in platoon columns. For 4 hours prior to their crossing, US-made M270 MLRS rockets had pounded Russian positions, command posts, ammunition depots and fuel storage facilities. Under the relentless pounding, some separatists and Russian soldiers began to flee in route. Oleh observed the panicked defenders as his company attacked their frontline positions. By the evening of 6 September 2022, Oleh's company had advanced 17km/11 miles, capturing the important road junction at Volohkiv Yar. In Volohkiv Yar, Oleh's men captured a Russian tank platoon of 4 tanks that had parked in the front yard of a civilian house. The crews were captured while drinking beer and talking about where to run. As the Ukrainian APCs arrived, the Russians surrendered. With Volohkiv Yar in Ukrainian hands, Oleh's company turned south toward Izyum and Balakliya. Based on his battalion's operation order, Oleh expected it would take 7 days to capture his objective, a ridge north of Izyum.

On or about 8 September, the Russian commanding general of the 1st Guards Tank Army realized he was about to be surrounded. Following Russian/Soviet doctrine he organized his twelve BTGs for a breakout of an expected encirclement. A rearguard was formed from the 386th Motorized Rifle Brigade (three BTGs). Between 9 and 10 September, the 1st Guards Tank Army's ten BTGs were forced to run a gauntlet of fire along the remaining road east, toward the Oskil River. To slow the advance of the lead UAF brigade advancing along the west bank of the Oskil Reservoir/River, 1st Guards Tank Army conducted a counterattack to protect the main hectic retreat out of the pocket.[16] With the failure to stop the UAF advance, Russian Command ordered a retreat to the east bank of the Siversky-Donets River and re-established a defence anchored on Lyman.

On 12 September 2022, six days after crossing the line of departure, Oleh's men occupied a check point north of Izyum. From that point he could observe the Russian vehicles fleeing east toward Lyman.

Upon entering the city the next day he discovered that, even though the Russians had been well-armed and supplied, they had surprisingly abandoned modern T-80 tanks and artillery in good working order.

It has been estimated that during the first fifteen days of the Kharkiv counteroffensive, the Russian 1st Guards Tank Army lost 65 tanks (T-72s/80s/90s) and 118 BMPs/BTRs had been either destroyed or captured. These losses were equivalent to the equipment of 4 BTGs. During the same operation it has been estimated that UAF lost 6 tanks (T-64s/72s/80s) and 10 BMPs/BTRs/BMDs.[17]

By taking the time and making the effort to shape the battlefield, the UAF had created the necessary manoeuvre space to threaten the 1st Guards Tanks Army at Izyum. The Russian artillery was neutralized by Western-supplied precision artillery and UAF commandos working in concert with Ukrainian partisans.[18] Between 10 and 12 September, the counteroffensive forced the Russians into a disorderly retreat, back to the international border or to the east bank of the Oskil River.

On 15 September 2022, President Zelensky visited the liberated city of Izyum. After the blitz, the UAF took an operational pause to move forward its logistics infrastructure and process the hundreds of PoWs and captured weapons and munitions.[19] The Kharkiv Battle Group used the pause to consolidate its gains and rest its troops. The Ukrainian counteroffensive had successfully pushed the Russian lines back 40km/25 miles, to the other side of the Oskil River. Unlike the challenges presented by the Dnipro River in Kherson, the Oskil River did not stop the Ukrainian advance because they had captured the bridges north of the Oskil Reservoir at Kupiansk, and most importantly they had captured the two bridges that crossed the centre of the reservoir. Bridgeheads were established in both locations and the Russians were pushed back from the eastern bank.

Chapter 23

Russian Mobilization

On 21 September 2022, Putin announced a partial mobilization of 300,000 men to increase troop strength and replace losses.[1] Ten days later, on 30 September 2022, Putin announced the (illegal) annexation of the Donetsk, Kherson, Luhansk, and Zaporizhzhia Oblasts. In conjunction with these actions, he issued another veiled nuclear threat.[2] These drastic measures followed 7 months of heavy losses of equipment and devastating casualties.

At the beginning of the invasion, Ukraine had immediately ordered a general mobilization of the country and spent the first half of the year expanding its manpower and forming highly motivated combat units, supported by the entire population and NATO. Putin shielded the general Russian population from realistic news and information about his 'Special Operation'. He did not mobilize the general reserve of former conscripts in an attempt to hide losses on the battlefield. With Russia limited to contract military personnel, the balance in military manpower quickly shifted to Ukraine's favour.

The replacement of heavy casualties was not planned for by the Russian military. Their assumption, even as late as March, was that Ukraine would collapse in the first week, or at worse the first month of the 'Special Operation'. High combat losses in its ground combat units were replaced with contract personnel from combat support and combat service support units. Eventually this source of manpower included security soldiers from the Strategic Rocket Forces. Gunners' mates from the Navy were soon assigned to command tanks.[3] It quickly became clear that this source of replacements would fall short of required qualified-manpower requirements.

Putin had five options to replace his losses: mobilize the Special Combat Army Reserve (BARS); create regional volunteer battalions; forcibly mobilize men from occupied Luhansk and Donetsk; increase dependence on mercenary groups such as Wagner; and/or partially mobilize former conscripts from the Reserve.[4] He would eventually execute all five options.

There is historic precedent for the successful employment of marginally trained conscripts in battle. During the June 1941 Nazi invasion, the Soviet Union suffered a series of major defeats on its border. Soviet first-strategic-echelon armies were nearly destroyed. The survivors rallied inside Russia and the second-strategic-echelon armies were built from trained reservists. These armies were soundly defeated, and the Nazis advanced on Moscow. In the following months, November and December 1941, the third-strategic-echelon armies defending the gates of Moscow finally halted the Nazi drive. This final defence was manned by survivors, reinforced with poorly equipped soldiers, literally off the street with little or no training, led by inexperienced officers. Lieutenants commanded battalions and captains commanded regiments and brigades, while majors lead divisions. The lesson learned by the Soviet Union was the criticality of having a fully trained and equipped reserve force, which they established during the Cold War period following the Second World War. This reserve force was periodically called up to conduct training by filling positions in the active-duty units.

Foolishly ignoring this hard-learned lesson, Russian leaders apparently thought they could repeat the success of the desperate defenders of Moscow, apparently believing that they could rely upon a mostly untrained reserve force to supplement its active military personnel. Based on this belief, and as a cost-saving measure, the Cold War Soviet reserve system inherited by Russia was disbanded, to be replaced by a greatly limited reserve force.

After 2013, the Russian reserve system was divided into the General Reserve and the Special Combat Army Reserve (BARS). Russia did not have the equivalent of American State National Guards, Army Reserve or British and Commonwealth Territorial troops, all of which receive yearly training with modern equipment. The massive Russian General Reserve did not formally train. Russian reservists were required to perform two years of conscript service in their teens or early twenties. After completing this initial period of conscript service, reservist training was complete and additional training was not provided. General Reservists remained in the system, subject to being called up till the age of 60, at which time their training would be forty years out of date.

The BARS programme was established by Putin in 2013 in an attempt to rectify the Russian armed forces' lack of trained manpower.[5] BARS soldiers were volunteers who had previously completed their conscript service. If found fit for service, after being medically and politically screened, they were contracted for three years and assigned to a military unit in their home oblast. BARS were issued modern kit and uniforms and were paid while performing training. As one would expect, Russian Cossacks were heavily represented in the BARS. The age limit for officers was no more than 47 years old for company grade (lieutenants and captains), no more than 52 years old for field grade (majors and lieutenant colonels) and a maximum of 57 years old for colonels. The upper age limit for soldiers was 42 years old, and 57 years old for warrant officers and sergeants. In February 2022, it was estimated that the BARS contained 100,000 soldiers, with 38,000 located within the Southern Military District bordering Ukraine, supporting the three CAAs in the district.[6]

BARS soldiers were called up in April 2022 to replace losses but appeared to have been deployed as battalions under their own officers instead of individual replacements. After two months in combat, some of the Southern Military District BARS were rotated out. There were many complaints from these now-veteran soldiers. They claimed that they had not received all their pay and benefits. Among their complaints was that they were disrespected, ill-informed, poorly equipped and that rations at the front were inedible.[7]

Russian law prohibited the deployment of conscripts outside of Mother Russia unless there was a declared war. The law, however, did not apply to separatist conscripts from the Donetsk People's Republic and Luhansk People's Republic. Technically, the LPR and DPR Armies fighting in Ukrainian Luhansk and Donetsk Oblasts were fighting to capture their own home territory. Large monetary bonuses were paid to DPR and LPR conscripts to join the contract army fighting at the front. Paramilitary groups and mercenaries were also hired to fight, but neither of these measures succeeded in sufficiently increasing manpower. Lacking sufficient numbers of trained troops, and unsuccessfully attempting to increase their number from existing resources, Russian leadership turned to the expedient of throwing undertrained volunteers into battalions.

Putin was reluctant to mobilize the Reserves, in order to keep the Russian population ignorant of battlefield losses. In June 2022, the Kremlin attempted to raise volunteer battalions of 400 soldiers, with one battalion provided by each of the 85 Russian oblasts. These soldiers were scheduled for 30 days of training and received salaries of $3,000 per month. In addition, they were to be awarded veteran status and benefits if they served in Ukraine. Volunteers were 18–60 years old and prior military experience was not required. Many veterans from the Afghan and Chechen Wars soon volunteered to fight in Ukraine. Former Airborne and Special Forces veterans stiffened the ranks. Compared to the general mobilization, these volunteer units were well-equipped with individual kit, such as helmets and body armour, from military bases in their home oblasts. To establish *esprit de corps* the battalions were named to reflect regional history, local heroes, and ethnic origins.[8]

Thirty days of training, at best, imparted basic soldier skills to the volunteers. Lacking trained NCOs, even the basic tactics of platoon operations were beyond the ability of these formations. Trained officers were in short supply and the complexities of maintenance and training in basic battle drills were neglected.[9] Like all Russian units, the volunteers drank too much and were ill-disciplined. At best the battalions became a patriotic ethnic minority crowd with rifles.[10]

Of the 85 battalions originally sought, only 40 were actually formed. The best use of these 40 battalions would have been to reinforce existing brigades or pairing a volunteer unit with a veteran BTG. In some cases, this was done where volunteers joined active units from their region, for example the Primorsky Tiger Battalion reinforced the 155th Guards Naval Infantry Brigade.[11] However, the majority of these volunteer battalions (16,000 men) were assigned to the newly raised 3rd Army Corps.

The Russian 3rd Army Corps was created in June 2022 as a command headquarters for the volunteer battalions and was subordinate to the Western Military District.[12] Initially, the Corps was organized with a Soviet-style motor rifle division, motor rifle brigade and artillery brigade. It was stationed in the northwest Rostov Oblast near the DPR border. Based upon Cold War Soviet standards it would have taken months of training to get 3rd Army Corps battalions and regiments combat ready. It would have required additional training to reach a standard to effectively fight as brigades, or to conduct coordinated corps level combat operations.

In response to the Ukrainian counteroffensive in September 2022, the 3rd Army Corps units were deployed piecemeal to the Kherson, Kharkiv, Melitopol, and Mariupol Sectors. Once committed to the front, they were poorly supported. In the case of the Bashkirs Regiment (2 volunteer battalions from the Belorestsk Oblast, commanded by a retired major), it was thrown into combat in the Kherson Oblast, near the dam on the Dnipro River. Barely supplied with food and ammunition, the Bashkirs suffered 200 KIA, including their commander, and 300 WIA.[13]

At the end of August, the 3rd Army Corps was sent to the Kharkiv Oblast. The Corps was well-armed with BMP-3s, T-80BVMs and T-90M tanks. Instead of shoring up the Russian lines, the Corps' vanguard was defeated and joined the general retreat from the oblast, abandoning its tanks, IFVs and APCs with the corps' distinctive circle-inside-a-triangle marking.[14] Survivors of these piecemeal deployments were sent to reinforce the units in the Donetsk and Zaporizhzhia Oblasts.[15]

The volunteer Chechen Army, commanded by Ramzan Kadyrov, began fighting with three or four battalions, that ultimately expanded into several regiments by November 2022. Ramzan Kadyrov had fought on the Russian side during the wars in Chechnya. His private army technically fell under the Russian Rosgvardia (internal security police). The main formations were the 249th, 141st and 78th Separate Motor Regiments. The 78th and 141st together mustered approximately 4,500 men, mounted in BTR-80 APCs armed with 30mm autocannons. The remainder of the Chechen units were equipped with small arms and mounted in light vehicles. Only Chechen units loyal to Kadyrov were allowed to be armed and fight in the 'Special Operation'. Kadyrov's Chechens provided Russia with motivated, well-trained but undisciplined soldiers, excelling at infiltration tactics. Chechens were a special case when it came to volunteer ethnic formations. Undisciplined, but motivated, they regularly posted TikTok videos on the internet.[16] During their operations, the Chechen units notoriously committed war crimes, including the 'filtration' of the forced deportation of Ukrainian civilians and murders in Bucha.

Early in the invasion, the Russians turned to mercenary groups to help make up the shortfall in combat troops. Named for Hitler's favourite composer, the most infamous was the Wagner Group. The Wagner Group entered the war early and suffered high casualties within the ranks of its expensive professional contractors. The Group's solution included recruiting inmates from Russia's extensive prison system. Yevgeniy Prigozhin, Wagner's CEO and close friend of Putin, began recruiting inmates in July 2022, and by year's end it was estimated that 40,000 inmates had been recruited. The convicts had been promised monetary rewards and pardons for fighting in Ukraine. The convicts were mostly committed to intense combat for 6 months. As expected, survival rate among the former inmates was low, with only two dozen of the first 350 living long enough to be pardoned in January 2023.[17]

After the successful Ukrainian Kharkiv and Kherson counteroffensives in August and September 2022, it became clear that Russia needed more men on short notice. While estimates varied, at the time of the annexation of the occupied oblasts, the Ukrainian Ministry of Defence estimated that the Russians had lost 50,000 killed in action, included in an estimated total of 200,000 casualties.

Putin obviously required more troops to sustain his 'Special Operation'. One way to increase troop strength was to overcome the legal prohibition of sending conscripts to fight outside of Russia in the absence of a declared war. To accomplish this, Putin worked with the Duma (Russian legislature) to change the facts to fit the law. If a legal fiction could be created that the Donetsk, Luhansk, Kherson, and Zaporizhzhia Oblasts were Russian territory, conscripts and mobilized reservists could be sent to fight in these contested regions.

Having fabricated a loophole in the law, Putin announced a partial mobilization of 300,000 men on 21 September 2022.[18] On 30 September, under the cover of sham referendums in occupied Donetsk, Luhansk, Kherson, and Zaporizhzhia Oblasts, Putin announced their annexation into the Russian

Federation. By annexation Putin converted the war zone into 'Mother Russia,' dissolving the legal restriction on deploying conscripts outside of Russia without a declared war.[19]

In addition to the annexation, the Duma enacted 'Stop Loss' legislation. The Russian 'Stop Loss' programme was more draconian than the US version enacted during the first decade of the twenty-first century. In the US version, soldiers were extended for a few months past their enlistment obligation, up to an additional year, to cover rotations into Middle East combat. Most of these volunteer soldiers had contracted for four years of active duty, with an additional obligation of four years in the Reserves. In the Russian programme, contracts were extended for the duration of the 'Special Operation.'[20] Contracted veterans, BARS, volunteers, convicts, mercenaries, and mobilized reserve soldiers were all under 'Stop Loss'. Without this programme Russia would have faced even more severe deficits in troop strength. The deficit would have been especially felt in the units consisting of experienced veterans who would have been discharged at the end of their contract.

The reservists mobilized in September either voluntarily reported to the induction centres or were dragged in handcuffs. Thousands of military-age men attempted to flee Russia. Many were rounded up at the jammed borders. Over 194,000 fled to Finland, Georgia, and Kazakhstan. Thousands departed Russia by air with one-way tickets.[21] Hundreds of protesters were arrested and sent to training bases. In the ensuing confusion, even those unqualified to serve were caught up. As an example, men in their 60s with medical issues, who should have been exempt, were pressed into service, only to be released later.

Whether voluntarily reporting to the induction centre or deposited by a police 'press gang', many mobilized reservists found they had to provide their own kit. Over 1,500,000 uniforms and sets of kit were missing from the warehouses. Many '*mobiks*', as these mobilized reservists are known, had to provide their own uniforms, body armour, helmets, and other kit. War profiteers made a fortune charging up to $350 for thermal underwear, as much as $600 for a military backpack and a whopping $810 for night vision devices. A set of substandard body armour originally costing $133, cost as much as $729 by October 2022. A good Army winter coat cost $2,188.[22]

The training of the *mobiks* was limited by Western standards. American Army Reservists and Army National Guard companies, battalions and brigades received two to six months post-mobilization training before deployment into a war zone, in addition to their annual thirty days of training. Replacement Army Reservists and Army National Guard soldiers received one month of post-mobilization training before joining their unit in a war zone. With most of Russia's Army trainers deployed to the front, the *mobiks* were lucky to receive three weeks refresher training. The shortage of training officers was so severe that Major General Binyukov was personally observed teaching *mobiks* marksmanship.[23] After three weeks of training the *mobiks* were formed into companies and battalions and sent to the front.

Conditions at the induction centres were covered in detail by Western media and Russian protest 'tweeters'. The sophisticated populations of St Petersburg and Moscow had been isolated from the news by Putin's policies restricting freedom of the press. Ethnic and racial minorities from outlying provincial oblasts had thus far provided most of the combat troops. Unknown to the general population of white Russians, they had suffered high casualties. The partial mobilization in September directly impacted the urbanized white Russian European populations of Moscow, St Petersburg, Tula, and Nizhny Novgorod (200km/124 miles east of Moscow). For the first time since the beginning of the 'Special Operation', Russia experienced a large-scale grass roots backlash, exactly what Putin had hoped to avoid.

Concerned Muscovites were only part of the story across the Russian oblasts. Reservists from several northern oblasts, including St Petersburg, were sent to Pechenga, near Murmansk, the training base of the 200th Motorized Rifle Brigade. Unlike other *mobiks* who reportedly had to supply their own equipment, the state-controlled Russian news media reported that, according to Governor Aleksandr Tsybuksky, mobilized soldiers were equipped with sleeping bags, blankets, boots, and gloves upon arrival. If true, the weapons, equipment and kit probably came from the warehouses of the Northern Fleet, commanded by Admiral Aleksandr. The critical strategic region's warehouses and armouries were reportedly full and well-maintained.[24]

While the mobilization did not appear orderly, it did provide badly needed emergency replacements for the Russian ground forces for the second half of 2022. Poorly trained, under-equipped and often badly led, *mobik* company and battalion combat efficiency was extremely low, as their combat record in the Donbas front soon demonstrated. Reportedly, *mobik* units suffered heavy casualties in their first week in combat.[25] However, if they were as bad as Western media and Ukrainian propaganda portrayed them, the war would have ended in 2022.[26]

Increased Russian troop strength slowed and ultimately stopped the Ukrainian counteroffensive in the Luhansk Oblast. After September 2022, battles in the oblast became a series of brigade-size thrusts and counterthrusts, with the frontline barely moving. Increased manpower in the Donetsk Oblast enabled Russia to pull its best units out of the line and focus efforts on capturing the city of Bakhmut.

Despite the numerous problems with the partial mobilization, it is estimated that 250,000 reservists were mobilized and sent to the front and performed combat, combat support and combat service support roles. This influx of manpower allowed the Russians to stabilize the fronts. These soldiers, initially, had little value in the offensive but could hold a defensive position. Some of the more capable *mobiks* were used as replacements in elite units like the 331st Airborne Regiment and 155th Naval Infantry Brigade.

It is important to note that the *mobiks* did not replace the annual conscription cycle for the Russian armed forces. These new conscripts were inducted in late 2022 and received a full three months of training. The *mobiks* bought time to allow these troops to be trained and equipped for a spring 2023 offensive.

Chapter 24

Liberation of Kherson

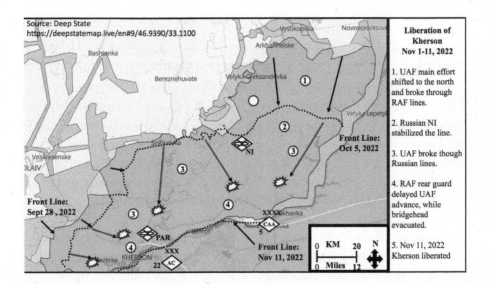

Source: Deep State
https://deepstatemap.live/en#9/46.9390/33.1100

Liberation of Kherson Nov 1-11, 2022

1. UAF main effort shifted to the north and broke through RAF lines.

2. Russian NI stabilized the line.

3. UAF broke though Russian lines.

4. RAF rear guard delayed UAF advance, while bridgehead evacuated.

5. Nov 11, 2022 Kherson liberated

In late September 2022, it was estimated that 20,000 Russians were dug in to defend the Kherson bridgehead. The 7th Guards Assault Airborne Division and BTGs from the 33rd Guards Motorized Rifle Regiment and 255th Guards Motorized Rifle Regiment were identified as being in place to defend the 120km/74 mile southwestern defensive perimeter, while the 34th and 205th Separate Motorized Rifle brigades, 126th Separate Coastal Defence (Naval Infantry) Brigade, 10th Special Purpose (Naval Infantry) Brigade and 140th and 227th artillery regiments defended the 100km/62mile northeastern perimeter. The 11th Separate Air Assault Brigade held the boundary between the two sectors. In addition to these formations several unidentified BTGs were present to reinforce the defence. Command and control, combat support and combat service support were provided by the 22nd Army Corps in the south and the 5th CAA in the north.[1]

The defenders consisted of some of the best Russian troops, but they were in a precarious position. They were at the end of the Russian main supply route that was dependent on the Antonivka Bridge, a nearby railroad bridge and the bridge over the Kakhovka Dam. The bridges had all been damaged by HIMARS strikes, especially the Antonivka Bridge, which had been rendered useless. A pontoon bridge had been erected next to the Antonivka Bridge, but it was being routinely bombarded by HIMARS. The heavy fighting between July and September 2022 had depleted the Russian ammunition supply on the west bank of the Dnipro and the resupply rate had been reduced to a trickle.

In late September 2022, Kyiv, frustrated with the lack of progress by the Kherson counteroffensive in OC-South, replaced Major General Andriy Kovalchuk with Brigadier General Oleksandr Tarnavasky, a trusted lieutenant of Colonel-General Syrsky.[2] This resulted in a change of both tactics and direction of the main effort.

Originally, OC-South's main effort had been to attack the west side of the bridgehead. The terrain was very complex, with irrigation ditches, tree lines, a small river, and small, interspersed villages, making it relatively easy for the Russian VDV paratroopers to defend. Brigadier Tarnavasky shifted the main effort to attack the perimeter from the north, down the west bank of the Dnipro River. The terrain was more open in the north and in theory more difficult to attack. The object of the attack was to bisect the bridgehead and trap the Russians west of the river. Probing attacks on the new axis started on 17 September, while pressure was maintained in the south.

Colonel Vadym Sukharevsky's 59th Motorized Infantry Brigade was assigned the mission to breach the Russian defences along the southern sector. The terrain between Mykolaiv and Kherson was perfect defensive terrain, flat farmland with few trees and concrete irrigation canals. The 59th first secured firing positions, so that HIMARS and other long-range artillery could target the bridges. Even though the Ukrainians fought against elite Russian air-assault troops, Sukharevsky's men had the advantage in that they were familiar with the countryside and had local contacts behind enemy lines. Despite heavy resistance, Sukharevsky was able to surprise the defenders and the 59th pushed the Russians back.

Ukranian Chief Yevhen Ignatenko, a platoon leader, had once operated a grain shipping business in the region. He used his knowledge of the terrain and civilian contacts to gather intelligence behind Russian lines. He modified civilian drones obtained from cigarette smugglers, transforming them into self-detonating explosives. Ignatenko used package-delivery drones to drop canisters into Russian trenches. The canisters only contained mercaptan, a chemical that released the foul odour associated with natural gas. This obviously caused panic in the trenches.

Sukharevsky was ultimately able to reduce the ability of the Russians to continue fighting by starving them of ammunition and supplies.[3] Sukharevsky credits this part of the successful counteroffensive to his artillery and innovative soldiers.

By mid-September 2022, Ukrainians conducted probing attacks in the northern part of the parameter. The Russian Naval Infantry holding the north conducted a spoiling attack on 28 September 2022, with little impact. On 10 October 2022, the northern Ukrainian brigades breached the Russian first defensive belt, resulting in a penetration 20km/12 miles deep near the Dnipro River. By 13 October the penetration was 40km/24 miles deep. The Russian Naval Infantry retreated, and the northern defences were pushed back 40km/24 miles. The Russians stabilized the line for a few days with their right flank anchored on the Dnipro River near the town of Velyka Lepetykha. This line held until 9 November 2022.[4]

On 9 November, Russian General Sergey Surovkin announced the withdrawal of his troops from Kherson. The heavy fighting had drawn down Russian ammunition stocks and the Naval Infantry, paratroopers and supporting troops on the front line were simply running out of bullets and food. A rear guard was organized and on the night of 10 November half the Russian troops crossed to the east bank. On the morning of 11 November, the rearguard infantry made a break for the river, abandoning their vehicles, including their tanks and APCs. Videos depicted the rearguard running across the damaged pontoon bridge. As they withdrew, Russian combat engineers blew up the Antonivka Bridge along with the railroad bridge and the bridges over the Kakhovka dam. The Ukrainians cautiously reoccupied Kherson on the same day.

On 14 November 2022, while still under threat of artillery and missile strikes, President Zelensky visited Kherson to celebrate its liberation. He thanked NATO and Western allies for their support and the US for the delivery of HIMARS. The civilian population, which had suffered under months of harsh Russian occupation, turned out to greet the president despite the threat of artillery strikes, mines, and booby traps.[5]

Skirmishes continued at the Kinburn Spit at the mouth of the Dnipro River estuary, and Ostriv Velykyi Potomkin Island, across from Kherson, throughout November and into January 2023, but major operations in the area ceased on 11 November 2022. The withdrawal of Russian troops from the west bank of the Dnipro ceded 40 per cent of the newly annexed Kherson Oblast back to the Ukrainians.[6] The Russians relocated their administrative capital to Henichesk, a port on the Sea of Azov. The destroyed bridges over the Dnipro River prevented the Ukrainians from pursuing the invaders and limited their counteroffensive options for the rest of 2022. While skirmishing continued for the rest of the year, both sides refocused their efforts on the Donbas Sector.

The Zaporizhzhia Sector remained relatively stable from late summer to December 2022. Flat, rolling farmland, dotted with villages would have been perfect tank country except for the winter weather. Mud and few all-weather roads rendered the sector unsuitable for mechanized operations until the winter freeze. To reinforce these natural obstacles, the Ukrainians heavily mined the

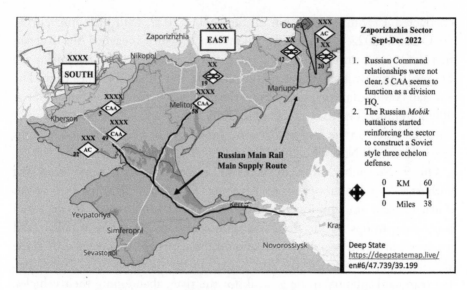

approaches to the town of Vuhleadr and other major defensive positions, and then positioned artillery to target the expected Russian axis of advance.

Vuhleadr defended the hinge of the Ukrainian defence where the Zaporizhzhia and Donbas Sectors converged. The town was surrounded by open fields stretching for kilometres, with little or no cover, a difficult area the Russians had to cross in order to assault the town.[7]

The shifting of Ukrainian and Russian mechanized and motorized forces out of Kherson Oblast during December 2022 was not followed by a large build-up of combat power in this region. A Ukrainian armoured thrust from the shores of the eastern edge of the Dnipro Reservoir to Melitopol would only need to travel 76km/47 miles. If Melitopol could be captured, the land bridge to Crimea would be cut. Undoubtedly aware of this threat, Russia built fortifications in depth along the projected Ukrainian axis of advance toward Melitopol. *Mobik* battalions began to occupy these fortifications in January 2023.

By 31 December 2022, Operational Group Vostok, commanded by Lieutenant General Rustam Muradov, with an estimated thirty-five BTGs and *mobik* battalions opposed the Ukrainians along the Zaporizhzhia Sector. The Ukrainians defended the sector with a total of nine brigades: three infantry, one mountain infantry, two motorized infantry, two mechanized infantry and one tank brigade, (totalling twenty-seven manoeuvre battalions and eighteen-plus artillery battalions). Operational Group Crimea defended the Dnipro River against OC South with twenty-one BTGs, including its *mobik* battalions. OC South defended the sector with ten brigades; five infantry, one tank, three mechanized and a security brigade (totalling thirty manoeuvre and twenty-one artillery battalions).[8]

Chapter 25

Battle of Donbas and the Fight for Bakhmut, August–December 2022

At the culmination of the Ukrainian counteroffensive, the Russians divided the Donbas into two sectors: Luhansk, and Donestk. The Russian Operational Group Voronezh controlled the Luhansk Sector. It was slowly reinforced and by December 2022 it consisted of a total of forty-five BTGs and battalions. These units were a mix of DPR, LPR, BARS, Naval Infantry, regular Army, *mobiks*, and VDV. Their supporting tanks ranged from T-72s to T-90s. Operational Group Don controlled the Donetsk Sector and commanded fifty-six BTGs including its battalions. These units were a mix of regular Army, *mobiks*, VDV, Naval Infantry, Wagner Group mercenaries, DPR, LPR, and BARS. Their supporting tanks ranged from T-64s to T-90s. Operational Group Don was the Russian main effort between October and December 2022. Its objective was to capture the fortified city of Bakhmut.

Battle of Bakhmut

With each defeat in 2022, Putin was forced to reduce his strategic objectives. After the defeat at Kherson, the Russians focused on the Donetsk and Luhansk Oblasts. In Luhansk, Russia was on the operational defensive, focused on preventing Ukraine from liberating the entire oblast. In the Donetsk Sector, Russia focused on capturing the fortified city of Bakhmut.[1]

The city of Bakhmut was located at one of many fortified road junctions in the Ukrainian second operational defensive echelon in the Donetsk Sector. With a pre-war population of 70,000 it was an administrative centre in the Ukrainian region of the Donetsk Oblast. The city was an urban agglomeration, with a river running through it. Dominated by high ground, it was a difficult location to attack.

While Bakhmut had no strategic significance during the May-July battles, capture of the city would have provided the Russians with a secure assembly area and positions from which to provide artillery support, for attacks on the fortified cities of Kramatorsk (35km/22 miles NW) and Slovyansk (38km/23 miles NNW) in the Ukrainian second defensive echelon. The roads from

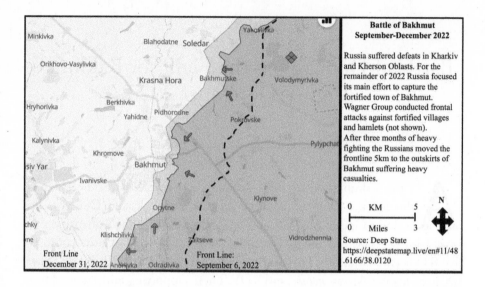

Battle of Bakhmut
September-December 2022

Russia suffered defeats in Kharkiv and Kherson Oblasts. For the remainder of 2022 Russia focused its main effort to capture the fortified town of Bakhmut. Wagner Group conducted frontal attacks against fortified villages and hamlets (not shown). After three months of heavy fighting the Russians moved the frontline 5km to the outskirts of Bakhmut suffering heavy casualties.

0   KM   5

0   Miles   3

Source: Deep State
https://deepstatemap.live/en#11/48
.6166/38.0120

Bakhmut lead deeper into Ukraine and would have provided the Russians several avenues of advance. However, each of these routes was easily blocked by fortified towns or cities.

The Russians had bombarded Bakhmut with artillery on 17 May 2022. During the first battle for the Donbas, Popasna had been captured on 22 May. Ukrainian forces had retreated 26km/16 miles to the second echelon fortified position in Bakhmut. Russian forces had advanced to the Bakhmut-Lysychansk highway, threatening to cut off the Lysychansk-Sievierodonetsk defensive zone. Withdrawal of the Ukrainian armed forces from the pocket, and the threatened counteroffensive in Kherson, made continuing the attack on Bakhmut irrelevant, as the fighting had moved east. However, the Russians continued shelling Bakhmut throughout June and July 2022.

With the September counteroffensive in Kharkiv, Russia prioritized its objectives and refocused on the capture of Bakhmut for the rest of the year. If Bakhmut, Kramatorsk, and/or Slovyansk had been captured in May, it would have isolated four Ukrainian brigades in the Donbas pocket. The failure of the Russians to capture these cities by May rendered them irrelevant and Bakhmut went from being key terrain in the Russian offensive to just another fortified city.[2]

However, after August 2022, Bakhmut became important once again, not for its military significance, but as a propaganda objective in the fight to capture the Donetsk Oblast. The importance of Bakhmut became strictly political, exaggerated by Putin's propaganda machine in an attempt to offset defeats and reverses in other sectors. Capturing Bakhmut became a symbolic objective.

The capture of Ukrainian Donetsk and Luhansk were Putin's ultimate strategic political and military objectives. The cities of Slovyansk and Kramatorsk were major operational objectives, required to secure the Donetsk Oblast. Before September, these cities could have been attacked from Izyum from the north, and Severodonetsk and Lysychansk from the east. The significant loss of Izyum in September prevented the Russians from capturing Slovyansk and Kramatorsk.

Initially, the capture of Bakhmut had been tactically important as it would have opened the rest of Ukrainian Donetsk to attack. In addition, capturing the city would have helped protect Russian Donetsk from the Ukrainian counteroffensive. Russian reasoning for the renewed frontal attack on Bakhmut in September was clearly prompted by the need to declare a victory, somewhere, anywhere, to demonstrate that Russia maintained the operational initiative.

Prigozhin, Wagner Group's CEO, stated that his goal was to turn Bakhmut into a modern Verdun and bleed Ukrainian forces through attrition. Ironically, however, like the Germans at Verdun in 1916, it was Prigozhin's mercenaries and Russian soldiers who suffered extreme heavy casualties at a higher rate than those suffered by the Ukrainian defenders.

The renewed Battle for Bakhmut commenced on 1 August 2022, when Wagner mercenaries and DPR militia launched a series of battalion-size attacks against villages south and east of Bakhmut, while intensifying airstrikes and shelling the city. This was a surprise to the Ukrainians because the city was heavily fortified and defended by two brigades. The Ukrainians had detected the massing of Russian forces but assumed they would bypass and attempt to encircle the city. They expected the Russians to attack the villages of Soledar to the north and Zaitseve and Opytne to the south.[3] Instead the Russian main effort conducted a series of frontal attacks along the strongest section of the Bakhmut frontline, defended by the 93rd Mechanized and 58th Motorized Brigades.

The frontal attacks on Bakhmut were the result of Prigozhin wanting to prove to Putin and Russian military leaders that his mercenaries were better trained and more capable than the Russian Army, which had just retreated from Kherson. Prigozhin was politically connected to General Sergei Surovikin, Russian Chief of Operations, and as a result he was given a free hand in the Bakhmut assault.

The approaches to Bakhmut were covered by villages, fortified into strong points, with interlocking fields of fire. Assaulting BTGs and later battalions, companies and small platoon and squad storm groups were subjected to flanking fire from the strong points and frontal fire from Bakhmut. A coordinated fire plan was required to suppress the strong points and allow the Russians to reach the defenders in the city. Unfortunately for the assault forces, Wagner mercenaries lacked the skill required to closely coordinate artillery and mortar fire with attacking infantry. Lacking NVGs, Russian infantry and mercenaries often attacked in daylight. The result was that their ground attacks were easily repelled, incurring heavy losses.

On 4 August Wagner mercenaries reached the outskirts of Bakhmut, while DPR and LPR battalions continued to push toward the city from the north and south. Fighting continued throughout September and October as both sides dug trenches, while heavy shelling and artillery duels became a daily occurrence.

The Wagner units were composed of 2 groups. The first group served as command and staff headquarters and planned the operations. They were equipped with encrypted communications and supported by well-paid contract combat troops. The second group was a regiment of 900 former inmates, which was basically employed as cannon fodder, dumped into the front lines after two-three weeks of poor training. This regiment suffered heavy casualties and was daily replenished by new inmate soldiers.

In order to break the stalemate and compensate for poor performance, the Russian armed forces and Wagner mercenaries resorted to German stormtrooper tactics from the First World War. Storm trooper groups of ten to twenty inmates were assigned narrow fronts and ordered to find weak spots in the Ukrainian lines. If successful, well-paid, follow-on, contract companies would assault through the gap. To succeed, stormtrooper tactics require highly

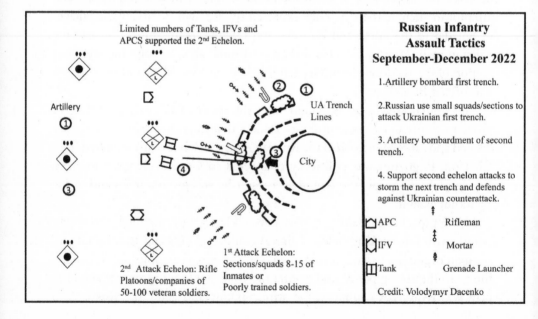

Russian Infantry Assault Tactics September–December 2022

Limited numbers of Tanks, IFVs and APCS supported the 2nd Echelon.

Artillery

UA Trench Lines

City

1. Artillery bombard first trench.

2. Russian use small squads/sections to attack Ukrainian first trench.

3. Artillery bombardment of second trench.

4. Support second echelon attacks to storm the next trench and defends against Ukrainian counterattack.

APC   Rifleman

IFV   Mortar

Tank   Grenade Launcher

1st Attack Echelon: Sections/squads 8-15 of Inmates or Poorly trained soldiers.

2nd Attack Echelon: Rifle Platoons/companies of 50-100 veteran soldiers.

Credit: Volodymyr Dacenko

trained and motivated soldiers, led by skilled junior officers, authorized to exercise initiative. Unfortunately for the Russians, most of the stormtroopers were under-equipped, poorly trained, and totally lacking in skilled junior officers. Heavy fighting continued through October-December 2022. Based on Wagner's propaganda, these battles were reportedly dominated by its mercenaries. In fact, the assaults were conducted not only by its mercenaries but included regular Russian troops and DPR soldiers.

Wagner Group tactics followed a set playbook. Stormtrooper groups formed the first echelon. Their attack along infiltration routes was plotted on Google Maps. The routes were specific, taking the tactical decision-making away from the assault leaders. A preparatory bombardment proceeded the attack. As the attack moved out, automatic grenade launchers and mortars provided fire support. The storm trooper groups then attempted to break into Ukrainian positions to create a breach for the follow-on second echelon to exploit. The second echelon was organized with Wagner Group contractors, who were well-equipped, trained, ably-lead, and well-paid.

If the defenders defeated the first echelon, they were subjected to a heavier bombardment before the second echelon attacked. Wagner's inmates could not retreat without orders. If a stormtrooper group made a breach, the second-echelon Wagner contractor unit, entered and exploited the breach. Using these tactics, the Wagner Group expended 50 to 100 soldiers a day and, according to their propaganda, took pride in the high casualty rates, which rarely moved the line a few metres. It was rumoured that Wagner Group used blocking forces with machine guns behind the inmates to ensure they would attack when ordered. Ukrainian soldiers reported repeated attacks over the same ground, littered with bodies from the failed attack the day before.[4] The majority of the causalities were suffered by the inmate troops. Russian armed forces troops used similar tactics, but with their own soldiers, rather than former inmates, making up the stormtrooper groups.

Despite Russia's superiority in artillery and months of bombardment, the ground attacks make slow gains. In November-December 2022, Wagner fighters were finally issued night vision devices (NVGs). This allowed them to use short-range infiltration tactics, like the Army and Spetsnaz reconnaissance platoons utilized, to creep up on Ukrainian positions before the assault.

Like the Imperial Germans during the First World War, the Ukrainians established a series of trench lines, bunkers, and/or fortified buildings throughout the Sector. Due to lethality of high-intensity combat in the Donbas, Ukrainian combined arms and infantry battalions were forced to defend a frontage up to 8–10km/4.9–6.2 miles wide. According to Russian doctrine (Ukrainian tactical doctrine has not been published in unclassified

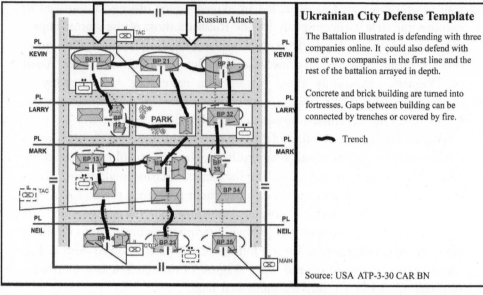

Ukrainian City Defense Template

The Battalion illustrated is defending with three companies online. It could also defend with one or two companies in the first line and the rest of the battalion arrayed in depth.

Concrete and brick building are turned into fortresses. Gaps between building can be connected by trenches or covered by fire.

↝ Trench

Source: USA ATP-3-30 CAR BN

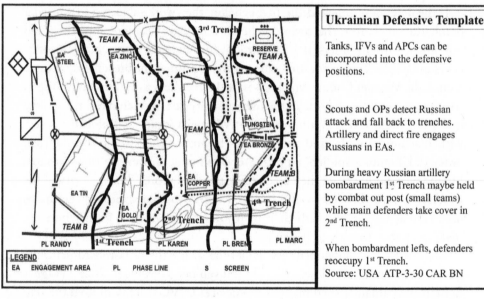

Ukrainian Defensive Template

Tanks, IFVs and APCs can be incorporated into the defensive positions.

Scouts and OPs detect Russian attack and fall back to trenches. Artillery and direct fire engages Russians in EAs.

During heavy Russian artillery bombardment 1st Trench maybe held by combat out post (small teams) while main defenders take cover in 2nd Trench.

When bombardment lefts, defenders reoccupy 1st Trench.
Source: USA ATP-3-30 CAR BN

sources), this was the frontage a brigade was expected to defend. The defensive zone was divided into a security zone, main defensive zone and rear area.

According to doctrine, a tactical combat security zone was to be established 2km/1.2 miles deep to provide early warning on expected avenues of enemy attack.[5] Snipers and observation posts, supplemented by drones, provided early warning. It also helped confuse the enemy as to the actual location of the defensive zone. The brigade may establish platoons from the second-echelon battalion into an expanded security zone.

Each company defensive zone consisted of platoon and squad strongpoints deployed in mutually supporting positions. When fully developed there were to be three to four trench lines. By doctrine, the company zone had a frontage of 3km/1.8 miles long and 3km/1.8 miles deep. Due to the need for dispersal, companies were required to defend a wider frontage. The first trench line was located at the forward edge of the defence zone.

Normally, the company would be orientated on a kill zone. However, with an extended frontal line, kill zones would be constructed on the avenues of approach into the company zone. Mines were placed forward of the first trench to reinforce the kill zone. The second trench was established 400–600m behind the first trench and, if terrain allowed, covered the approaches to the first trench and provided overwatch of the obstacles in the kill zones. A third trench was to be arrayed 600–1,000m behind the second. This trench would be used to organize a counterattack in the event of an enemy penetration. A fourth trench was to be established 600–1,000m behind the third. Communication trenches were to be dug to provide cover for soldiers moving between the trench lines. If in an urban area the four defensive lines could include buildings, maintenance tunnels, salt mines and/or other dominating terrain. In Bakhmut the lines included the garbage dump as a dominating terrain feature.

The company zone should have primary, alternative and supplementary positions providing a 360-degree defence. The supplementary position defends the flanks and rear of the position. By doctrine there would be a 2km/1.2 mile gap between company zones, which was within effective range of autocannons, ATGMs and the 125mm tank cannon of T-64s, T-72s, T-80s and T-90s.[6] With the extended front required for survival on the Ukrainian battlefield, this gap could be as much as 3–4km/1.8–2.4 miles wide, covered by a supplementary position. Coordinated crossfire from tanks (effective range 4km/2.4 miles) and ATGMs (effective range of Javelins and TOW IIs was 3,900m) of the companies on both sides would cover the gap. Detailed fire plans for artillery and mortars were required to cover the avenues of approach and dead ground leading into the company defensive zone.

The battalion would normally be deployed in two defensive echelons. Two reinforced companies manned the first echelon, and the second echelon would include the third company, a platoon-size tank reserve, mortars, ADA and other fire support and combat service support assets. This defensive doctrine made it extremely difficult for partially trained Wagner fighters and Russian infantry battalions to capture and hold the first trench line.

When a bombardment commenced most Ukrainians fell back to the second trench, while friendly artillery and mortars were massed against the attackers. The Wagner fighters often gained the first trench, and the illusion of small incremental gains was reported in Russian propaganda. A local counterattack then pushed the exhausted attackers out of the first trench. If the counterattack failed, then the first trench become a Russian position. Toward the end of the year, the invaders had succeeded in penetrating the edge of Bakhmut, but instead of defensive trenches, the invaders encountered heavily fortified buildings.

This simplification of the ebb and flow of trench and urban combat in and around Bakhmut illustrates why the Wagner fighters and Russian soldiers suffered such high casualties. The better-trained, better-equipped, and highly motivated Ukrainians suffered heavy casualties, but not on the scale of the poorly trained and poorly led invaders.

Between October and November, the garbage dump in Bakhmut, located on high ground on the southeast corner of the city became key terrain and was hotly contested. Other key landmarks and buildings were captured at the expense of hundreds of Russian soldiers and mercenaries, only to be lost to a well-timed counterattack. After suffering extremely heavy casualties, Wagner fighters finally breached the lines around Bakhmut's southern flank on 28–29 November 2022, but counterattacks by the Ukrainian National Guard's 4th Rapid Reaction Brigade, 57th Brigade, and militia contested every inch and recovered the lost ground.

Drones were extensively used by both sides. They directed artillery, conducted reconnaissance, and dropped hand grenades. Cheap gyrocopters helped fire teams and squads root out soldiers in trenches and bunkers. The Ukrainians used precision-guided munitions to maximize their limited artillery ammunition.

If Russia could have established air superiority over Bakhmut, the balance of combat power would have shifted to the invaders. However, the integrated Ukrainian air defence over the Donbas prevented the Russian air force from providing the close air support needed by the ground forces. The result was higher Russian casualties for marginal gains on the ground.

By the end of December 2022, it was estimated that Ukraine had deployed 10 brigades or 30,000 personnel into the Bakhmut Sector. The initial defenders were the 93rd Mechanized and 58th Motorized Brigades. Between August and December 2022, Ukraine reinforced the Bakmut Sector with National Guard and Territorial brigades. Each brigade deployed a battalion to the front line that was then rotated every week or two.[7]

Despite Prigozhin's grandstanding in the media, claiming sole credit for each limited success in the battle for Bakhmut, the fighting force clearly included the regular Russian combat, combat support, combat service supports, VDV and Spetsnaz soldiers in far greater numbers than the mercenaries.

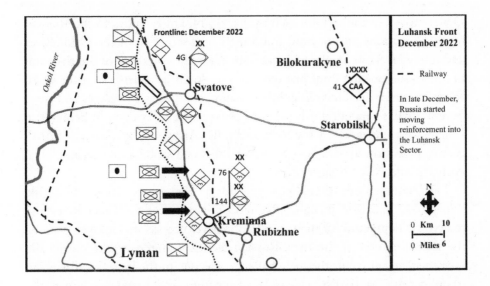

By the end of December, Prigozhin's Wagner Group had not proven superior to the Russian Army. Elite VDV paratroopers from the 217th Airborne and 106th Parachute Regiments (98th Airborne Division) were committed to the battle and the main effort shifted from encircling Bakhmut from the north, to assaulting and capturing Soledar.[8]

In early January 2023, as the Battle for Bakhmut continued to rage on, Russian General Surovikin was replaced by General Valery Gerasimov, who was then assigned Chief of Operations in Ukraine. Gerasimov initially helped plan the 'Special Operation'. Even though Surovikin had proven to be competent, and had a good relationship with Prigozhin, Gerasimov was senior and had closer ties with the Kremlin. This reassignment may have reflected the internal conflict caused by Prigozhin taking credit for successes that were, at least in part, made possible by the regular Army.[9] In a sea of bureaucratic generals, General Surovikin will probably rise to high command again in 2023.

Despite heavy casualties suffered by the Russians and gross expenditure of ammunition and other supplies, after five months of heavy fighting victory was elusive. Operationally, the Ukrainians had committed ten brigades to the defence of the sector, instead of preparing for the spring-summer 2023 counteroffensive. Weather limited cross-country mobility and would have curtailed manoeuvres if the Russians could have penetrated Ukrainian lines. Operationally, five months of fighting at Bakhmut tied down the reserves of both sides, hampering preparations for winter and spring 2023 offensives.

The Kharkiv counteroffensive succeeded in pushing the invaders east of the Oskil River, into the Luhansk Oblast. After the operational pause from the counteroffensive, the newly established front line ran north, from the Siversk-

Donets River, in the vicinity of Lysychansk, 143km/88 miles to the Russian border. Locations on the front line varied in distance from the Oskil River and reservoir. At some places it was only 20km/12 miles east of the river and in other locations the front line was as far as 46km/28 miles east of the Oskil River and reservoir. The rolling hill terrain was dotted with villages and trees. Several small rivers ran north to south between the hill ridges. In September, Luhansk was defended by the Russian regular Army, and by December 2022, they were reinforced with BARS, *mobiks*, DPR and LPR battalions, and VDV Airborne and Naval Infantry BTGs.

The Ukrainian operational objective was to liberate the city of Starobilsk, a major rail and road junction, 94km/58 miles east of the Oskil River and reservoir. They continued their counteroffensive success into October, pushing the front line east of the river. Russian tactical counter-attacks slowed the Ukrainian advance, but the real challenge was due to the increase of Russian troop density, as BARS and *mobik* companies and battalions joined the front line.

By 31 December 2022, Operational Group Voronezh (probably the 41st CAA) commanded forty-five BTGs or battalions, with the 4th Guards Tank Division headquarters controlling the northern half of the sector. The identified defending elements from north to south were the 18th Motor Rifle Division, 423rd Guards Motor Rifle Regiment, 5th BARS, 234th Airborne Assault Regiment, 74th Separate Guards Motor Rifle Brigade, 35th Separate Guards Motor Rifle Brigade, 488th Motor Rifle Regiment and the 30th Separate Motor Rifle Brigade.[10]

After September 2022, the fighting developed into a series of tactical battalion and regimental (three battalions) attacks and counterattacks, with the objective of capturing key hills and ridgelines that dominated the villages. Despite improved C2 and *mobik* battalions increasing troop strength, the Russians were only capable of tactical offensive actions.[11]

The heaviest fighting took place near Kreminna, 80km/50 miles north of Bakhmut, when Ukrainian paratroopers attempted to capture the city. Heavy Russian infantry counterattacks from the 144th Guards Motor Rifle Division stalled the Ukrainian advance. *Mobik* companies led assaults in the first echelon. Like at Bakhmut, if a breach in the Ukrainian lines could be created, the second echelon of experienced soldiers moved in.[12] Fighting continued into the new year, without significant gain by either side.

Chapter 26

Threat of Nuclear War: The Potential Use of Tactical Nuclear Weapons

With the successful Ukrainian counteroffensives in the Kherson and Kharkiv Oblasts and the routing of the Russian Army at Izyum, Putin became desperate, not only to recover loss of face internationally but to maintain his power base at home. His response to disasters on the battlefield was to mobilize an additional 300,000 men between the ages of 18 and 50 years, annex occupied Ukraine into the Russian Federation, and threaten the use of tactical nuclear weapons to defend 'Mother Russia' (including the newly, illegally annexed Ukrainian territory).

The Cold War generation of the 1950s and 60s lived under the constant threat of strategic nuclear war. Unannounced drop drills in schools were conducted, as students scrambled under flimsy decks for the illusion of protection. By the mid-60s the threat of strategic nuclear war may have receded from frontline news but, for the military, fighting a ground tactical nuclear war remained a real threat until the breakup of the Soviet Union in 1990.

Between 1970 and 1990 the public remained mostly naive while NATO forces and their Soviet and Warsaw Pact opponents trained for conventional, chemical, and tactical nuclear warfare in Central Europe. This threat only seemingly receded with the breakup of the Soviet Union and Warsaw Pact in 1990.

Ukraine was a nuclear power in 1992, but it lacked the funds, facilities, and expertise to maintain its nuclear arsenal.[1] Signing various international treaties and agreements, Ukraine agreed to relinquish its nuclear arsenal to Russia and signed the Non-Proliferation Treaty as a non-nuclear weapons state in 1994. The last nuclear weapon was transferred to Russia by 1996.[2] Ukraine was given various assurances by the US, UK, France, Russia, and other signatory countries that Ukraine's independence, sovereignty, and existing borders would be respected.[3] These assurances were breached when Russia annexed Crimea in 2014, and again by the Russian-led insurgency in the Donbas.[4]

Potential use of nuclear weapons falls into two categories: tactical and strategic. Tactical weapons are designed to destroy a battlefield target such as a specific bridge or a munitions depot. Strategic weapons are designed to

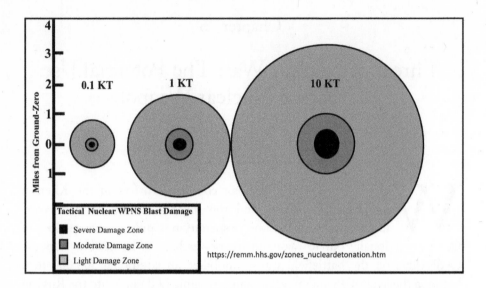

strike the enemy's homeland, such as levelling a city, and are launched by intercontinental ballistic missiles or strategic bombers and submarines. There are no small nuclear weapons.[5] Any standard Russian 152mm howitzer can fire a small-yield nuclear weapon (1 kiloton = 1,000 pounds of TNT conventional explosives) at a target up to 17 km/10 miles away that would produce damage beyond that of conventional weapons. The fireball, shock wave and deadly radioactive fallout would contaminate air, soil, and water over a large area.[6]

Tactical nuclear weapons basically fall within the 0.1 KT to 10 KT range. A smaller 'nuke' (0.1–1 KT) can be fired from standard 152mm and 155mm howitzers, while the large-yield nukes can easily be delivered by aircraft or tactical missile. Most government statistics published describe 10 KT weapons. While the blast effects are the short-term killers, deadly radiation poisoning from fallout would linger for decades.

To put these raw statistics into human terms a 10 KT nuke detonated over Kyiv would cause over 1,000,000 casualties from blast effects. Within 48 hours the radioactive fallout would travel over 80km/50 miles downwind from ground zero, causing devastating long-term health impacts from cancers and other medical conditions caused by radiation poisoning. Eventually wind and other climatic conditions would carry the radiation poisoning throughout Europe and Russia, poisoning the air, destroying crops, and contaminating the land.

The best example of projected contamination is not secret government tests but rather the April 1986 meltdown of the Chernobyl nuclear reactor. This nonexplosive nuclear event deposited radioactive materials over much of Europe as well as Russia.[7] But for the heroic Soviet technicians who entered

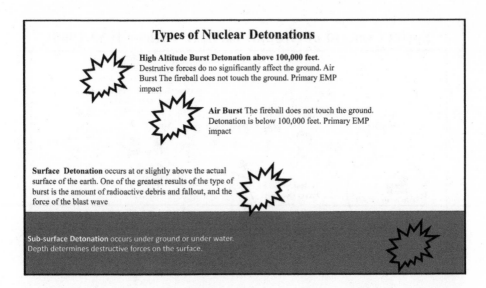

the facility to contain the meltdown, facing certain death from radiation poisoning, the environmental disaster and long-term deaths from cancers in Europe would have been much worse.[8] Despite their valiant efforts, these heroes failed to prevent radiation poisoning from spreading to other countries. Based upon the far-reaching effects of the meltdown at Chernobyl it is likely that any use of tactical nuclear weapons would risk impacting NATO countries.

In theory there are methods of limiting radioactive fallout, primarily by determining the location of detonation. There are four basic tactics for detonation: high air (above 100,000ft), air (below 100,000ft), ground and subsurface. Smaller tactical nuclear weapons are ground detonations. They are referred to as 'dirty bombs' because the ground is incinerated and produces the maximum amount of radioactive fallout.

NATO and the Soviet bloc both planned to use tactical nuclear weapons in the opening weeks of a potential Third World War. Between 1950 and 1990 various tactical doctrines were developed prescribing how the Soviet bloc would blow through NATO defences and reach the Rhine. NATO developed battle plans including the use of tactical nuclear weapons to halt rampaging Soviet tank armies. Even if the war did not escalate into a strategic exchange, Germany, as the expected battlefield, would have been reduced to ash and all of Europe and Russia would have been contaminated from radioactive fallout.

Original Soviet doctrine envisioned tactical nuclear weapons blowing a hole in NATO lines and destroying targets along the axis of advance. Tank armies would assault through the breach, along the path of nuclear destruction and contamination to their objective. In theory Russian soldiers would have been protected by over-pressure systems in their tanks and BMP infantry fighting

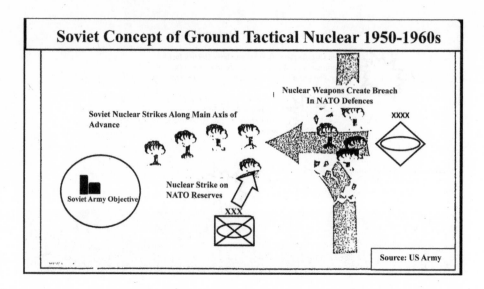

vehicles. The illusion of protection by over-pressure systems in armoured vehicles was copied by NATO armies, along with individual protective clothing for soldiers (MOPP gear).

As these two charts demonstrate, Soviet tactics were refined to plan for the use of tactical nuclear weapons to protect its flanks as it advanced rather than to create a forward passage through contaminated ground. The remaining problem was that troops on both sides of the conflict would be poisoned by radioactive fallout even if they did not enter the zones of destruction.

The one inescapable conclusion for anyone trained to fight in a tactical nuclear environment is that if you survived the attack, you would later die from radiation poisoning. Putin absurdly discounted this basic fact of nuclear warfare when he threatened to use nuclear weapons. On 24 February 2022, with total disregard for the welfare of his troops, Putin ordered his soldiers to seize and occupy all the Chernobyl nuclear power plants. During their occupation they transported vehicles and soldiers through contaminated areas totally disregarding warnings from Ukrainian technicians. Unprotected Russian soldiers dug defences in the surrounding contaminated forest and will likely suffer the ill effects of radiation poisoning.[9]

However inherently dangerous, an enemy may consider the use of tactical nuclear weapons when fighting for national survival.[10]Putin claimed that the annexation of occupied Ukraine incorporated these oblasts into 'Mother Russia', so that any use of nuclear weapons would be for national survival or defence. While the world did not recognize this land grab or the sham referendums authorizing the annexations, the propaganda was broadcast to the Russian population, which would conceivably support the use of nuclear weapons in defence of their homeland.

There are several conceivable situations in which Putin would use tactical nuclear weapons; primarily to affect the course of fighting on the ground, secondly to retaliate for Ukrainian strikes into 'Mother Russia', and finally to raise the stakes and persuade Ukraine to surrender. It is also possible that, if Putin is politically threatened at home, he would want to put a quick end to his 'Special Operation'.[11]

Putin could send a warning by detonating a low-yield warhead above Novaya Zemlya, the old Soviet Artic test site. While radioactive fallout would be negligible, the psychological impact would serve as a warning of things to come.

Alternatively, he could order an air atmospheric detonation above Ukraine. The primary affect would be an electromagnetic pulse that would disrupt civilian and military infrastructure. This option would disrupt communications in Ukraine as well as NATO countries but would also impact Russian tactical military communication.

Another possibility is a ground detonation in Ukraine against a military or logistical target in sparsely populated Western Ukraine, between Lviv and Kyiv. The fire ball would ignite wildfires throughout the area and the radioactive fallout would extend to NATO countries and Belarus, as well as Russian territory.[12] A less disastrous option would be to strike a UAF forward supply dump, defensive position, or village.[13]

The expected response by NATO nuclear members would be proportionate to the provocation. One option would be to stay the course by increasing

Soviet/Russian Concept for Tactical Nuclear War 1970-2022

Soviet/Russian tactical nuclear manoeuvre doctrine evolved by 1970.

1. Tactical nuclear weapons still would be used to break NATO lines.
2. Nuclear weapons would be used to protect the flanks of the penetration.
3. NATO operations reserves, C2, supply depots and airfields would targeted.
4. Soviet/Russian mechanized forces axis of advance **no longer** advanced through areas devastated by tactical nuclear weapons

Source: US Army

sanctions and increasing military support to Ukraine, while building international support to completely isolate Russia. Experts believe that, if Putin employed a nuclear option, the world, including China, would turn against him.

NATO could launch a conventional armed response. This could be in the form of establishing a 'No Fly Zone' over Ukraine, establishing a haven within Ukraine for refugees, and/or protecting Kyiv and Black Sea ports with anti-missile and anti-aircraft batteries.

The ultimate option would be to respond by launching a proportionate nuclear attack. Unless a NATO country was directly attacked, its nuclear members (US, UK, and France) would not have an obligation to respond with nuclear weapons. NATO long-range, precision-guided conventional munitions could sever all rail links delivering supplies to the Russians. Cut off from all rail supply routes and lacking sufficient wheeled vehicles, the Russian forward-deployed BTGs in Ukraine would literally 'wither on the vine' and freeze during the winter. Opinions are mixed as to what the appropriate response to Russia's use of tactical nuclear weapons should be.[14]

The fallout from any nuclear attack in Ukraine posed a very real problem for 'Mother Russia'. It is unknown whether radiological fallout over a NATO country would be considered an 'attack' under Article 5.[15] Article 5 of the NATO Charter views an 'armed attack' on one member of the alliance as an attack on all 30 members.[16] Since the US was the best equipped, any state in the alliance would be under the protection of its nuclear umbrella.[17] The effects of radioactive fallout carried downwind might very well be considered an attack within national borders.[18] Neighbouring Poland (a NATO member since the fall of the Soviet Union) would definitely view the fallout as a direct attack.

The Biden administration has not yet provided Ukraine with ATACMS missiles (with a range of 482km/300 miles). Both the HIMARS and MRLS systems provided to Ukraine can fire these missiles with minor modification. These missiles were probably in the NATO ammunition dumps and could have been provided to Ukraine within days if not hours. ATACMS would allow the UAF to strike high-value targets inside 'Mother Russia', such as command posts, ammunition dumps, logistical hubs, air defence complexes, airfields, and ballistic missile launchers.[19]

Despite bellicose speeches and threats Putin was deathly afraid of ATACMS. Theses missiles could destroy all Russian supply lines within Ukraine. Putin lacked the air defence assets to defend every little bridge over every creek and small river that his supply routes cross.

With ATACMS, the UAF could reach military targets well within 'Mother Russia'. If Putin deployed tactical nuclear weapons, and if a NATO member were impacted there is no reason the US would refrain from arming the UAF with conventional ATACMS. Frankly, with the shaky Russian supply situation, ATACMS were more of a threat to the Russian Army than tactical nuclear weapons are to the Ukrainian defenders.

Historically, the only country to detonate nuclear weapons in war was the US. Atomic bombs were dropped on Japan in the Second World War to destroy the cities of Hiroshima and Nagasaki. Those early atomic bombs were 15 KT and would be considered large tactical weapons in the twenty-first century. The pre-raid population of Hiroshima was 255,000. The blast and resulting fire killed or wounded 135,000. The pre-raid population of Nagasaki was 195,000 and the blast and resulting fires killed or wounded 64,000. These casualty rates do not reflect the terrible long-term impact of radiation poisoning on the survivors and their descendants.[20]

Throughout the 1960s and 1970s a great number of books and articles were published second guessing President Truman's decision to deploy atomic weapons. The most extreme position of this debate was taken by Gar Alperovitz in his book *Atomic Diplomacy: Hiroshima and Potsdam*.[21] Alperovitz argued that dropping the bombs was racially motivated rather than the result of overriding military considerations. He further points out that the US Joint Chiefs were convinced that Japan would surrender without dropping the bomb and without the necessity of a land invasion.[22] Other authors have added to Alperovitz arguments that the spectre of bigotry was an additional motivation for the use of the bomb against Japan.[23]

From the very beginning of the Second World War, claimed racial superiority and ethnic cleansing were at least partly motivating the economic and political actions of Nazi Germany, Imperial Japan, and fascist Italy. From the beginning there was an ethnic and cultural conflict between the Western Democracies and their Axis rivals. Yet opponents of the use of the bomb by America paint the act as particularly sinister, alleging that it was racially motivated:

Race-tinged revenge may have shaped the United States' decision to firebomb Tokyo and to detonate atomic bombs over Hiroshima and Nagasaki Japan, killing hundreds and thousands of civilians and leaving those cities in ruins.

Yet as distasteful as those bombing campaigns are today to most citizens of liberal democracies under [seventy] years of age, the Combined Bomber Offensive in Europe and the bombing of Japan reflect not only a sense of moral conviction on the part of the West but a belief that such attacks would end the war that daily grew more horrible for soldiers and civilians alike.[24]

The racial motivation argument ignores the devastating effect of war, whether killing by nuclear weapons or conventional weapons. When conventional bombers attacked Dresden, Germany on 13–14 February 1945, the city was levelled, with as many as 135,000 killed and hundreds of thousands more wounded or displaced.[25] Of course the significant difference was Germany was spared the horrific after-effects of radiation poisoning causing death and birth defects generations after the blast.

US Secretary of War Stimson and General Marshall, Army Chief of Staff, were unconvinced that the naval blockade, conventional bombing or even the atomic bomb could force the Japanese to unconditionally surrender.[26] He was not entirely wrong. Even after the bombs were dropped, not all Japanese leaders were ready to surrender. On 9 August 1945, despite the fact that the Japanese were besieged on the Home Islands, 73 of their 76 major cities had been destroyed through conventional and atomic bombardment, 300,000 of their civilians had been incinerated in their cities, 2,500,000 homes had been destroyed, and 8,000,000 refugees were facing starvation, the war nearly continued. The Japanese governing cabinet was not unanimous in deciding to surrender. A strong minority from the military favoured continuing the war. On 14 August 1945, with the threat of a military coup, Emperor Hirohito gave his cabinet instructions to surrender.[27]

The 15 June 1945 US casualty estimate for a potential invasion was 40,000 killed, 150,000 wounded, plus 3,500 missing, for a total US casualty estimate of 193,500.[28] Other casualty estimates raised the number to 500,000.[29] This total does not include the casualties to the Japanese military or civilian population. In the battles for Iwo Jima and Okinawa the destruction of the defending garrisons was almost complete. In the battle for Okinawa the civilian population of 450,000 shielded the defending garrison with the resulting death of 150,000 civilians.[30]

Putin rattled his nuclear sabre. As unthinkable as nuclear war was, his threats were particularly worrisome as the war continued and his battlefield losses persisted. Arguably the Third World War was already being fought by proxies, Western alliances against the Russian state. Many soldiers within the Russian Army aired their belief that Ukrainians were 'subhuman'. Considering that Putin publicly promoted and even awarded officers who had committed war crimes against Ukrainian civilians, Putin may indeed have a racial/ethnic motivation for using nuclear weapons in Ukraine. If true, Putin may have had less reluctance than otherwise to use the bomb in Ukraine.[31]

The more compelling reason for why Putin may have considered using nuclear weapons is a belief that it would have ended the war and quickly forced Ukrainians to the negotiating table. As battlefield losses and Russian

KIAs mounted, Putin's position at home may have been threatened. More and more internal disputes between Prigozhin as CEO of the Wagner Group and the Russian Army were publicly aired. More and more Putin faced public protests against the war at home and internal pressure at the highest level to end his 'Special Operation' quickly.

Putin's use of nuclear weapons would clearly have saved Russian lives on the battlefield and ended the war faster than conventional weapons, removing threats to Putin's position of power at home. The obvious disadvantages would have been the horrific after-effects of radiation poisoning that could have very well spread throughout Europe as well as across Russia. The radiation would have rendered the once-fertile fields of Ukraine incapable of growing the wheat the world depended upon. Much like the after-effects of the disaster at Chernobyl, radiation sickness throughout that part of the world would have been felt for decades. The Chernobyl clean-up alone involved more than 500,000 personnel and cost Russia an estimated 18,000,000,000 roubles, almost $68,000,000,000 in 2019 dollars. The deadly impact in Russia would have very likely more than offset the potential lives saved in continued fighting in Ukraine. In addition, any use of a nuclear weapon would have most definitely triggered a proportionate response by the world. Among the devastating impacts of any use of nuclear weapons, perhaps the most significant impact would have been the danger to the already delicate worldwide climate, that was already being damaged by the impacts of Putin's 'Special Operation'.

Chapter 27

Twenty-first Century Holodomor: Putin's Terror Campaign

Captured Russian war plans and other documents revealed Putin's Stalinist-type scheme to control Ukraine once it was occupied. The population would be divided into four categories. Those who should be killed, those who needed to be suppressed and intimidated, those who would remain neutral or could be encouraged to collaborate, and those prepared to collaborate.[1] It was expected that by D+10 the Russian Army would transition to occupation duty and those marked for death could be rounded up by FSB VDV death squads and army patrols.[2] Included in the category of those who 'should be killed' were military and civilian leaders, down to village, town and oblast councils, police chiefs and junior army officers. The plan was similar to the 1939 Soviet occupation of Poland, where 22,000 Polish military officers, police, government officials, and intelligentsia were marched into a forest and executed.[3] In other words, a proper occupation plan that would have made Stalin proud. In a twist of irony, on 2 April 2010, Putin and Polish Prime Minister Donald Tusk officiated at a ceremony commemorating that massacre.[4]

Included in the 'Special Operation' war plan was the goal of controlling central Ukrainian heating, electricity, transportation hubs and the banking industry to suppress the Ukrainian population. The task of capturing power stations, including the nuclear power plants, airfields, centralized water distribution facilities, the central bank and parliament was given to the VDV, and special forces.[5]

These premeditated war crimes against the Ukrainian people resonate with Putin's fear of Ukraine's liberal democracy as a threat to his autocratic regime.[6] The plan imitates Stalin's occupation of eastern Poland in 1939 and his control of Eastern Europe between 1945 and his death in 1953. By implementing this war plan Russia became a terrorist state and the FSB and VDV became terrorist organizations equivalent to Hitler's Gestapo (secret police) and Schutzstaffel (SS).

During Putin's 'Special Operation' Russian soldiers have reportedly committed 66,000 war crimes against individuals, including rape, torture, and murder. Many of these war crimes are well-documented, with photographic evidence posted on the internet by the proud perpetrators and daily interviews of witnesses and victims provided to the international press. President Zelensky has made justice for the victims one condition for eventual peace with Russia. Ukraine's Prosecutor, General Andriy Kostin, firmly declared 'we have to win in both battles – in the fight for our territory and in the fight for justice.'[7]

Mass graves have been located in almost all towns, villages and cities once occupied by Russian forces. Modern technology, including satellite footage was used to locate and document mass graves. The liberation of occupied territory enabled investigators to document first-hand accounts and forensic evidence within days and weeks of the crimes being committed. Every liberated region revealed new mass graves, and torture chambers. Detailed examination of the bodies needs to be conducted to determine the circumstances of death, and Ukrainians hoped to identify individual perpetrators from evidence gathered in each location after liberation. The task was herculean and would not be completed for months or years.

By the end of 2022, only 86 indictments against individual Russian soldiers had been filed, ranging from looting, rape, torture, and murder. One case against a battalion commander cited him for ordering his troops to fire on fleeing civilians. By the end of 2022, Ukrainian investigators had identified 250 individual perpetrators. Only 18 of the 250 were in custody as prisoners of war. These 18 have been convicted of war crimes, the rest were tried *in absentia*.[8]

Debriefings of Ukrainian PoWs released in prisoner exchanges have not been released to the public. Released Ukrainian soldiers have not given interviews about their treatment as a PoW, with one exception. Captain Hotskiy, of Snake Island fame, was captured and held prisoner, but subsequently released as part of a prisoner exchange. Many of his soldiers and border guards were still in Russian custody when he was released and he did not give an interview as to his treatment. Father Vasyl Vyrozub, an Orthodox priest, was also captured when the Russians stormed Snake Island. He was also subsequently released and was willing to talk about his experience as a PoW.

On 25 February 2022, a Ukrainian naval officer requested that Father Vyrozub join two other clergymen and a doctor and journey to Snake Island. The party was to bring back the bodies of the presumed-dead garrison. He was guaranteed that the Russian Navy had approved the trip.

The red-painted rescue boat sailed 144km/90 miles from Odesa to Snake Island, passing a cargo ship that was on fire, having been hit by a missile. As the small boat approached the island, the Russians told them to wait for inspection. A Russian boat filled with Spetsnaz approached and they were boarded. They were informed that everyone had left the island and had been taken into custody. Father Vyrozub tried to hide his phone because it contained photos of him with several Ukrainian generals. The chaplains and the doctor were loaded on a cutter and transported to Sevastopol. A Spetsnaz officer told him that he would remain in custody until the 'Special Operation' was completed. He was assured the war would be over in seven days.

Upon arriving in Sevastopol, Vyozub and two dozen other non-combatants were searched and then transported to a watch tower. Vyozub's phone was probably discovered. Vyozub was interrogated three times a day for eleven days. The Russians did not believe that he had gone to the island on his own accord to render last rites to the dead Ukrainians. They thought the three priests and the doctor were on a secret spy mission. While incarcerated, he was interrogated by the FSB, Russian military intelligence, and local prosecutors. He was accused of being a spy and a 'fascist'. In March, Vyozub and 200 detainees were flown to Stary Oskol, a Russian city north of Belgorod, and placed in a detention centre.

At the detention centre Vyrozub was tortured. He was held in a cell with the two other priests and the doctor who had accompanied him to Snake Island. Professional interrogators tortured him. He was beaten and shocked with electric cattle prods. In late March, he was stripped of his clothes and put in a freezing punishment cell for three days. It was too cold to sit, lie down or sleep. He assumed he was going to die. In April, the two other priests and the doctor were released. Vyrozub was freed during a prisoner exchange in May. He had lost 15kg/33lbs due to the poor food.[9] The Russian treatment of Vyrozub while in custody was a clear violation of international rules of war. The proper treatment of PoWs had been routinely ignored by the Soviets and it is clear from Vyrozub's statement that nothing has changed in the new Russian state.

The initial invasion of Ukraine caused 4.1 million civilians to flee their country seeking the safety of Europe. Early in the invasion, Russia opened 'humanitarian corridors' to provide safe passage for civilian refugees. The eastern corridor first made available was ostensibly to move non-combatants from Mariupol and other besieged towns in Eastern Ukraine out of the combat zone. Russia offered other corridors from the Kyiv region into Russia and Belarus, but they were rejected.[10]

Ultimately the refugees were misled. Instead of reaching safety, civilians and children were gathered and illegally transported into Russia. Refugees had to pass through Russian 'filtration stations' at the border. These stations were intelligence-gathering operations. Refugees were not treated kindly. Treatment ranged from interrogations and data collection to strip searches and torture. Many refugees were transported to detention centres within Russia. Estimates varied between 900,000 to 1,600,000 Ukrainians being illegally deported into Russia, often to cold, isolated eastern regions. Just in the month of July 2022, more than 1,800 children were separated from their families or taken from captured Ukrainian orphanages and sent into Russia. Russia's UN ambassador, Vassily Nebenzia, admitted that 3,700,000 Ukrainians, including 600,000 children had been taken into Russia or separatist areas but denied they were being kept in prisons.[11] UN investigators verified that civilians passing though 'filtration centres' were subjected to violations of basic human rights.[12] As of the end of 31 December 2022, there were not any reports regarding the whereabouts of these illegally deported refugees.

Russian military doctrine included targeting civilians and civilian infrastructure to encourage an enemy to surrender. The conduct of the Russian military in Chechnya and Syria demonstrated that not only was this an accepted method of warfare, but Russian generals were promoted and received commendations for their efforts in implementing this directive. Russian pilots bombed civilian targets with impunity. This doctrine of targeting civilians was in direct violation of international laws defining war crimes and crimes against humanity.

Like Hitler's blitz on Great Britain in 1940, Putin's initial missile campaign targeted legitimate military and political targets. The Russian invasion began with a heavy cruise- and ballistic-missile barrage, that averaged 24 missiles per day for the first 3 weeks of the war, but it increased steadily. Between February and May, more than 2,000 missiles of various types were launched. Between 24 and 28 February 2022, the strikes targeted Ukrainian ADA facilities, C2 nodes and other military targets.

The most important targeting information was provided by human intelligence (HUMINT). Agents recruited within Ukraine by Russian intelligence services (FSB, GRU and SVR) reported target locations. During the 'Special Operation' these quislings provided targeting information to their handlers.[13] They also identified and located the Ukrainians to be individually targeted and killed.

In June 2022 the Russian bombardment strategy changed to striking fuel storage faculties, refineries, and key railway infrastructure. By this stage in the war Ukrainian ADA had been reorganized and redeployed to cover key cities and facilities. Interception rates, from 20 to 30 per cent in April, rose to 50 to 60 per cent in June. Coupled with the higher interception rates, Russia started to run low on missile stocks with expenditure far exceeding production rates. Between June and September 2022, launch rates were reduced back to twenty-four per day.

To remedy the reduction in missile stocks, Russia converted anti-ship and large anti-air missiles to land-attacks. In addition, Russia entered a deal with

Iran to secure large numbers of Shahed-136 loitering kamikaze drones. The Shahed-136 has a range of 1,000km/621 miles and a speed 150–170kmh /93–105mph, with a warhead of 20–40kg. What, if anything, Iran received in return was not disclosed. They did not need oil or gas.

Putin believed the billion-dollar Kerch Strait Bridge, not within range of Ukrainian HIMARS, was not in danger. The only weapons that could threaten the bridge were Ukrainian fighter bombers, but Russia's intergrated ADA system and jet fighters negated that threat. The Kerch Strait Bridge linked Crimea with Russia's Kerch Peninsula and was the main supply route for the Russian army in Kerson Oblast. On 8 October 2022, a truck laden with explosives, planted by Ukrainian naval commandos, stopped in the middle of the bridge. By coincidence or not, a train loaded with fuel was stopped on the bridge for an extended period of time. When the truck exploded, sections of the bridge collapsed into the water, setting the railway tanker cars on fire. No one claimed responsibility for the explosion. Traffic by road and rail was stopped. Putin ordered the bridge to be fully repaired but the work was not expected to be completed until July 2023.[14]

The successful Kharkiv counteroffensive rattled Putin and his generals. The successful commando raid on the Kerch Strait Bridge embarrassed Putin. His reaction was like Hitler's reaction to the British bombing of Berlin during the Battle for Britain. Hitler shifted his bombing campaign from destroying military targets, to terror bombing London. Putin shifted his missile bombardment to striking civilian infrastructure.

Prior to this event, the Russians deliberately bombed hospitals, a maternity ward and a theatre used as a civilian bomb shelter. With their quisling forward observers, the Russians had to have been aware that these locations were non-military targets. Before the bombing of the bridge, Russia had targeted several individual civilian buildings. As retaliation for the bombing of the Kerch Strait Bridge, Russia openly admitted to targeting civilian infrastructure for its terrorizing effect.

On 9 October 2022, General Segey Surovikin was named Commander of the 'Special Operation'. Surovikin was one of the generals who masterminded the terror campaign against Syrian civilians.

On 10 October 2022, a barrage of cruise and ballistic missiles was launched, along with Shahed-136 loitering drones, targeting the national Ukrainian power grid. Despite more than half the incoming missiles being shot down the power grid was severely damaged.[15]

After 10 October, the Russians continued to launch massive attacks against the Ukrainian power grid.[16] On 14 October Ukrainian Foreign Minister Dmytryo Kuleba stated that the strikes on the energy facilities were 'war crimes, planned well in advance and aimed at creating unbearable conditions for civilians.[17] On 1 December, Russian Foreign Minister Sergey Lavrov countered, justifying the attacks because the electric power grid supported the Ukrainian armed forces.[18] This was a valid point, since many Ukrainian trains operated on electric power, and the UAF used rail to move troops and supplies from one embattled sector to another.

However, Russian lawmakers Andrey Gurulyov and Konstantin Dolgov made it clear that Putin and the Russian government were knowingly committing war crimes. During an interview they advocated freezing and starving the Ukrainian population, forcing as many as possible into exile by making survival in the cities impossible.

Gurulyov said 'the absence of electricity means the absence of water, the absence of refrigeration, absence of sewer. One week after all electricity is cut off, the city of Kyiv will be swimming in shit.... There will be a clear threat of an epidemic.'[19] Upon review, American Chief of Staff General Milley stated that the Russian campaign of targeting the electric grid with winter coming on was a terror tactic designed to cause maximum suffering of the Ukrainian civilian population to defeat Ukrainian morale.[20]

Russian doctrine envisioned infliction of civilian casualties as a way to quick victory. The Russian political and military leadership believed they could compel Ukraine to sit down at the negotiating table.[21] The result of this mindset was to justify an increase in Russian attacks on civilian infrastructure in direct proportion to Russia's failures on the battlefield.

Putin hoped his attacks on civilian infrastructure would make life miserable enough for Ukrainians that they would admit defeat. Putin and his cronies missed the lesson of the Great Patriotic War, that terror bombing only solidifies the civilian population and their will to resist.

Ukraine lobbied the international community to create a special tribunal, as was established to prosecute war crimes in Rwanda and Yugoslavia.[22] Ukraine developed cases against high-level Russian officials that were provided to the Hague's International Criminal Court.

While international laws protecting civilians during war and the list of 'crimes against humanity' were primarily developed in the twentieth century, there was no permanent international criminal court to prosecute until 1998, when the 'Rome Statute' established the International Criminal Court (ICC). The document reflected consensus in the international community on crimes against humanity, war crimes, genocide, and ethnic cleansing.[23]

Russia originally signed the Rome Statute in 2000, but thereafter failed to ratify the treaty and remained outside the court's jurisdiction. In 2008 the Kremlin received a negative court ruling against its invasion of Georgia. The court also ruled against the Kremlin on its occupation of Crimea in 2014.[24] In 2016, Putin formerly withdrew from the Rome Statute. While Russia did not recognize the jurisdiction of the ICC, the court nevertheless opened investigations into the war crimes alleged to have been committed by Russians in Ukraine.[25]

Ukraine signed the Rome Statute in 2000, and even though its legislature never ratified the treaty, it filed charges against Russia with the ICC.

The US helped negotiate the accord but did not formally join the ICC. The US position was that it can and does investigate and prosecute its people for violation of the crimes enumerated under the Rome Statute. An ICC prosecutor with too much power could conceivably violate an America citizens' rights under the US Constitution. Nevertheless the US stated it would assist the ICC to investigate the crimes alleged against Russia.[26]

Many of the alleged crimes against humanity were verified by international agencies. The ability of the ICC to bring the alleged perpetrators to trial was limited, especially if they remain inside Russia, and outside of the ICC's jurisdiction.

On or about 23 November 2022, the EU Parliament adopted a resolution declaring that because of the brutal war of aggression against Ukraine, 'Russia was a State Sponsor of Terrorism.' The resolution highlighted the deliberate attacks and atrocities committed by Russian forces and their proxies against civilians in Ukraine. It specifically concluded that the destruction of civilian infrastructure for the purpose of terrorizing the civilian population was a violation of international and humanitarian law amounting to acts of terror and constituting war crimes. The Parliament recommended that the Council add the Russian paramilitary organization Wagner Group, the Chechnya 141st Special 'Kadyrovites' Motorized Regiment and other Russian-funded armed groups, militias, and proxies to the EU list of terrorists. The resolution further isolated Russia by stripping it of membership in international organizations, reducing diplomatic ties to a minimum, and enacting a ninth sanction package. While the EU did not officially add Russia to the list, the resolution encouraged member states to take such action.[27]

To punish Russia, Putin, and the oligarchs for the unlawful invasion of Ukraine, the international community imposed economic and political sanctions. These sanctions included restrictions on transactions with Russian banks as well as transactions with the Russian government. Over $330,000,000,000 of Russian government and oligarch funds were frozen and there was a move in the international community to transfer these funds to Ukraine to help rebuild the country after the war. Export controls targeting Russia's defence, aerospace, and maritime industries were implemented. A wide range of commercial and industrial operations were banned. A ban was also passed on the importation of Russian petro-chemical products and suspension of normal trade relations with Russia and its ally Belarus. In addition, the US banned investment in Russia, export of luxury goods, secondary market transactions, entrance and use of US airspace and ports, and a prohibition of trade or investment in Russian occupied Ukraine.[28]

International sanctions targeted Putin individually, the oligarchs, individual members of the Duma and senior military leaders of the Russian armed forces. Thousands of Russian miliary officers and governmental officials have been banned from entry into the US. The EU, NATO, and allied countries around the world, including Switzerland, have enacted similar sanctions. Two days after the invasion, the German government suspended the certification of the Nord Stream 2 pipeline. On 5 December 2022, the EU banned most Russian oil imports and joined the US, UK, Canada, Japan, and Australia in setting a global price cap of $60 per barrel on Russian oil. They also banned their nationals from providing sea transport services for oil, that would have violated the price cap.[29]

It will take decades for the victims of Putin's twenty-first century Holodomor to receive justice. It will take decades to locate the millions of adults relocated into Russia, assuming they were not executed. The thousands of Ukrainian children shipped to Russia will probably be assimilated into local society and never repatriated. While the sanctions imposed will impact Russia's economy and its ability to wage war for years to come, they will not address compensation for the war crimes committed. A few low-ranking soldiers may be captured in battle and tried for their offences, however the officers and officials giving the orders will remain unpunished as long as they remain in Russia. Like the Nazi war criminals, it will take decades for the victims of Putin's twenty-first century Holodomor to received justice.

Chapter 28

Rush to Join NATO

One of Putin's strategic goals in invading Ukraine was to stop the western expansion of NATO. He expected this show of military might would dissuade countries near the borders of Russia from applying to join the alliance. His aggressive actions and nuclear posturing backfired. On 18 May 2022, Finland and Sweden simultaneously tendered official letters of application to join NATO as full members.[1] These progressive democracies were part of the European community and recognized that Russia's illegal invasion of Ukraine upset the security of Europe. For decades both Finland and Sweden have worked with NATO. Finland shares a long border with Russia and Sweden is just across the Baltic Sea from St. Petersburg.

NATO members have historically been concerned with the security of its northern Arctic flank. By joining NATO, Finland and Sweden would be in position to secure the north. As of the twenty-first century, only Norway, supported by the US and British Fleets, stood watch in the north. Other NATO-member naval assets were available to supplement the defence, but it remained the mission of the larger US and British fleets to provide ships and Marines. Applications to join NATO by Finland and Sweden served to strengthen NATO as Russia's conventional strength was being depleted in battle. In return Finland and Sweden were to gain the protection of NATO's nuclear umbrella.[2]

Finland had once been included in Imperial Russia but had become autonomous with its own senate and institutions during the 1850s. Friction developed in the 1890s when the Russian government decided Finns should become 'more Russian' and pressured them to disband their legal system and adopt Imperial institutions.

The Russian Empire went to war against the Austro-Hungarian and German Empires in 1914. Finnish Field Marshal Carl Gustaf Emil Mannerheim rose to prominence during the fighting on the eastern front. With the disintegration of the Russian Empire in 1917, and the following Civil War, Mannerheim joined the 'Whites' fighting against the Bolshevik 'Reds'. Mannerheim created a Finnish Army that defeated the 'Reds' and was eventually instrumental in securing independence for Finland.

In 1939, Stalin decided that the Soviet Union required strategic territory in Finland to protect Leningrad (St. Petersburg). The Soviet army invaded the tiny country but was soundly defeated during the Winter War. The Soviets quickly reorganized and invaded once again, finally forcing Finland to the negotiating table. The subsequent peace talks resulted in the Soviet Union acquiring land along Finland's border with the Soviet Union. In 1941, Finland joined the Germans in invading the Soviet Union and both were defeated in 1945. Finland suffered over 200,000 casualties and lost more territory.

While the Soviet Union absorbed Lithuania, Estonia, and Lathia, it did not absorb Finland. However, it imposed reparation payments and several harsh conditions including requiring Finland to remain neutral and precluding Finland from joining any alliance. These limitations on Finish foreign policy ended with the dissolution of the Soviet Union and Finland joined the EU.

Finland came to be concerned that it was on Putin's list to be absorbed into a reconstituted Russian Empire, causing Finland to seek closer ties with NATO. Seeking interoperability with NATO, Finland joined as an 'Enhanced Opportunity Partner'.[3]

Sweden based its historic policy of neutrality on tradition rather than treaty. In 1810 King Karl XIV Johan changed Sweden's foreign policy from one seeking military conquest of neighbouring countries to one of neutrality. Sweden had maintained its neutral status through the decades.

In 1994, Sweden joined the Partnership for Peace to establish a relationship with NATO. Swedish armed forces increased their interoperability with NATO and adopted alliance standards, with English as its operational language. It participated with NATO-led operations in Bosnia, Herzegovina, Kosovo, Afghanistan, Libya, and Iraq. Sweden participated in collective defence exercises in 2013.

In response to Russia's annexation of Crimea in 2014, Sweden became not a full member of NATO, but along with Australia, Finland Georgia, Jordan, and Ukraine became an 'Enhanced Opportunity Partner'.[4] The 'Enhanced Opportunity Partner' programme developed interoperability between NATO members and partners.[5] Sweden also established close defence cooperation agreements with Norway, Denmark, the UK, USA, and Finland.[6]

Considering the change in the security environment after Russia's invasion of Ukraine, Sweden determined it was in its best interest to join NATO as a full partner with the protection of Article 5, rather than just an 'Enhanced Opportunity Partner'.[7] The actions of Russia during the twenty-first century gave rise to a long-term deterioration of the security of Europe and the world. The new security environment had long-term implications for countries in the Euro-Atlantic area. Due to Sweden's opposition to the invasion, and its support of Ukraine, potential Russian retaliatory action against Sweden could not be ruled out. Russia's aggression against a NATO 'Enhanced Opportunity Partner' did not trigger Article 5 protection. NATO's collective defence obligations did not include partners. Joining NATO was Sweden's only guarantee of joining the collective defence of Europe.[8]

As the Russian invasion unfolded, NATO reinforced its collective defence abilities by reinforcing Estonia, Latvia, and Lithuania. Multinational battle groups were deployed to Poland, Bulgaria, Romania, Slovakia, and Hungary. Almost immediately NATO poured military aid into Ukraine, proving that NATO would honour its commitment to members, even if contrary to the economic interest of an individual member, such as Germany.

Finland had a world class army larger in number when fully mobilized than the UK. Its artillery was world class and had a higher ratio of artillery to manoeuvre units when compared to most NATO countries. Finland had a small army of 23,000 soldiers and an air force of 3,083. Its reserve force contained 285,000 soldiers. It maintained a fleet of 200 Leopard IIs (some of which were sent to Ukraine), 203 IFVs, 600 APCs and 700 artillery pieces, supported by 55 F-18s with F-35s on order. The Finnish navy had 4,700 sailors and consisted primarily of patrol boats and small surface combatants for coastal defence.[9] This force was maintained through conscription, refresher training and a mobilization infrastructure that could mobilize its reserve manpower quickly. Every major structure in the country was built as a bomb shelter.

Sweden fielded a world-class military.[10] It was small but technologically advanced and supported by an advanced defence industry and exceptional

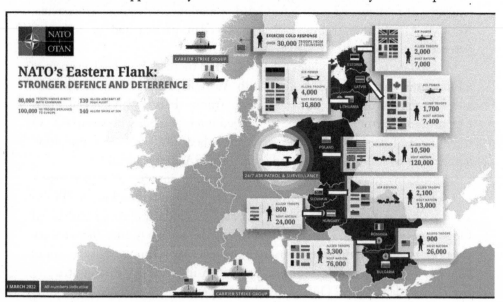

intelligence service. Its 14,600 active-duty troops were backed up by 10,000 reservists. It was a world leader in the international development, manufacture and exportation of highly advanced weapons. The 7,000 strong army fielded Leopard 2A tanks, and Patriot missile batteries. The air force included 2,770 personnel operating over 100 JAS 39 Gripen jets. The Gripen was designed to require little maintenance and could operate on short take-off and landing strips. The Swedish navy's 2,100 sailors operated advanced Gotland diesel-electric submarines and patrol boats.[11]

Turkey and Hungary objected to the applications by Finland and Sweden to join NATO as full members. All current members must agree to the acceptance of new members. The objection by Turkish President Recep Tayyip Erdogan surprised NATO members, since prior discussions had not signalled an issue. Ankara had previously supported NATO expansion. Erdogan's objection was primarily based on Sweden's favourable support of Turkish Kurds and the prior refusal of both Finland and Sweden to sell arms to Turkey.

Turkey historically opposed Kurdish demands for statehood and had fought against the Kurdistan Workers' Party (PKK) for decades. Turkey labelled the PKK a Terrorist Organization.[12] It had been estimated that since 1984 between 30,000 and 40,000 on both sides had died in the fighting between the PKK and Turkish government. The PKK had carried out a large number of attacks within Turkey.

Nearly 20 per cent of Turkey's population of 84,000,000 were Kurdish. Like the Armenians within Turkey, the Kurds had been subjected to massacres during the First World War and in the years following the establishment of the Turkish State in 1923. Spread out between Turkey, Syria, Iraq and Iran, Kurds have been heavily persecuted and marginalized by all four countries. Saddam Hussein's chemical attacks against the Kurds in the 1980s reportedly killed 200,000. The Kurds in all four countries advocated an independent Kurdistan, carved out of Turkey, Syria, Iraq, and Iran. The Kurds had participated in a local insurgency over the past forty years against Turkey. Erdogan's government was not pleased that the Kurds were portrayed as 'good guys' in 2017 when they helped the West suppress the ISIS uprising in Syria and Iraq.[13]

Sensitive to human rights and the right of minorities, Sweden had accepted 100,000 Kurdish refugees. Its parliament had 6 Kurdish deputies. Because of harsh Turkish policies toward the Kurds, both Finland and Sweden had imposed restrictions on the sale of weapons to Ankara. Erdogan considered Sweden a 'nesting ground for terrorists' and objected to both Finland and Sweden becoming full members because both countries had refused to sell Turkey weapons.[14]

Turkey had previously caused friction within NATO. In 2019 the US blocked sale of its F-35 fighters to Turkey because Erdogan's government had purchased Russian-made S-400 ADA missiles. In September 2022, Turkey sent a formal request to buy forty new upgraded F-16 jets and eighty kits from the US to modernize its existing aircraft. As of 2022 the US had refused to grant Turkey's request.[15]

The main issue was that NATO members differentiated between the two linked Kurdish groups Turkey was fighting against. Turkey, the US, and EU agreed that the PKK was a terrorist organization. In 2014 the US and European partners supplied arms to the PKK's Syrian affiliate the YGP, to fight ISIS. Turkey considered the YGP a branch of the PKK. Alarmed by the arming of its opponents, Turkey entered Syria and pushed the YGP away from its border. In response, many EU countries, including Finland and Sweden, restricted weapon sales to Turkey.[16]

Erdogan had transformed Turkey's parliamentary democracy into a presidential government with few checks and balances. His growing authoritarianism and suppression of critics has undermined the country's civil liberties. Erdogan's goal was to dismantle the secular Turkish society created by Mustafa Kemal Ataturk at the end of the First World War and establish an Islamic religion-based state in its place. The response was a failed military coup in 2016 that was supported by the Kurdish groups. Afterward Erdogan developed a close relationship with Putin, resulting in the ADA sales.[17]

Despite Erdogan's cooling toward NATO, he did close the Bosporus Strait to Russian naval ships at the beginning of Putin's 'Special Operation'. Additionally, Turkey shipped substantial military aide to Ukraine. Erdogan must have been mindful of domestic polls that show 58 per cent of the Turkish public support NATO membership and its actions.

Hungary's opposition to Finland and Sweden joining NATO as full members was unfounded and roused the anger of its neighbours, Poland, Czech Republic, and Slovakia. These countries exerted political pressure on Budapest to change position and in November 2022, Budapest announced that Hungary would support the applications of both Finland and Sweden.[18]

At the close of 2022, Turkey had withdrawn its objections to Finland's application, but not Sweden's bid for NATO membership. It is foreseeable that in 2023 a negotiated solution may be reached since Turkey wants cooperation from the US on the sale of military upgrades and the US supports Sweden's application. The end result might be an increase in NATO membership along Russia's borders, the very threat that Putin feared.

Chapter 29

Lessons Learned and the 2023 Offensives

One of the constants of history is that a nation rarely goes to war until it has convinced itself that victory is attainable and worth the cost.[1]

War is never worth the cost. High intensity warfare is ugly and destructive and those that start it eventually regret it. Aggressors like Putin assumed they could achieve their objectives quickly. History teaches that the failure to achieve victory with a lightning strike often results in stalemate and a prolonged war of attrition. At the close of 2022 Russia and Ukraine were locked in a war of attrition.

Putin's invasion failed to achieve all but one of his objectives, capturing a land bridge to Crimea. Putin failed to affect a regime change and failed to capture Kyiv. Putin failed to defeat the Ukrainian armed forces. Putin did succeed in expanding and uniting NATO. With the failure of the Russian armed forces to achieve air superiority, combined with its many defeats on the battlefield, Russia lost face and the ability to intimidate its neighbours. Europe cut the strands of Putin's petrochemical trap and the resulting sanctions disrupted Russia's economy. His sole victory by the end of 2022 was capturing a land bridge to Crimea, but his hold on the peninsula was tenuous at best. Kyiv was in position to cut the water supply to Crimea at will and there remained a real threat of the Ukrainian armed forces recapturing the peninsula. Finally, heavy losses in weapons and ammunition left Russia with under-equipped and poorly trained battalions for its projected 2023 offensives, despite deploying hundreds of thousands of newly mobilized troops.

The first year of the war was shaped by several factors, the primary of which was Russia's failure to achieve air superiority over Ukraine. This caused a disconnect between Russian air and ground forces, resulting in an over-reliance on artillery to support ground attacks. The derailing of the ground offensive was the CAAs' inability to execute combined-arms operations. The failure was due to their lack of brigade and division headquarters, that would have provided staff capable of utilizing the seven battlefield functions properly. Well-executed offensive combined-arms tactics were required to defeat defensive combined-arms tactics. Survival on the ground required dispersal, entrenching and high operational tempo.[2]

Both sides were handicapped by the lack of secure rear areas within the Ukrainian theatre of operations. A secure rear area provides combatants with a safe location to resupply, re-arm and perform maintenance in relative safety so that the fight can continue. A secure rear area is effective only until one side achieves air superiority, which can threaten or destroy the opponent's rear-area sanctuary. Once a combatant's secure rear area is compromised the war is lost. The short Arab-Israeli wars of 1967 and 1973 demonstrate this principle. The Israelis quickly gained air superiority and took out the Arab sanctuaries, leaving them unable to resupply. The wars were each over within a few weeks.

The existence of sanctuaries in a theatre of operations prolongs high intensity warfare. During the Korean War (1950–1953) the UN had air superiority over the peninsula, but UN policy prevented its combined air fleets from attacking north of the Yalu River into Chinese Manchuria. China was then able to mass supplies along the river and infiltrate them across the river at night. Because the UN combat forces were prevented from cutting the Chinese lines, the war turned into a battle of attrition that dragged on for three years.

Due to modern technology, satellites, drones, EW, and human intelligence both Russia and Ukraine had a full real-time view of the chess board. If a target could be located, it could be destroyed by missiles, rockets, artillery and infrequently by aircraft. As an example, the Russians used a ballistic missile to strike the International Legion's staging area outside Lviv, a few kilometres from the Polish border. Neither combatant had secure rear areas within the theatre of operations, but they were able to establish sanctuaries outside of Ukraine.

The Kremlin had relatively safe troop-assembly areas inside Russia. In addition, except for war material in Crimea, its supply dumps, rail infrastructure and war industry were mostly safe within its borders. Ukrainian drones and commandos were able to strike a few targets up to 600km/372 miles inside Russia and suspicious fires erupted at Russian industrial complexes as far away as the Ural Mountains (1,835km/1140 miles east of Kharkiv). These limited high-profile attacks had very little impact on Russian operations.

Ukraine received much support from various sources, including Eastern European NATO members, many of which provided repair facilities and Lend Lease staging areas, outside of the theatre of operations. Other NATO members provided safe training bases and instructors for Ukrainian soldiers. Russia conducted constant cyber-attacks, targeting technology used by the countries that supported Ukraine. Russia's cyber-attacks targeted NATO satellites and critical infrastructure.[3] Unlike a direct missile strike, these cyber-attacks were more of an annoyance, mostly because they encountered sophisticated cyber defences. An overt strike against any of these faculties would have triggered Article 5 and a direct response by NATO.

At the beginning of 2022, Russia had the capability to gain air superiority over Ukraine. Based on Russia's assumption that the war would be over quickly, the Russian air force (VKS) was constrained by Moscow to preserve infrastructure to be acquired. The VKS had 300 jet fighter bombers within striking range of Ukraine, but it appears most of them stayed on the ground during the first days of the invasion. Attack and transport helicopters conveyed paratroopers to landing zones near Kyiv. In the absence of the jet fighters, Ukraine was able to provide limited low-level close air support to ground units. Ukraine was also able to intercept Russian attack helicopters. The sight of Ukrainian aircraft during those first few days was a morale-booster and helped unify resistance across the country. The inability of Russia to execute an intensive SEAD (suppression of enemy air defences) campaign, provided opportunities for Ukrainian troops with MANPADS to engage Russian helicopter gunships.[4]

There were several additional factors that prevented Russia from gaining air superiority during the early days of the invasion. The first was the limited quantity of air-delivered precision guided munitions (PGMs) available to most VKS fighters. During combat operations over Syria only the SU-34 pilots regularly used PGMs. The lack of PGMs, combined with the lack of targeting pods prevented pilots from engaging targets at long range. As a result, the VKS generals were reluctant to commit the bulk of their strike aircraft before political approval for unguided munitions was authorized. A final factor was the low number of flight hours VKS pilots receive each year. Pilots averaged 100–120 flight hours per year. Compared with the Royal Air Force and US Air Force fighter pilots who struggled to maintain proficiency flying 180–240 flight hours yearly. Both the US and UK air forces had access to modern high-fidelity simulators for additional training. It appeared VKS pilots did not have access to these high-quality training aids. Based on the lack of funding for flight hours and high-quality training it was impossible for VKS pilots to remain competent for complex operations.[5]

Once the Ukrainian ADA recovered from the shock of the first days of the war, it established effective integrated air defence over the major cities and infrastructure. Tactical ADA units and MANPADS protected ground units, supply dumps and headquarters. By the end of April 2022, Ukrainian ADA claimed to have shot down 171 aircraft, 150 helicopters and 165 UAVs (drones). By end of 2022, that number increased to 278 aircraft, 261 helicopters and 1,506 UAVs.[6] While Ukrainian estimates of Russian aircraft lost were on the high side, the figures help explain why the VKS stopped trying to dominate the sky over Ukraine and in 2022 its battlefield strike capability was limited.

In 2022, it was evident that the VKS's attempt to effectively suppress air defence over Ukraine was a failure. This failure forced the jets and helicopters to operate at safer low altitudes. Despite being outmatched at the technical level and heavily outnumbered, Ukrainian fixed-wing and rotary-wing aircraft periodically contested the sky at low altitudes and attacked Russian ground forces. The large number of Ukrainian MANPADS made Russian low-altitude attacks costly. As a result, air attacks by Russian jets and helicopters were significantly reduced after April 2022.[7]

Russia was ultimately unable to effectively employ its overwhelming numbers of superior multi-role jet fighters. Russia was relegated to using its strategic bomber fleet to fire cruise and ballistic missiles from Russian airspace. For the last six months of 2022, the VKS operated in small numbers, flying low to minimize losses from Ukrainian ADA. This reduced pilot situational awareness and limited their ability to acquire targets. It also put them within range of MANPADs. During NATO's air war over Kosovo in 1999, NATO had air superiority and flew above 10,000ft, out of MANPAD range. To successfully impact ground operations the VKS likewise needed to operate above MANPAD range (10,000ft).[8]

To break the deadlock on the ground, Russia needs to gain air superiority in 2023. To accomplish this task the VKS needs to execute a massive SEAD campaign over the battlefield to provide air support to a ground offensive. Considering the limited air campaign in 2022, Russia had the time to develop SEADs and stockpile PGMs required for such a campaign. The VKS had the time to focus on pilot training.

With the marginalization of the VKS, the ground war was primarily fought by combined-arms operations with artillery dominating the battles. Combined-arms tactics synchronize battlefield operating systems (command and control, intelligence, manoeuvre, fire support, air defence, mobility/counter mobility/survivability, combat service support) to enable commanders to build, employ, direct, and sustain combat power.[9] The Russians thought they found the solution to the organization of the optimum formation of combined-arms operations in the development of the BTG.

The modern BTGs made their début in limited numbers during the Donbas fighting in 2014–2015. These combined-arms formations, equipped with modern weapons and technology were fully manned by contract soldiers. Their performance on the battlefield was adequate but not dominating. The BTGs required additional logistical support from division or CAA to make them truly independent command formations.[10] The successful combat performance of the BTGs in 2014–2015 indicated that all components of the combined-arms team had trained together for months before crossing into Ukraine.

In 2022 however, the mass of BTGs committed to the 'Special Operation' were undermanned, poorly led, inadequately equipped, and not trained to fight as a combat arms team. The notable exception were the naval infantry and paratroopers. The BTGs had been thrown together resulting in company and battalion command teams intermingled, crewed with personnel from different units. The commanders were unfamiliar with their subordinates. The intermixing of units caused logistical and communication problems. Most of these problems could have been avoided if the BTGs had conducted combined-arms training while sitting for weeks and months in their assembly areas near the Ukrainian border. While the media was full of photos of Russian tanks and soldiers on the firing ranges, there was no footage of BTGs conducting combined-arms manoeuvres. Proficiency at individual soldier and crew training is only the first step in combined-arms training.[11] The subsequent performance of the BTGs during the 'Special Operation' demonstrated that BTGs and Army staffs had not diligently performed combined-arms map or communication exercises, let alone field exercises. Expecting an easy operation, the bureaucratic Army generals neglected to train their attached BTGs and ignored the maxim: 'The more you sweat in peace, the less you bleed in war!'

Keeping the details of the 'Special Operation' secret, the BTGs charged across the border in administrative formations. Columns tried to bypass strongpoints, only to expose their flanks to Ukrainian fire. The columns were often ambushed while rolling through unsecured towns. Lacking full complements of infantry to secure or capture buildings and strong points, tanks and other armoured vehicles were ambushed and destroyed. The BTGs were too small to absorb losses and continue to function. The tank and infantry companies took a disproportionate percentage of losses, rendering the BTG combat ineffective while their artillery and other combat support units remained operational. As the war progressed, the battalion and company commanders leading from the front were eliminated, to be replaced with junior leaders with even less experience at coordinating the combined arms BTGs. During the various reorganizations over 2022, BTGs were slowly disbanded. The artillery batteries were stripped and formed into artillery groups, and battalions of tanks and infantry were reformed. Brigade and regimental headquarters were deployed to coordinate combined-arms operations.

The Ukrainians entered the war with traditional, but uniquely Ukrainian, combined-arms organizations. In the Regular and Reserve Army and National Guard, brigades provided command and control for three to five task organized combined arms battalions (CABs). All battlefield operating systems were coordinated within the CABs and their brigade HQs coordinated the efforts of multiple CABs. Initially, the Territorials, international legions, and militia were fielded as infantry companies and battalions with limited combat service and combat service support.

The manoeuvre element of combined-arms tactics was the infantry and tanks, while the fire support was provided by artillery and mortars. In the tooth-to-tail ratio, approximately 30 per cent of the soldiers within the battalion fell within the combat arms. The majority of those were infantry. Infantry does most of the direct fighting and suffers the most casualties. The only way to capture an objective is for infantry to capture the ground. This often requires clearing trench lines, bunkers, or buildings. The rest of the combined-arms team create conditions for the foot soldier to do his job. In the past, the poorly trained conscript infantry could do the job, but at a higher casualty rate. During the Second World War, the Soviet Army was poorly trained but highly motivated conscript soldiers defeated the better trained Nazi Army. However, in today's advanced technological environment, infantry combat requires trained, well-equipped and motivated soldiers.

In Ukraine the infantry was armed with an assault rifle, high-tech anti-tank weapons, drones, computers, encrypted radios, and various types of grenades. If part of a mechanized or motorized unit, each infantry squad/section had a supporting IFV or APC. Each soldier wore body armour capable of stopping close-range machinegun bullets, as well as small shrapnel from an artillery or mortar burst. When on the move, the IFVs and APCs protected the tanks and other armoured and unarmoured vehicles by suppressing enemy infantry and ATGM positions.

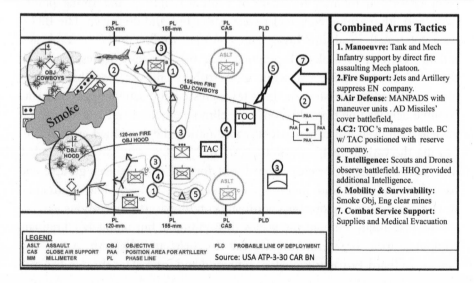

Combined Arms Tactics

1. **Manoeuvre:** Tank and Mech Infantry support by direct fire assaulting Mech platoon.
2. **Fire Support:** Jets and Artillery suppress EN company.
3. **Air Defense:** MANPADS with maneuver units . AD Missiles' cover battlefield,
4. **C2:** TOC's manages battle. BC w/ TAC positioned with reserve company.
5. **Intelligence:** Scouts and Drones observe battlefield. HHQ provided additional Intelligence.
6. **Mobility & Survivability:** Smoke Obj, Eng clear mines
7. **Combat Service Support:** Supplies and Medical Evacuation

LEGEND
ASLT   ASSAULT
CAS   CLOSE AIR SUPPORT
MM   MILLIMETER
OBJ   OBJECTIVE
PAA   POSITION AREA FOR ARTILLERY
PL   PHASE LINE
PLD   PROBABLE LINE OF DEPLOYMENT
Source: USA ATP-3-30 CAR BN

The IFV/APC protected its mounted infantry squad from small arms and artillery fire. In close terrain or towns and villages, infantry dismounted to clear the area, protected from enemy fire by the IFVs and APCs.

In the absence of air support, the Russian and Ukrainian armies were both forced to revert to artillery as the traditional source of massed firepower. From the start of the war, artillery remained the 'Queen' on the Ukrainian chess board. The Ukrainian General Staff gave artillery, not NLAWs or Javelin AGTMs, credit for the victory before the gates of Kyiv. The NATO ATGMs were key factors in the victory, but it was general and precision-guided artillery strikes that disrupted Russia's supply lines, destroyed trucks, IFVs, APCs and killed the enemy. It was artillery that gave Russia the 'pyrrhic' victory mid-year in the Donbas, and it was artillery (HIMARS) that created the conditions for the successful Kharkiv and Kherson counteroffensives. At the end of the year, artillery allowed Russia to make small, costly gains in the Battle for Bakhmut.

Drones were instrumental in guiding and directing the artillery duel. They were a combat multiplier in all aspects of combined-arms tactics. Military and civilian drones flooded the battlefield. Daily videos showed modified civilian drones dropping hand grenades on helpless Russian soldiers or down open hatches of armoured vehicles. Small gyrocopters assisted infantry squads to clear trenches and small drones assisted company and battalion commanders to see the battlefield. Larger armed military drones assaulted supply columns and unprotected armoured vehicles. Naval drones provided the Ukrainians the ability to attack the Black Sea Fleet in their home port. Kamikaze drones of various sizes loitered for hours above the battlefield, searching for targets, and long-range drones allowed Ukraine to strike airfields 600km/373 miles inside Russia.

Drones were the most effective in spotting for artillery. Drones flew over the battlefield searching for targets. Some relayed their discoveries to firing batteries and/or painted the target with laser designators for precision strikes, allowing tanks to be destroyed by artillery. Without precision munitions, it would have normally required a massed, high-volume artillery strike, such as a 'battalion six' (18 guns firing 6 rounds each or 108 shells) to destroy or disable a single tank. Lighter armoured vehicles such as the IFVs and APCs were easily damaged by standard artillery rounds. Inside many sets of body armour is a printed label warning that 70 per cent of all death and wounds are caused by shrapnel.[12]

Countermeasures to drones were quickly developed. The oldest defence to aircraft flying slow and low over the battlefield was individual soldiers shooting them down with rifles and/or machine guns from armoured vehicles. MANPADs were used against larger drones, resulting in artillery batteries being issued these weapons. The drone threat resulted in the development of anti-aircraft artillery, equipped with auto-cannons being introduced onto the battlefield. Both sides began to employ older Soviet ground-mounted ZU-23–2 anti-aircraft guns, self-propelled 2K22 Tunguskas, German Gepard flakpanzers, and the always field-expedient heavy machine guns mounted on trucks.[13] These weapons did not eliminate the threat of tactical drones but denied them unhampered access to the battlefield and protected ground units.

In addition to the foot soldiers, the most recognized component of the combined-arms team was the tank. By 1 April 2022, Russia had lost 614 tanks. By November 2022 the number had increased to 2,840. These figures included destroyed and captured vehicles. The heavy Russian tank losses during the first part of the war immediately reignited the debate as to whether tanks had become obsolete in high-intensity war.

After the initial tank battles in the 'Special Operation', analysts and so-called media military experts, questioned whether the age of the tank had passed. They urged the same argument as armchair generals made when, in 1918, German large calibre anti-tank rifles were developed and deployed to counter Allied tanks. Cheap anti-tank weapons would make the tank obsolete. This was an argument first raised by budget-conscious politicians over a century ago and rejected by most combat veterans.[14]

Despite these arguments regarding the future role of a heavy armoured tank, the Second World War saw tremendous tank-dominated battles throughout Europe, Ukraine, and Russia. In close terrain they were employed as infantry support weapons and in open terrain their speed provided fast manoeuvrability, allowing deep penetrations, following the infantry as it punched through the enemy frontline. Some of the largest tank battles in history occurred in Ukraine or in the now-Russian-controlled steppes around its border. Arguably the largest tank battle in history was fought during the Second World War at Kursk in 1943.

The Nazis attacked the Kursk Salient in July 1943, with 780,000 men, 2,928 tanks, and 9,966 guns, howitzers, and mortars. The Soviets defended the salient with 1,426,000 men, 5,128 tanks and 25,000 guns, howitzers, and mortars. Many large tank engagements took place over a week of heavy fighting. The largest occurred on 12 July 1943, during the sub-battle for the town of Prokhorovka, in Russia. The Soviet 5th Guards Tank Army attacked with 500 tanks and assault guns. The II SS Panzer Corps defended with 200 tanks and assault guns on a 4km/2.4mile front. A total of 700 heavily armoured tanks were squeezed almost side by side, fighting along a relatively short front, with approximately 8m between each Soviet tank and 20m between the Nazi tanks. The battle raged between 05:30 and sundown, often at point blank range. The

Nazis held their ground with the loss of 60–80 tanks damaged or destroyed. The Soviets lost 222 tanks. The tank battle resulted in a Soviet victory and the initiative shifted from the Nazis to the Soviets.

As the Nazis were pushed back westwards through Ukraine, hundreds of thousands of men and thousands of tanks engaged in numerous smaller tank battles as the invaders were driven back into Poland and Hungary. Compared to the huge numbers of tanks battling in the Second World War, the numbers of tanks shooting it out during the 'Special Operation', over much of the same terrain, seem relatively small, and yet the tank battles were just as decisive.

Toward the end of the Second World War, cheap, light anti-tank weapons like the US Bazooka, the British PIAT and the Nazi Panzerscheck and Panzerfaust, could destroy most tanks in close terrain. These anti-tank weapons were all relatively short ranged. Infantry armed with these weapons had to get very close to heavily armoured Tiger, Jagdtiger and Stalin tanks to attack the flanks and rear of these tanks.

Despite the development of cheap, lightweight anti-tank weapons, both sides in the Cold War invested heavily in tanks, IFVs and APCs. Towed anti-tank guns, lacking the mobility of tanks, were phased out. Lightly armoured, self-propelled anti-tank guns and tank destroyers, along with light and heavy tanks, were phased out in favour of one class, the main battle tank. The heavily armoured main battle tank, with a high-velocity, large-calibre main gun, was very mobile and effectively replaced the other vehicles as being redundant.

Arguments against the battle effectiveness of tanks resurfaced during and after the 1973 Israeli Yom Kippur War. The Egyptians had created a bridgehead on the Israeli side of the Suez Canal in an attempt to capture the Sinai Peninsula. They had established a defence integrating new Sagger wire-guided, anti-tank missiles (ATGMs) and rocket-propelled anti-tank grenades (RPGs). The Saggers provided infantry with the capacity to engage tanks at a distance of between 500 and 3,000m. The RPGs covered the 500-meter dead zone. On 8 October 1973, two Israeli tank brigades attempted to break through to the strong points along the Suez Canal

Attacking without artillery or infantry support, the Israelis expected the Egyptians to be routed as they charged across the open desert. In 1967, the Egyptian infantry had been armed with 100mm anti-tank guns that could not penetrate the frontal armour of the Israeli Centurion and M-48 tanks beyond 1,000m.[15] The Israeli veterans of the 1967 war expected the Egyptians to break and run as they closed with their positions. Both Israeli tank brigades were rendered combat ineffective after losing ninety tanks within twenty-minutes. A week later, the Israeli combined-arms counterattack, led by tanks, crossed the Suez Canal and trapped an Egyptian army. A second tank-led combined-arms attack drove deep into the Egyptian rear, destroying ADA batteries. The attack returned control of the air to the Israeli Air Force, and once again the tank attack was decisive.

It was soon seen that the ATGMs did not render tanks obsolete for a modern battlefield. Both NATO and the Soviet Union invested heavily, improving ATGMs and tanks as the Cold War progressed. Wire-guided ATGMs dominated the development of ground anti-tank weapons. Toward the end of the Cold War, newer systems like the US Hellfire, shifted from wire- to laser-guided missiles.

In 2006, at Wadi Saluki, Hezbollah engaged an attacking Israeli tank battalion, supported by infantry and artillery, on a battlefield that was favourable to Hezbollah's ATGMs. Hezbollah held the high ground and was forewarned that the Israelis were coming. The Israelis attacked with twenty-four modern Merkava Mark IVs supported by infantry and artillery. The position was defended by 14–20 Kornet first-line ATGMs. The Russian-made Kornet was a laser-guided ATGM, first introduced in combat in 2003, during the US invasion of Iraq. The Kornet disabled two M1A1 Abrams tanks and a Bradley IFV.[16]

During the Wadi Saluki engagement, the Israeli tanks rushed into battle without properly coordinating the attack with supporting infantry and artillery. The Merkava tanks fought the battle unsupported. Hezbollah fired swarms of missiles at the tanks. It was later estimated up to seventy missiles were fired. The Israeli tanks failed to fire their smoke (phosphorus) grenade launchers which would have interfered with the guidance of the missiles. The result was eleven tanks hit, some more than once. Three tanks had their armour penetrated and seven crewmen were killed, but no tanks were irretrievably destroyed.[17]

Flash forward to April 2022, Russia had lost 605 tanks and a combined total of 1,723 IFVs and APCs. These figures represented not only vehicles destroyed, but also those captured intact or disabled but repairable. Based upon media representations and viral videos posted on the internet, these losses were due to modern 'fire-and-forget' ATGMs such as NLAWs and Javelins. By the end of the year, information was not yet available as to which weapon system destroyed the tanks. These new weapons targeted the weakest part of the tank, its relatively thin armour on the top, at ranges similar to the range of its cannon, 2–4kms/1.2–2.4 miles.

In theory a $30,000 modern ATGM could neutralize a multi-million-dollar main battle tank. However, the 2022 expenditure rate of the modern ATGMs does not equal one shot per one tank or IFV disabled or destroyed.[18] The high loss rate of T-72 tanks and BMP IFVs was a result of the lethality of the new generation of the ATGMs combined with the Russians' inability to successfully coordinate combined-arms operations.

Despite the deadly nature of the twenty-first century battlefield, tanks will not disappear, because they alone provide a mobile weapons platform with the ability to engage a target with a large-calibre cannon quickly, cheaply, and accurately out to a range of 4,000m. Modern tanks are capable of firing a selection of shells, specially designed for different targets. Besides other armoured vehicles, tanks can engage helicopters, troops in trenches, and infantry in the open. Due to the speed of a tank round, no target can react fast enough to avoid being hit once a round is fired. Under battle conditions, a tank gunner generally requires less than 10 seconds to acquire a target and fire. The only salvation for the target is if the gunner did not properly aim before firing. Stabilized modern NATO tanks are as accurate on the move as they are when stationary. An average crew can effectively engage targets out to 2,500m. A well-trained crew can effectively engage targets out to 4,000m. No other military vehicle or weapons platform system currently on the battlefield can provide the immediate, accurate firepower of the tank.

Older tanks, like the T-62 and Leopard I, have weaker armour than modern tanks and relatively smaller main guns. However, their armour is heavier than

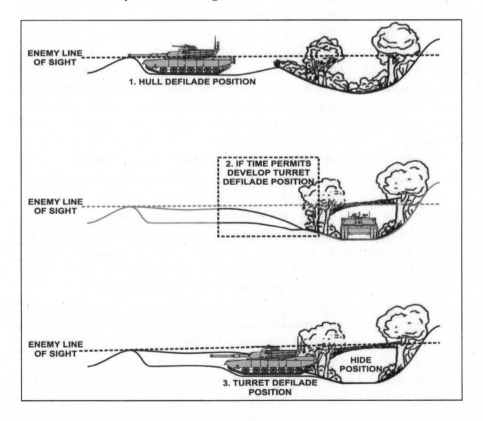

the newest IFV. The main gun on the older tanks may not be able to penetrate the frontal armour of a T-80, M1A1 Abrams, or Leopard II A4 tank. However, this was not particularly an issue on the battlefields of Ukraine. There have been far fewer battalion-size mass tank battles than were seen in the Second World War. Most tank engagements have been part of combined-arms battles where artillery and ATGMs augmented the limited number of tanks.

The first line of protection for a tank in a combined-arms battle operation should be the infantry and artillery. These supporting arms should ideally neutralize enemy infantry, tanks and ATGMs. The second line of defence always lies with the skill of the crew. Fully trained tank crews need to spend hours conducting berm drills, where a tank hides in a turret-down or hide position as the commander searches for targets. When a target is located, it should only take ten seconds to roll up into a hull-down firing position, fire and return to the hide position. The tank may remain exposed for an additional four seconds if two targets are identified. If a platoon of four tanks effectively executes this drill, an enemy tank company could lose eight of its ten tanks in less than fourteen seconds. Finally, if the tank is fired upon by an ATGM, it should immediately fire its phosphorous smoke grenades. This smoke screen disrupts the homing signal on the newest generation 'fire-and-forget' ATGMs and obscures the target from wire-guided munitions.[19]

In the offensive, tanks rely on the combined-arms team for protection. Trained tank sections and platoons use movement techniques to cover each other as they bound from one covered position to another. Artillery and engineers lay smoke to cover movement when protective terrain is not available. Specially equipped tanks and combat engineer vehicles clear lanes through minefields, allowing tanks and IFVs to close on an objective, covered by smoke.

The final line of protection is the tank's armour, heavier in the front than on the sides, rear or top. The front has the heaviest armour to protect the crew from direct frontal attack. Studies from past combat indicate that the front of the tank took the hit 60 per cent of the time. Reactive armour is designed to negate the ATGM's high-explosive, anti-tank (HEAT) warhead. Newer tank models are equipped with jammers to interfere with an ATGM's targeting system. Finally, a tank is such a large combat vehicle that hits on its weakly armoured parts may often not disable or destroy its fighting ability.

The heavy losses of Russian tanks can be attributed to marginally trained tank crews and battalion commanders inadequately trained in combined-arms tactics. The T-72 series tank's unprotected ammunition storage compartment in its turret, contributed to a high proportion of catastrophic vehicle destruction and crew deaths. This design defect, compounded with the real issue of lack of training resulted in huge tank losses and deaths.

The Battle of Wadi Saluki demonstrated that when combined-arms coordination fails, the fight degenerates into a duel between tanks and ATGMs. Survival and success on the battlefield ultimately depend upon the training and nerve of the combatants. Despite heavy tank losses, no other weapon has the capabilities of a heavily armoured modern tank with its high velocity large calibre cannon. It was no surprise that Ukraine requested an additional 500 modern tanks from NATO for its Spring-Summer 2023 counteroffensive. Ukraine continues to train its troops in combined-arms tactics.

The Russians began refurbishing their 800 old, Soviet-era T-62 tanks (20 tank battalions), due to be ready for service in late spring 2023. When these tanks are ready, the 125,000 soldiers conscripted in the normal bi-yearly October-November process will be fully equipped and deployable. These soldiers were projected to complete training by March-April 2023 and will probably join frontline units as replacements, in time to oppose the Ukrainian counteroffensive.

Russia's real 'Achilles' heel' remains logistics. Getting beans, bullets and fuel to the front, and wounded troops transported back to hospitals, was problematic during the first year of Putin's 'Special Operation'. With a pre-war economy the size of Italy's, Russia was greatly impacted by sanctions imposed by the West. Worldwide restrictions on imports continued throughout 2022, limiting the availability of basic materials required to manufacture weapons and ammunition. Unable to significantly increase its production of ammunition and equipment, Russia was reliant upon its Soviet Cold War-era stockpiles.[20] Its large Cold War stockpile of conventional artillery ammunition had been greatly depleted and consumption rate far exceeded Russia's yearly production.[21] The Russian armed forces' supply of precision-guided munitions was, toward the end of December 2022, nearly depleted. Russia fired approximately 3,100 of its estimated 4,000 stockpiled cruise and theatre ballistic missiles. Russian pre-invasion production rates of these high-tech missiles was significantly less than the US.

During the first year of the war, it was estimated that Russia had fired over 2,000,000 artillery shells. At best, by switching munition factories to increased war-level production, Russia would only be able to produce 100,000 replacement artillery shells per year. This production rate was similar to US peacetime yearly production of 100,000 shells per annum. Each round cost about $850, with precision shells costing as much as $2,700. While Russia had a superiority in munitions over Ukraine, Putin reduced his conventional munitions stockpile to dangerously low levels.[22] Russia needed to maintain a sufficient reserve of conventional artillery munitions in case of a NATO intervention. Having a massive stockpile of shells is one thing, transporting them to the firing batteries is another.

Russia relied on rail to transport needed munitions to the theatre of operations, resulting in massive ammunition depots at the railheads in or near the frontlines. Trucks transported the ammunition to the firing batteries along the main supply routes. The massive depots were perfect targets for Ukrainian HIMARS rocket artillery. By the end of 2022, HIMARS, rockets and commando raids had destroyed fifty large ammunition depots. The Russians were forced to relocate depots beyond HIMARS range or further outside the theatre of operations into Russia. Ukraine requested extended-range HIMARS rockets to target these logistics centres. Their request had not been granted as of the end of 2022.

The Russian armed forces had a shortage of trucks when it invaded Ukraine in February 2022. By the end of 2022, Russia had lost 3,021 irreplaceable supply and fuel trucks, complicating the supply and distribution of ammunition to the Russian firing batteries on the front lines. Complicating the supply problem further, Russian truck convoys needed to cross partisan-controlled areas and travel within the range of HIMARS.[23]

With serious logistical problems expected to continue into 2023, Russia may well turn to its aligned neighbours, Kazakhstan, Kyrgyzstan, China and Iran, for resupply. China would definitely expect something tangible in return, such as access to Siberian resources. Iran would probably provide drones and other high-tech support, but would no doubt seek Moscow's assistance in procuring nuclear materials.[24]

By the end of 2022, both sides were expected to assume the offensive in 2023. Putin's objective would be to capture the Ukrainian-controlled remainder of Donets and Luhansk Oblasts. The objective of Ukraine's counteroffensive would be to cut the Crimea land bridge, starving the Russian occupiers of supplies and recapturing the peninsula.

Putin's 'Special Operation' proved to be a disaster for Ukraine, Russia and the world. Attempting to bring Ukraine into its sphere of influence, Russia had only succeeded in destroying the illusion of its invincibility. By the end of 2022 Russia had gutted its army, lost most of its semi-modern operational fleet of tanks and armoured vehicles, depleted its arsenal of conventional and precision munitions, and ruined its economy. It will take years, if not decades to rebuild its economy and ground forces. Its Stalinist policies and state-sponsored war crimes in occupied Ukraine will prevent a lasting peace between the two countries. The hatred will last decades.

On the other side of the war, Ukraine suffered untold horrors. Thousands have been raped, tortured, captured and killed among both its military force and civilian population. In addition, hundreds of thousands of Ukrainians have disappeared, being vectored into Russia after fleeing toward the illusion of safety. Thousands of Ukrainian children were literally kidnapped and may never be seen again. Millions of civilians left their homes, seeking shelter outside the war zone. Hundreds of Ukrainian cities, villages and towns have been reduced to rubble. Bridges, dams, airports, and roads have been destroyed. Its nuclear reactor facility has been seriously compromised and its national power grid was significantly degraded. The once-fertile farmlands that produce wheat for the world have been damaged. Despite billions in economic and humanitarian aid from NATO and its Western Allies, it will take decades for the Ukrainian economy to recover. It will take decades for Ukraine to get justice for the war crimes committed against its population.[25]

By the end of 2022 it was expected that war would eventually end in a negotiated peace or more probably a ceasefire, like in Korea. As long as Putin and the *siloviki* and their successors are determined to politically and economically dominate the former Soviet Republics there will be no lasting peace. History will record that the one thing Putin clearly accomplished along with destroying much of Ukraine was destroying the myth of Russian invincibility.

Notes and References

Introduction
1. McMaster, H. R., *Battlegrounds* (p. 13). HarperCollins. Kindle Edition.
2. My comrades and I are in our late 60s and early 70s. Too old for frontline service.
3. Staff 'Invasion of Ukraine, D+15, Sitrep, (#200)', The Five Coat Consulting Group, https://www.thefivecoatconsultinggroup.com/the-coronavirus-crisis/ukraine-context-d15

Chapter 1: A Short History of Ukraine
1. https://www.britannica.com/place/Kyiv/History
2. Ibid.
3. Oleg Sukhov, 'Ukraine's victories from Kyivan Rus to 2022 Battle of Kyiv,' *The Kyiv Independent*, 5 November 2022. https://kyivindependent.com/national/ukraines-victories-and-achievements-from-kyivan-rus-to-2022-battle-of-kyiv
4. Kyivan-Rus, *Britannica*.
5. Ibid.
6. Ibid.
7. Staff, 'History of Moscow', *Britannica*, https://www.britannica.com/place/Moscow/History
8. 'Medieval Origins of Ukraine', Kings and Generals Research Project. https://www.youtube.com/watch?v=3uyHWEOoPnM
9. https://www.britannica.com/place/Kyiv/History
10. 'Medieval Origins of Ukraine', Kings and Generals Research Project.
11. Oleg Sukhov 'Ukraine's victories from Kyivan Rus to 2022 Battle of Kyiv,' *The Kyiv Independent*, 5 November 2022. https://kyivindependent.com/national/ukraines-victories-and-achievements-from-kyivan-rus-to-2022-battle-of-kyiv
12. https://www.britannica.com/place/Kyiv/History
13. Oleg Sukhov (2022) '
14. Ibid.
15. Alina Selyukh, Elissa Nadworny, Brian Mann, 'Ukraine agonizes over Russian culture and language in social fabric,' *NPR*, 2 June 2022. https://www.npr.org/2022/06/02/1101712731/russia-invasion-ukraine-russian-language-culture-identity
16. Balint Stork, 'Geopolitical Situation of Ukriane and Its importance', https://securityanddefence.pl/pdf-103292-36222?filename=Geopolitical%20situation%20of.pdf
17. 'Holodomor, The Ukrainian Genocide', University of Minnesota, Holocaust and Genocide Studies. https://cla.umn.edu/chgs/holocaust-genocide-education/resource-guides/holodomor, https://holodomormuseum.org.ua/en/the-history-of-the-holodomor/
18. *Mr Jones* was written by Andrea Chalupa, directed by Agnieszka Holland and starred James Norton, Vanessa Kirby and Peter Starsgaard.
19. Oleg Sukhov (2022).
20. Ibid.
21. https://www.britannica.com/place/Ukraine/Soviet-Ukraine-in-the-postwar-period
22. Pavlo Savchenko, 'The Insurgent Movement in Ukraine During 1940s-1950s: Lessons Learned from the Case Study of the Ukrainian Insurgent Army', US Army Command & General Staff College, Fort Leavenworth KS, August 6, 2012. https://apps.dtic.mil/sti/citations/ADA562947
23. John S. Harrel, *Soviet Cavalry Operations During the Second World War and the Genesis of the Operational Maneuver Group*. (Pen & Sword, 2017).
24. The author and his friends were in Ukraine as part of the staff for the California Army National Guard's 2nd Brigade, 40th Infantry Division (Mechanized) participating in the NATO exercise Rapid Trident 97.

25. Mark Kramer, 'The Transfer of Crimea from Soviet Russia to Soviet Ukraine, 1954', Wilson Centre, downloaded 10/22/2022. https://www.wilsoncenter.org/publication/why-did-russia-give-away-crimea-sixty-years-ago?gclid=CjwKCAjwzNOaBhAcEiwAD7Tb6Oqgr4SSzL4J6yEjEz7KfwiSDsBXwoi3Zdy_fzW2FSchugLP6fHnVxoCSpQQAvD_BwE

26. 'Why Ukrainians and Russians are not one people, and why Russians are not Ukraine's indigenous people,' Ukraine Crisis Media Centre, 7 July 2021. https://uacrisis.org/en/ukrainians-russians-not-one-people

27. 'Ukraine's Struggle for Independence in Russia's Shadow,' Council on Foreign Affairs, 2022. https://www.cfr.org/timeline/ukraines-struggle-independence-russias-shadow

Chapter 2: Partnership for Peace
1. 'NATO U.S. Assistance to the Partnership for Peace', US Government Accounting Office, 20 July 2001. https://www.gao.gov/products/gao-01-734, 'NATO Partnership for Peace', US State Department Archive. https://1997-2001.state.gov/regions/eur/nato_fs-pfp.html

2. 'Partnership for Peace Programme,' NATO, 23 March 2020. https://www.nato.int/cps/en/natohq/topics_50349.htm

3. 'State Partnership Program, Partner Focused, Strategically Aligned', US National Guard Bureau homepage. https://www.nationalguard.mil/leadership/joint-staff/j-5/international-affairs-division/state-partnership-program/, https://www.nationalguard.mil/Portals/31/Documents/J-5/InternationalAffairs/StatePartnershipProgram/Securing-the-Nation-One-Partnership-at-a-Time.pdf, 'Partnership for Peace programme', North Atlantic Treaty Organization homepage. https://www.nato.int/cps/en/natohq/topics_50349.htm 'Ukraine's Struggle for Independence in Russia's Shadow 1991–2022', Council on Foreign Relations. https://www.cfr.org/timeline/ukraines-struggle-independence-russias-shadow

4. Ibid.

5. This was the author's experience in 1997.

6. 'Ukraine's participation in UN peacekeeping activities', Permanent Mission of Ukraine to the United Nations webpage. https://ukraineun.org/en/ukraine-and-un/peacekeeping-activities/

7. Staff, 'Partnership Interoperability Initiative,' NATO, 22 February 2022. https://www.nato.int/cps/en/natohq/topics_132726.htm

8. Ibid.

9. Ukrainian PfP Training Centre. https://www.nato.int/structur/nmlo/links/yavoriv-training-centre.pdf

10. Jim Garamone, 'Ukraine-California ties show worth of National Guard Program', National Guard Bureau, 21 March 2022, https://www.nbclosangeles.com/news/politics/newsconference/newsconference-california-national-guard-trains-ukrainian-military/2861957/https://www.nationalguard.mil/News/Article/2972128/ukraine-california-ties-show-worth-of-national-guard-program/

11. Interview with Major General (Ret) David Baldwin.

Chapter 3: Ukraine: Terrain and Weather
1. Climate Change Knowledge Portal. https://climateknowledgeportal.worldbank.org/country/ukraine

Chapter 4: Twenty-first Century Warfare
1. https://www.dictionary.com/browse/war

2. Francis Miyata, 'The Grand Strategy of Carl von Clausewitz,' US Army War College, 26 March 2021. https://warroom.armywarcollege.edu/articles/grand-strategy-clausewitz/

3. Major Amos C. Fox, 'Russian Hybrid Warfare and Its Relevance to The U.S. Army's Infantry', *Infantry Magazine*, April-July 2016.

4. Andrew Monaghan, 'The "War" in Russia's Hybrid Warfare,' *Parameters* 45(4), Winter 2015–16, pp 65–74.

5. Fox (2015)

6. Ibid, p3.

7. Koffler, Rebekah, *Putin's Playbook* (Kindle Locations 570–571). Regnery Gateway. Kindle Edition, July 2022

8. Andrew S. Harvey, PhD, 'The Levels of War as Levels of Analysis,' *Military Review*, November-December 2021, pp 75–81. https://www.armyupress.army.mil/Portals/7/military-review/Archives/English/ND-21/Harvey-Levels-of-War-1.pdf

9. Scott Nicholas Romaniuck, 'Military Strategy and the Three Levels of Warfare,' *Defence Report*, 2017. https://defencereport.com/wp-content/uploads/2017/11/Romaniuk-Military-Strategy-and-the-Three-Levels-of-Warfare.pdf

10. *FM 3-0 Operations*, (Department of the US Army: Washington D.C., October 2022), 1–10 to 1–13. https://irp.fas.org/doddir/army/fm3-0.pdf

11. Gustav Gressel, 'Combined forces: Russia's Early Military Failures in Ukrane,' *European Council On Foreign Relations*, 15 March 2022

12. Douglas A. Macgregor, *Breaking the Phalanx, A New Design for Land power in the 21st Century*, (Praeger: Westport, Connecticut, London, 1997).

13. FM 3-0

14. ADP 3-90 *Offense and Defence*, (US Army, July 2019) 3-90 3-1 to 3-2, https://irp.fas.org/doddir/army/adp3_90.pdf

15. *Russian New Generation Warfare Handbook* (US Army, December 2016), 7–10.

16. Ibid, 7.

17. Isabelle Khurshudyan, Mary Ilysushina and Kostuantyn Khudiv, 'Russia and Ukraine are fighting the first full-scale drone war,' *The Washington Post*, 2 December 2022.

18. Arwa Mahdawi, 'Russian Black Sea flagship damaged in Crimean drone attack, video suggests,' *The Guardian*, 30 October 2022. https://www.theguardian.com/world/2022/oct/30/russias-black-sea-flagship-damaged-in-crimea-drone-attack-video-suggests

19. Howard Altman, 'Ukraine's Shadowy Kamikaze Drone Boats Officially Break Cover', *The War Zone*, 11 November 2022. https://www.thedrive.com/the-war-zone/ukraines-shadowy-kamikaze-drone-boats-officially-break-cover

20. Mark Trevelyan, 'Moscow says three killed in Ukrainian drone attack on air bases deep inside Russia,' *Reuters*, 5 December 2022. https://www.reuters.com/world/europe/three-killed-fuel-tanker-explosion-russian-airfield-2022-12-05/

21. Brian Clark and Timothy A. Walton, 'Arm Ukraine to fight drones from the air,' *The Hill*, 28 November 2022. https://thehill.com/opinion/international/3749292-arm-ukraine-to-fight-drones-from-the-air/

Chapter 5: Road to War

1. McMaster, *Battlegrounds*, 15.

2. Koffler,(Kindle locations 578–579).

3. McMaster, *Battlegrounds*.

4. Koffler,(Kindle locations 589–590).

5. 'Putin's Messianic Mission, The autocrat's Darwinian worldview was shaped by a grim childhood, the KGB and Fall of the Berlin Wall,' *The Week*, 25 March 2022, p 11; Nataliya Bugayova, *How We Got Here With Russia, The Kremlin's Worldview*, ISW, Reuters, 2019, pp 16–22. https://www.understandingwar.org/sites/default/files/ISW%20Report_The%20Kremlin%27s%20Worldview_March%202019.pdf

6. Andrei Illarionov, 'The Siloviki in Charge', *Journal of Democracy*, April 2009, pp 69–72.

7. Koffler, (Kindle location 769).

8. Ibid.

9. Ibid, (Kindle location 818).

10. Ibid.

11. Ibid, (Kindle location 1398).

12. With the illusion of Russian invincibility destroyed during the Kharkiv counteroffensive and its war stocks of ammunition being consumed at an alarming rate, Azerbaijan took advantage of the situation and invaded the contested region of Armenia on 12 September 2022. Putin rejected Armenia's request for military assistance. Armenia was a signatory to Russia's Collective Security Organization while Azerbaijan was not. This refusal to assist degrades Russia's influence in the region. Members of the organization were obligated to assist each other if attacked. Russia brokered a ceasefire on 13 September 2022 that almost immediately fell apart. Russia's failed attempt to convince both parties to cease fighting demonstrated its loss of credibility in the region. EU leaders eventually brokered

a shaky ceasefire and deployed observers who were still in place in December 2022. Guy Faulconbridge (ed), 'Russia tells Armenia and Azerbaijan: cease hostilities,' Reuters, 13 September 2022, https://www.reuters.com/world/russia-tells-armenia-azerbaijan-cease-hostilities-2022-09-13/; Report Nagorno-Karabkh, 'Averting a New War between Armenia and Azerbaijan', International Crisis Group, Report No. 266, 30 January 2023, https://www.crisisgroup.org/europe-central-asia/caucasus/nagorno-karabakh-conflict/266-averting-new-war-between-armenia-and-azerbaijan

13. Koffler, (Kindle location 1409).
14. Matthew Karnitschnig 'Putin's Useful German Idiots, *Politico*, 28 March 2022.
15. Ibid.
16. It is a very good war movie and I have watched four times.
17. Tara John and Tim Lister, 'A Far-right battalion has a key role in Ukraine's resistance. Its neo-Nazi links have given Putin ammunition', CNN, 9 March 29 2022.
18. Bohdah Marusyak, 'Their Business Is Death,' Promote Ukraine Media, November 26, 2022. https://www.promoteukraine.org/their-business-is-death/
19. https://thehill.com/policy/international/596649-putins-nazi-claims-jeered-in-west-but-stoke-russian-pride, https://www.nbcnews.com/think/opinion/ukraine-has-nazi-problem-vladimir-putin-s-denazification-claim-war-ncna1290946, https://www.jta.org/2022/02/27/opinion/what-putins-talking-about-when-he-talks-about-denazification. Confidential note drawn up in Goring's Headquarters on 20 June 1940 (Main Commission for Investigation of Nazi War Crimes in Poland-600/40 x/VIII).

Chapter 6: Putin Tests NATO and EU Resolve

1. https://www.nato.int/cps/en/natohq/topics_50349.htm
2. Hugh Williamson, 'Germany blocks ex-Soviets' NATO entry', *Financial Times*, 1 April 2008. https://www.ft.com/content/ab8eb6a6-ff44-11dc-b556-000077b07658; Robert Marquand, 'NATO divided over Ukraine, Georgia membership bids', *Christian Science Monitor*, 28 March 2008. https://www.csmonitor.com/World/Europe/2008/0328/p01s01-woeu.html; Staff, 'NATO denies Georgia and Ukraine, BBC News, 3 April 2008.
3. Dr. John J Mearsheimer, 'The Causes and Consequences of the Ukraine War,' Belfer Centre, Harvard Kennedy School for Science and International Affairs, 23 June 2022.
4. Mearsheimer, 'The Causes and Consequences of the Ukraine War,' (2022).
5. 'Georgia Army National Guard Soldiers Arrive in Georgia for International Military Exercise,' *NGB*, July 2008. https://www.nationalguard.mil/News/Article/573370/georgia-army-national-guard-soldiers-arrive-in-georgia-for-international-milita/
6. John Vandiver, 'US Troops Still In Georgia', *Stars and Stripes*, 12 August 2008. https://www.stripes.co_Ken/news/u-s-troops-still-in-georgia-1.81903
7. Martin Malek (March 2009), 'Georgia & Russia: The "Unknown" Prelude to the "Five Day War"', *Caucasian Review of International Affairs* 3 (2), pp 227–232. Archived from the original on 15 June 2014. Retrieved June 15, 2022.
8. As an example, the introduction of the After Action Review (AAR) after every flight improved pilot performance and squadron proficiency without the expenditure of additional money. Interview with Maj Gen(Ret) Baldwin.
9. 'Ukraine crisis: Timeline', BBC, 13 November 2014. https://www.bbc.com/news/world-middle-east-26248275
10. 'Ukrainian ex-leader Viktor Yanukovych vows fightback', BBC, 28 February 2014. https://www.bbc.com/news/world-europe-26386946
11. 'Ousted Ukrainian President Warns of Civil War', *Sputnik International*, 3 November 2014. https://sputniknews.com/20140311/Ousted-Ukraine-Leader-Warns-of-Civil-War-Threat-188313017.html; Olena Goncharova, 'Yanukovych says he is clean, unlike the current government', *Kyiv Post*, 24 December 2014. https://www.kyivpost.com/article/content/kyiv-post-plus/yanukovych-says-he-is-clean-unlike-the-current-government-376021.html
12. Dmytro Putiata, Andrii Karbivnychyi and Vasyl Rudyka, 'Ukraine's Armed Forces on the Eve of the Conflict', *Defence Industry of Ukraine*, 12 March 2020. file:///Users/johnharrel/Desktop/Russian%20Invasion%20Ukraine%20Project/Rus%20Invasion%202014/2014%20Ukraine's%20Armed%20Forces%20on%20the%20Eve%20of%20the%20Conflict%20-%20Militarnyi.html

13. Ibid.
14. Russian spelling vs the Ukrainian.
15. Putiata (2020).
16. Dmytro Putiata, 'Ukraine's Armed Forces on the Eve of the Conflict (2014)', *Defense Industry of Ukraine*, 12 March 2020.
17. In the news broadcasts Russian special forces did not completely change out of their unforms.
18. John S Harrel, *Soviet Cavalry Operations During the Second World War & The Genesis Of The Operational Manoeuvre Group* (Barnsley: Pen & Sword, 2019).
19. Staff, 'Zabrodskyi's Raid: The First Major Ukrainian Counteroffensive', *Weapons and Warfare, History and Hardware of Warfare,* 27 August 2018. https://weaponsandwarfare.com/2018/08/27/zabrodskyis-raid-the-first-major-ukrainian-counteroffensive/
20. Interview with MG(Ret) Baldwin.
21. 'Satellite images show Russian military build-up along Ukraine border', Reuters, 20 April 2021.   https://www.reuters.com/news/picture/satellite-images-show-russian-military-b-idUSRTXBN4Y0
22. Mearsheimer, (2022)..
23. 'Russia recognizes independence of Ukraine separatist regions,' *DW,* 21 February 2022.https://www.dw.com/en/russia-recognizes-independence-of-ukraine-separatist-regions/a-60861963
24. Task Force Orion, 27th Infantry Brigade Combat Team, New York Army National Guard in February 2022 was given the mission of training, equipping and mentoring UAF soldier. Jim Garmone, 'U.S. Troops to Deploy to Europe, Guardsmen Reassigned Out of Ukraine', *US Department of Defense,* 12 February 2022. https://www.defense.gov/News/News-Stories/Article/Article/2933203/more-us-troops-to-deploy-to-europe-guardsmen-reassigned-out-of-ukraine
25. Interview with MG(Ret) David S. Baldwin.

Chapter 7: The Ukrainian Armed Forces (UAF)

1. David M. Herszenenhorn and Paul Mcleary,'Ukraine's "Iron General" is a hero, but he's no star,' *Politico,* 8 April 2022. A defending NATO company is trained to defeat an attacking Soviet-style battalion.
2. Luis Martinez, 'Trump admin approves new sale of anti-tank weapons to Ukraine', ABC, 2019.https://abcnews.go.com/Politics/trump-admin-approves-sale-anti-tank-weapons-ukraine/story?id=65989898; https://www.defensenews.com/congress/2019/09/25/what-you-need-to-know-about-the-us-aid-package-to-ukraine-that-trump-delayed/
3. 'What Russia Faces: Primer to Ukraine's Ground Forces.' https://www.youtube.com/watch?v=U26SNwTH8p0&t=301s
4. https://www.youtube.com/watch?v=7_hf65lQf-k&t=610s, https://www.youtube.com/watch?v=U26SNwTH8p0
5. Sakshi Tiwari, 'Meet Elite British Commndos-The SBS-That "Helped" Ukraine To Snatch Back Snake Island From Russia', *The Eurasian Times,* 4 February 2023. https://eurasiantimes.com/meet-elite-british-commandos-the-sbs-that-helped-ukraine-to-snatch/; Editor, 'Its official: SAS troops are training Ukrainian soldiers', *Forces Penpals,* 16 April 2022. https://forcespenpals.net/gb/news/sas-troops-training-ukrainian-sodliers/
6. The ex-commandos were each paid £600 per day. Marco Giannangeli, 'Ex-SAS heros teach Ukrainian troops to "fight smart" in war against Russia', *Express,* October 2022. https://www.express.co.uk/news/world/1686495/ukraine-russia-war-sas-teaches-Ukraine-troops-putin
7. Five Coat Consulting.
8. Charlie Dunlap, JD, 'The Ukraine Crisis and the international; law of armed conflict (LOAC): some Q&A'. *Lawfire*https://sites.duke.edu/lawfire/2022/02/27/the-ukraine-crisis-and-the-international-law-of-armed-conflict-loac-some-q-a/
9. https://tass.com/world/1419543
10. Emily Crawford,'Armed Ukrainian Citizens: Direct Participation in Hostilities, Levees en Masse or Something Else?', *EJIL:TALK, Blog of the European Journal for International Law,* 1 March 2022. https://www.ejiltalk.org/armed-ukrainian-citizens-direct-participation-in-hostilities-levee-en-masse-or-something-else/
11. Convention (III) relative to the Treatment of Prisoners of War, Geneva, 12 August 1949, Article 4/A(6). https://casebook.icrc.org/glossary/levee-en-masse

12. Jann Kleffner, 'Ukraine Symposium-Ukraine Levee en Masses and the Obligation to Ensure Respect for LOAC (Law of Armed Conflict), Lieber Institute West Point, 14 April 2022'. https://lieber.westpoint.edu/ukraines-levee-en-masse-obligation-ensure-respect-loac/
13. Herszenenhorn (2022). A defending NATO company is trained to defeat an attacking Soviet-style battalion.
14. Interview with General (Ret) Mark Hertling: 'Russia's Army is Awlful', https://www.youtube.com/watch?v=fZ5-xCMIMQs&t=195s, Richard D. Hooker, 'The Ukrainian Military must reorganize to defeat Russia', *Atlantic Council*, 30 August 2022, Interview with MG(Ret) David S. Baldwin.
15. Interview with MG(Ret) David S. Baldwin.
16. Jack Watling and Nick Reynolds, 'Ukraine at War, Paving the Road from Survival to Victory,' *Royal United Services Institute for Defence and Security Studies*, 4 July 2022.
17. Christopher Woody, 'unpredictability of Ukrainian troops, top enlisted leader says,' *Insider*, 2 August 2022. https://www.businessinsider.com/russian-forces-cant-cope-with-ukrainian-ncos-enlisted-leader-says-2022-8.
18. 'Building a corps of professional Non-Commissioned Officers in Ukraine,' NATO homepage. https://www.nato.int/cps/en/natohq/news_129998.htm; 1st LT Kayla Christoper, USA, 'Building NCOs in Ukraine', *US Army*, 22 April 2017. https://www.army.mil/article/186536/building_ncos_in_ukraine; SGT Alexander Rector, 'New York Army National Guard Soldiers mentor and learn in Ukraine', *NGB*, 22 June 2018, https://www.nationalguard.mil/News/Article/1557426/ny-army-guard-soldiers-mentor-and-learn-in-ukraine/
19. Watling (2022).
20. https://www.forbes.com/sites/davidhambling/2022/05/12/drones-give-ukrainian-artillery-lethal-accuracy/?sh=38c74be5424b
21. https://www.nbcnews.com/news/world/ukraine-army-uses-guns-weapons-drone-combo-rcna27881
22. https://www.atlanticcouncil.org/blogs/ukrainealert/the-ukrainian-military-must-reorganize-to-defeat-russia/
23. Nicholas Kristoff, 'Ukrainian Women Fight for Their Own Liberation,' *New York Times*, 3 December 2022. https://www.nytimes.com/2022/12/03/opinion/ukraine-women.html
24. Francesca Ebel, 'Hell on Earth: Ukrainian Soldiers Describe Eastern Front', Military.com, 4 July 2022. https://www.military.com/daily-news/2022/07/04/hell-earth-ukrainian-soldiers-describe-eastern-front.html,https://www.google.com/search?q=Ukrainian+Woman+platoon+commanders+TGF&client=safari&rls=en&ei=hP6dY5jsFazNkPIPwI6y8A8&ved=0ahUKEwiYvvzmmIH8AhWsJkQIHUCHDP4Q4dUDCBA&uact=5&oq=Ukrainian+Woman+platoon+commanders+TGF&gs_lcp=Cgxnd3Mtd2l6LXNlcnAQAzoKCCAAQRxDWBBCwAzoFCAAQogQ6CgghEMMEEAoQoAFKBAhBGABKBAhGGABQ1wpY6B5gvzJoAXABeACAAY8BiAHcCpIBBBDAuMTGYAQCgAQHIAQLAAQE&sclient=gws-wiz-serp#fpstate=ive&vld=cid:218eab4d,vid:X-dJ0butbVg
25. Illia Ponomarenko, 'Regular Kyivans get ready to help repel Russian attack,*Kyiv Independent*, 21 Febuary 2022. https://kyivindependent.com/national/regular-kyivans-get-ready-to-help-repel-russian-attack
26. Staff, 'Azov regiment expands to brigade within National Guard of Ukraine,' Yahoo News, 9 February 2023.
27. Staff, 'Ukraine civil war fears as volunteer units take up arms', *The Guardian*, May 2014.
28. Vasco Cotovio, 'Russian nationals fighting for Ukraine vow to resist Moscow's forces "until the end"', CNN, 6 December 2022.
29. Staff, 'Switching Sides: The Elusive "Russian Legion" Fighting with Ukraine', *The Moscow Times*, 8 August 2022.
30. Joseph McDonald, interview: 'A British Volunteer Back from the Front: Ukraine' Parts I, II, YouTube Video, March 2022.
31. https://www.navalnews.com/naval-news/2022/01/analysis-russia-to-dominate-the-black-sea-in-case-of-ukraine-conflict/
32. Ukrainian Air Force (2022) https://www.wdmma.org/ukrainian-air-force.php, Tyson Wetzel, 'Ukraine air war examined: A glimpse at the future of air warfare,' *Atlantic Council*, August 2022. https://www.atlanticcouncil.org/content-series/airpower-after-ukraine/ukraine-air-war-examined-a-glimpse-at-the-future-of-air-warfare/

33. Sebastien Roblin, 'Ukraine is quietly using its Mi-24 "flying tanks" helicopters to batter Russian force, *Insider,* 27 April 2022. https://www.businessinsider.com/ukraine-is-using-mi24-flying-tank-helicopters-to-fight-russia-2022-4

34. David Axe, 'Ukraine's Best Fighter Pilots Are Preparing for War, But will They Fight', *Forbes,* 4 February 2022. https://www.forbes.com/sites/davidaxe/2022/02/04/the-ukraines-best-fighter-pilots-are-preparing-for-war-but-will-they-fight/?sh=4c6282f6408b, Maj. Matthew Mutti, USAF, 'National Guard forces train for safer skies in Europe, NGB, July 18, 2021. https://www.nationalguard.mil/News/Article/575141/national-guard-joint-forces-train-for-safer-skies-in-europe/.

Chapter 8: Russian Armed Forces

1. 'First Chechen War', https://en.wikipedia.org/wiki/First_Chechen_War#cite_note-Gall-42

2. Emma Graham-Harrison, 'Russian airstrikes in Syria killed 2,000 civilians in six months', *The Guardian,* 2016. https://www.theguardian.com/world/2016/mar/15/russian-airstrikes-in-syria-killed-2000-civilians-in-six-months

3. Peter Young, 'Russia committing war crimes by deliberately bombing civilians and aid works, says Amnesty International', *Independent* 2016. https://www.independent.co.uk/news/world/middle-east/russia-civilians-war-crimes-amnesty-international-a6887096.html

4. 'General who lead Syrian Bombing is New Face of Russian War', Associated Press, 20 October 2022. https://apnews.com/article/russia-ukraine-putin-mikhail-gorbachev-syria-middle-east-c2582dabed6158f058e58d2e2bc0d4cf

5. During the Second World War, the Soviet command headquarters for army groups were titled 'Fronts'. They normally were provided geographical names such as the 1st Ukrainian Front.

6. Dr. Lester W. Grau and Charles K. Bartle, *The Russian Way of War* (US Army Foreign Military Studies Office, 2016), p 29.

7. Lester (2016), p 31

8. Ibid, p 32.

9. 'Invasion of Ukraine, D+89 Sitrep (#215)', The Five Coat Consulting Group, 24 May 2022.

10. 'BTG, OoB, Crowd Source BDA in Ukraine (#199)', Five Coat Consulting Group, 8 March 2022. https://www.thefivecoatconsultinggroup.com/the-coronavirus-crisis/perspective-ukraine

11. Staff, 'Zabrodskyi's Raid: The First Major Ukrainian Counteroffensive', *Weapons and Warfare,* 27 August 2018.

12. Lester W. Grau and Charles K. Bartles, 'Getting to Know the Russian Battalion Tactical Group', RUSI, 14 April 2022. https://rusi.org/explore-our-research/publications/commentary/getting-know-russian-battalion-tactical-group

13. This is an average number. Each tank types fuel consumption varies based upon weight, engine, terrain and weather.

14. 'The World's Biggest Fuel Consumer', *Forbes,* 5 June 2008. https://www.forbes.com/2008/06/05/mileage-military-vehicles-tech-logistics08-cz_ph_0605fuel.html?sh=369f3437449c

15. Aleksey, Khloptov, 'The USSR's Hungriest Tank', *Tank Archive,* 1 March 2021.

16. Alex Vershinin, 'Feeding the Bear: A Closer Look At Russian Army Logistics and the Fait Accompli', *War on the Rocks,* 23 November 2021. https://warontherocks.com/2021/11/feeding-the-bear-a-closer-look-at-russian-army-logistics/

17. During the siege of Grozny in the Chechen wars the Russians were firing 4,000 shells or 50 truck loads a day. During the Russo-Georgian War in 2008, the Russians expended their entire basic load of ammunition in 12 hours.

18. *Russian New Generation Warfare Handbook* (US Army, Asymmetric Warfare Group, Version 1, 2016), p 30.

19. Kateryn Stepanenko, Frederick W. Kagan and Brian Babcock-Lumish, 'Reserve, And Mobilization', *ISW,* 5 March 2022. https://www.understandingwar.org/backgrounder/explainer-russian-conscription-reserve-and-mobilization

20. Grau (2016), p 3–9

21. Stavros Atlamzoglou, 'The Russian Military's Weak NCO Corps on Display in Ukraine,' *Sandboxx*, 5 April 2022. https://www.sandboxx.us/blog/the-russian-militarys-weak-nco-corps-on-display-in-ukraine/

22. Gil Barndollar, 'The Best or Worst of Both Worlds?', *CSIS*, 23 September 2020. https://www.csis.org/blogs/post-soviet-post/best-or-worst-both-worlds

23. Captain Nicola J. Fiore, USA, 'Defeating Russian Battalion Tactical Group', *Armor Journal*, Spring 2017, https://www.benning.army.mil/armor/earmor/content/issues/2017/spring/2Fiore17.pdf

24. Michael Kofman and Robert Lee, 'Not Built For Purpose: The Russian Military's Ill-Fated Force Design', *War on the Rocks*, 2 June 2022. https://warontherocks.com/2022/06/not-built-for-purpose-the-russian-militarys-ill-fated-force-design/ 'All metal, no manpower- Russian Infantry shortages and mobilization in Ukraine', *Perun*. https://www.youtube.com/watch?v=AKewF8_SiIs&t=209s

25. 'Russian Airborne Force Structure (and its Flaws)', *Battle Order* https://www.battleorder.org/post/vdv-video, Jorgen Elfving, *An Assessment of the Russian Airborne Troops and Their Role on Tomorrow's Battlefield*, (Jamestown Foundation: Washington DC: 2021).https://jamestown.org/wp-content/uploads/2021/04/Jorgen-Russian-Airborne-Troops.pdf?x39384

26. 'Soviet Naval Infantry', *Weapons and Warfare*, 26 June 2020. https://weaponsandwarfare.com/2020/06/26/soviet-naval-infantry/

27. Each platoon has one officer and three nine-man squads. Each squad has a staff sergeant, two sergeants and six soldiers. The platoon sergeant commands the Bradley IFV when the infantry dismount.

28. 'US Army Stryker Rifle Platoon (Current)', *Battle Order* https://www.battleorder.org/us-stryker-platoon-2019, ATP 3-21/8 *Infantry Platoon and Squad*, (US Army: 2016). Each platoon has one officer and three nine-man squads, each of one staff sergeant, two sergeants and six soldiers. The platoon sergeant normally commands the Stryker APCs.

29. Nicholas Drummond, 'The Universal Infantry Battalion,' https://wavellroom.com/2019/08/29/the-universal-battalion-possible-future-infantry-unit-structures/

30. Catherine Harris and Fredrick W. Kagan, 'Russia's Military Posture: Ground Forces Order of Battle', *ISW*, March 2018, p 21.

31. 'Russian Marines at Palmyra', *Inform Napalm*, 18 April 2016. https://informnapalm.org/en/russian-marines-palmyra/; Askai707, 'Russia's 61st Seperate Naval Infantry Brigade in the Donbas', *Bellingcat*,15 November 2016. https://www.bellingcat.com/news/uk-and-europe/2016/11/15/russias-61st-separate-naval-infantry-brigade-donbass/

32. Dr. Lester W. Grau and Charles K. Bartle, *The Russian Way of War* (US Army Foreign Military Studies Office, 2016), p 32.

33. Lester (2016).

34. *'Little Green Men': a primer on Modern Russian Unconventional Warfare, Ukraine 2013–2014* (US Army Special Operations Command: Fort Bragg), p 43.

35. Dr. Christopher Marsh, *Development in Russian Special Operations* (Canadian Special Operations Command: Ottawa, 2017).

36. Marsh, *Development in Russian Special Operations (2017)*, pp 20–27; *'Little Green Men'*, pp 42–43; Hall Gardner, 'Hybrid Warfare: Iran and Russian Versions of "Little Green Men" and Contemporary Conflict', *NATO Research Paper No. 123*, December 2015. https://www.ndc.nato.int/news/news.php?icode=885.

37. 'Ukraine crisis: Thousands of Russians' fighting in east.' BBC, 28 August 2014. https://www.bbc.com/news/world-europe-28963310

38. 'Russia and the Separatists in Eastern Ukraine', Crisis Group, Kyiv/Brussels, 5 February 2016. https://www.refworld.org/pdfid/56b843194.pdf

39. Galeotti, Mark, *Armies of Russia's War in Ukraine* (Oxford: Osprey Publishing, 2019), p 30.

40. LTC Amos C. Fox, USA, 'Reflections on Russia's 2022 Invasion of Ukraine: Combined Arms Warfare, The Battalion Tactical Group and Wars In A Fishbowl', *AUSA*, 29 September 2022. https://www.ausa.org/publications/reflections-russias-2022-invasion-ukraine-combined-arms-warfare-battalion-tactical

41. *Little Green Men*, pp 40–43.

42. 'Band of Brothers: The Wagner Group and the Russian State,' *CSIS*, 21 September 2020.https://www.csis.org/blogs/post-soviet-post/band-brothers-wagner-group-and-russian-state.
43. Ibid.
44. Ibid, Eleanor Beardly, 'An ex-member of one of the world's most dangerous mercenary group goes public', *NPR*, 6 June 2022. https://www.npr.org/2022/06/06/1102603897/wagner-group-mercenary-russia-ukraine-war
45. Christopher Faulkner and Marcel Plichta, 'Win, Lose, Or Draw, the Wagner Group Benefits From the War in Ukraine', *Lawfare*, 23 October 2022. https://www.lawfareblog.com/win-lose-or-draw-wagner-group-benefits-war-ukraine
46. Sherryn Groth, 'Who's behind Wagner, the most notorious mercenary group in the world?', *The Sydney Morning Herald*, 9 October 2022. https://www.smh.com.au/world/europe/who-s-behind-wagner-the-most-notorious-mercenary-group-in-the-world-20220722-p5b3pm.html
47. Ragip Soylu, 'Wagner Group lures foreign mercenaries with bumped-up salaries as Russia suffers losses', *Middle East Eye*, 6 October 2022. https://www.middleeasteye.net/news/wagner-group-russia-foreign-mercenaries-salaries-suffers-losses
48. Lynne O'Donnell, 'Russia's Recruiting Afghan Commandos', *Foreign Policy*, 25 October 2022.
49. Arwa Mahdawi, 'We thieves and killers are now fighting Russia's war: How Moscow recruits from its prisons', *The Guardian*, downloaded 14 January 2023. https://www.theguardian.com/world/2022/sep/20/russia-recruits-inmates-ukraine-war-wagner-prigozhin, https://www.bbc.com/news/world-60947877
50. https://www.wdmma.org/russian-air-force.php
51. Keir Giles, 'Assessing Russia's Reorganization and Rearmed Military', *Carnegie Endowment for International Peace*, 3 May 2017. https://carnegieendowment.org/2017/05/03/assessing-russia-s-reorganized-and-rearmed-military-pub-69853
52. Russian Air Force (2023), *WDMMA*, 17 December 2022. https://military-history.fandom.com/wiki/Russian_Navy#The_Black_Sea_Fleet
53. 'Russian Black Sea Fleet's Warships Return to Naval Bases after massive drills', TASS, 31 January 2022. https://tass.com/defense/1395149
54. https://warontherocks.com/2022/04/the-russo-ukrainian-war-at-sea-retrospect-and-prospect/
55. https://www.navalnews.com/naval-news/2022/01/analysis-russia-to-dominate-the-black-sea-in-case-of-ukraine-conflict/

Chapter 9: The Effect of Russian Corruption and Deceptive Reporting

1. Aleksandra Klitina, 'How the National Anti-Corruption Bureau Works During Wartime', *Kyiv Post*, 17 January 2023. https://www.kyivpost.com/post/11228
2. Tor Bukkvoll, *Russian Mmilitary Corruption-Scale and Causes*, FORSVARETS FORSKNINGSINSTITUTT (FFI) Norwegian Defense Research Establishment, 11 November 2005, p 22.
3. Staff, 'Russian corruption: A factor in the war in Ukraine?', *GlobalData*, 19 July 2022; Tor Bukkvoll, *Russian Military Corruption – Scale and Causes*, pp 19–21.
4. 'How Corruption Destroys Armies – Theft, Graft, and Russian failure in Ukraine' *Perun*, 6:48. https://www.youtube.com/watch?v=i9i47sgi-V4; Stefan Hedlund, 'The collapse of the Russian military machine', *GIS*, 2 May 2022.
5. Staff, 'A Most Reliable Ally: How Corruption in the Russian Military Could Save Ukraine', *OCCRP*, 13 April 2022.
6. 'Bukkvoll (2005), pp 12–17.
7. Lasha Tchanouridze, 'Corruption in Russia and War in Ukraine,' Norwich Record, Summer 2022.
8. Ibid.
9. Staff 'Where did the equipment disappear to? Russian MP says 1.5mln military uniforms are missing', *Novaya Gazeta Europe*, 2 October 2022. https://novayagazeta.eu/articles/2022/10/02/where-did-they-disappear-to-russian-local-pm-says-1-5-mln-military-uniforms-are-missing-news

10. David Hambling, 'New Russian Soldiers Issued Fake Body Armor', *Forbes*, 19 October 2022.   https://www.forbes.com/sites/davidhambling/2022/10/19/new-russian-soldiers-issued-with-fake-body-armor/?sh=7ff7d83714f0

11. Stefan Hedlund, 'The collapse of the Russian military machine', *GIS*, 2 May 2022

12. Bukkvoll (2005).

13. This happened to my brigade in Kosovo. A civilian contractor shipped diesel fuel to my base which was delivered at a few degrees higher in temperature than was specified. When the fuel cooled to the proper temperature, several hundred gallons of diesel disappeared. A quick investigation by my provost marshal ended with the contractor being required to make up the shortfall under threat of prosecution.

14. 'How Lies Destroy Armies, Lies Coverups & Russian Failure in Ukraine', *Perun*. https://www.youtube.com/watch?v=Fz59GWeTIik

15. Douglas Birch, 'In Russia, the truth is optional', *Baltimore Sun*, 8 August 2022. https://www.baltimoresun.com/news/bs-xpm-2006-08-27-0608250029-story.html.

16. Christopher Bort, 'Why The Kremlin Lies: Understanding Its Loose Relationship With the Truth', *Carnegie Endowment for International Peace*, 1 January 2022. https://carnegieendowment.org/2022/01/06/why-kremlin-lies-understanding-its-loose-relationship-with-truth-pub-86132

17. 'How Lies Destroy Armies', *Perun*, video.

18. Ibid.

19. Alia Shoaib, 'How the Russian officer elite was decimated in Ukraine – 29 generals and commanders who were killed in action', *Insider*, 31 December 2022. https://www.businessinsider.com/ukraine-russian-officer-elite-decimated-9-who-were-killed-in-combat-2022-3

20. Joshua Rudolph and Norman L. Eisen, 'Ukraine's Anti-Corruption Fight Can Overcome US Skeptics', *Just Security*, 10 November 2022. https://www.justsecurity.org/84076/ukraines-anti-corruption-fight-can-overcome-us-skeptics/

21. Andriy Yermak, 'Why Ukraine sanctioned Putin's ally Medvedchuk', Atlantic Council, 26 February 2021. https://www.atlanticcouncil.org/blogs/ukrainealert/why-ukraine-sanctioned-putins-ally-medvedchuk/.

22. Steve Inskeep, 'Ukrainian officials fired after probe shows their workers collaborated with Russia', *NPR*, 18 July 2022. https://www.npr.org/2022/07/18/1111985737/ukrainian-officials-fired-after-probe-shows-their-workers-collaborated-with-russia

23. Staff, 'US Plan to Counter Illicit Diversion of Certain Adavanced Conventional Weapons in Eastern Europe', US Dept. of State news release, 27 October 2022. https://www.state.gov/u-s-plan-to-counter-illicit-diversion-of-certain-advanced-conventional-weapons-in-eastern-europe/

24. Anna Myroniuk and Alexander Kherbet, 'Investigation: International Legion soldiers allege light weapons misappropriation, abuse by commanders', *The Kyiv Independent*, 30 November 2022. https://kyivindependent.com/investigations/investigation-international-legion-misappropriation

25. Caitlin Doornbos, 'US troops checking Ukraine weapons delivery sites against theft threat', *New York Post*, 1 November 2022. https://nypost.com/2022/11/01/us-troops-checking-ukraine-weapons-delivery-sites-against-theft-threat/

26. Oleksky Bobrovnikov, 'Explained: What We Know About Two Major Corruption Scandals in Ukraine's Ministries', *The Kyiv Post*, 23 January 2023. https://www.kyivpost.com/post/11435

27. Asami Terajima, 'Ukraine war latest: Bakhmut 'increasingly isolated' as Russia appears to make progress on encircling the city', *The Kyiv Independent*, 7 February 2023. https://kyivindependent.com/national/ukraine-war-latest-bakhmut-increasingly-isolated-as-russia-appears-to-make-progress-on-encircling-the-city

28. Staff, 'Explained: What Do We Know About Latest Searches and Dismissals of Ukrainian Officials', *The Kyiv Post*, 1 February 2023. https://www.kyivpost.com/post/11740

29. Alisa Orlova, 'Mass Resignation Rock Ukrainian Government Amid Corruption Scandals', *The Kyiv Post*, 24 January 2023. https://www.kyivpost.com/post/11458

30. Matthew Loh, 'Zelenskyy fired 9 top officals after reports that members of his government went on vacation to Spain and France and took bribes during the war', *Insider*, 24 January

2023. https://www.businessinsider.com/zelenskyy-fires-top-officials-corruption-scandal-vacation-war-2023-1

31. Staff, G7 Ukraine Support Group, University of Toronto, http://www.g7.utoronto.ca/ambassadors/ukraine.html

32. Staff, 'Fighting Corruption is Vital to Increased Foreign Aid to Ukraine-G7 Ambassadors', *Kyiv Post*, 28 January 2023. https://www.kyivpost.com/post/11607, Staff, 'G7, EU ambassadors expect Ukraine to resume education, anti-curruption program,' *Ukrinform*, 7 February 2023. https://www.ukrinform.net/rubric-economy/3661954-g7-eu-ambassadors-expect-ukraine-to-resume-education-anticorruption-program.html

33. Staff, 'Oleksandr Kubrakov presents strategic directions of reconstruction to G7 ambassadors', *The Odessa Journal*, 2 February 2023. https://odessa-journal.com/oleksandr-kubrakov-presents-strategic-directions-of-reconstruction-to-g7-ambassadors/

Chapter 10: Ukrainian and Russian Armed Forces' Combat Capabilities Compared on the Eve of the Invasion

1. Seth G, Jones 'Russia's Ill-Fated Invasion of Ukraine: Lessons in Modern Warfare', *CSIS*, 1 June 2022. https://www.csis.org/analysis/russias-ill-fated-invasion-ukraine-lessons-modern-warfare

2. Alex Vershin, 'Feeding the Bear: A Closer Look at Russian Army Logistics and the Fait Accompli', *War on The Rocks, Texas National Security Review*, 23 November 2021.

3. https://www.janes.com/docs/default-source/ukraine-conflict/equipment-profile_report_280222.pdf?sfvrsn=c51c7182_1, https://www.janes.com/defence-news/news-detail/russian-build-up-on-ukrainian-border-enters-new-stage-analysis; https://taskandpurpose.com/analysis/russian-military-generals-killed-ukraine/?amp

4. Two Soviet tank divisions would contain twenty tank battalions, and twelve motorized infantry battalions.

5. The 4th Rapid Reaction Brigade consists of: brigade HQ, two light infantry battalions, one tank battalion (T-64s), one artillery battalion, one AA missile battalion and support units.http://eu.eot.su/2016/06/19/president-of-ukraine-to-send-national-guard-militants-to-donbass-for-combat-trial-run/

6. Myhaylo Zabrodsky, Jack Watling, Oleksander V Danylyuk and Nick Reynolds, *Preliminary Lessons in Conventional Warfighting from Russia's Invasion of Ukraine: February-July 2022* (RUSI: London, 2022) p 11.

7. Zabrodsky (2022), p 22

8. Zabrodsky (2022), p 22

9. Leslie Gornstein, 'Russian's invasion of Ukraine: Weapons and movement of the massive military building up', CBS News, 26 February 2022. https://www.cbsnews.com/pictures/ukraine-russia-military-photos/27/

10. Thomas Frank, 'Assets, $300 billion of Moscow Bank Funds', CNBC News, 29 June 2022.https://www.cnbc.com/2022/06/29/doj-says-allies-have-frozen-30-billion-of-russian-oligarch-assets.html

Chapter 11: Putin Invades and Stumbles

1. Staff, 'Invasion of Ukraine, D+15, Sitrep, (#200)', The Five Coat Consulting Group, https://www.thefivecoatconsultinggroup.com/the-coronavirus-crisis/ukraine-context-d15. 'The Member-States of the Eurasian Economic Union are the Republic of Armenia, the Republic of Belarus, the Republic of Kazakhstan, the Kyrgyz Republic and the Russian Federation', http://www.eaeunion.org/?lang=en#about.

2. Pavel Baev, 'Russia's War in Ukraine, Misleading Doctrine, Misguided Strategy', *Etudes De L'IFRI No 40*, October 2022, p 16.

3. In American terminology 'Movement to Contact' formation.

4. Deep State Map. https://deepstatemap.live/en#8.5/51.1387/31.7520

5. Zabrodsky (2022), p 22.

6. Ibid.

7. Deep State Map. https://deepstatemap.live/en#8.5/51.1387/31.7520

8. Staff Reporters, 'President Putin's February 21, speech to the nation -full text', *The Rio Times*, 24 February 2022.

9. Dan Rice, 'The Untold Story of the Battle for Kyiv', *Thayer*, 2 June 2022.
10. 'Russian-Ukraine Warning Update: Initial Russian Offensive Campaign Assessment, 24 February 2011', *Institute of the Study of War.*
11. Rice, (2022).
12. KI Staff, 'SBU: Antonov officials suspected of obstructing Hostomel Airport defence in early 2022, Kyiv Independent, 10 March 2023. https://kyivindependent.com/sbu-former-antonov-state-enterprise-officials-suspected-of-obstructing-hostomel-airport-defense/
13. https://www.ukrinform.net/rubric-ato/3420446-ukrainian-armed-forces-take-control-of-hostomel-intelligence.html, https://www.criticalthreats.org/analysis/russia-ukraine-warning-update-initial-russian-offensive-campaign-assessment
14. Dan Rice (2022).
15. Deep State Historical interactive map. https://deepstatemap.live/en#8.25/51.3033/31.4892
16. Alex Vershinin, 'Lessons From the Battle for Kyiv', *Russia Matters*, 21 April 2022. https://www.russiamatters.org/analysis/lessons-battle-kyivA
17. Tom Cooper, 'Russian Heliborne Assault on Antonov / Hostomel Airport seems to have Failed', 2022. https://www.youtube.com/watch?v=QlttS0N7uVA
18. Tom Cooper (2022).
19. https://twitter.com/karhunen_timo/status/1511993188566843393?lang=en
20. https://www.aberfoylesecurity.com/?p=4812
21. Zabrodsky(2022), p 22.
22. Vershinin (April 2022), Zabrodsky (2022), p 28.
23. James Marson, 'The Ragtag Army that won the Battle of Kyiv and Saved Ukraine', *Washington Post*, 20 September 2022; Zabrodsky (2022), p 28.
24. Phil Helsel, 'Ukrainian forces blow up bridges to impede Russian forces interior ministry says', https://www.nbcnews.com/politics/politics-news/blog/russia-ukraine-conflict-live-updates-over-100-people-killed-hundreds-n1289845/ncrd1289864#blogHeader; Vincent Mundy, 'Ukraine's Hero River, helped save Kyvi. But what now for its newly restored wetlands?', *The Guardian*, 11 May 2022. https://www.theguardian.com/environment/2022/may/11/ukraine-hero-irpin-river-helped-save-kyiv-but-what-now-for-its-newly-restored-wetlands-aoe; Oleksii Vasyliuk and Eugene A. Simonow, 'Plans to rebuild Ukraine shaped by solutions for Irpin', *Reserchgate*, 9 September 2022, https://www.fox5atlanta.com/news/ukrainian-marine-sacrifices-himself-to-blow-up-bridge-ukrainian-military-says; Brendan Cole, 'Ukraine Forces Blow Up Bridge Near Kyiv to Halt Russian Tank Advance', *Newsweek*, 5 February 2022, https://www.newsweek.com/russia-ukraine-kyiv-bridge-blown-explosion-invasion-tank-advance-1682560
25. The flooded area was controlled by observation posts.
26. https://www.researchgate.net/publication/363405887_Plans_to_rebuild_Ukraine_shaped_by_solutions_for_Irpin; Staff, 'After dam breaks saved capitol. Dozens of houses still underwater in flooded village of Demydiv', *The New Voice of Ukraine*, 3 May 2022. https://english.nv.ua/nation/village-in-kyiv-ukraine-flooded-to-defend-capital-in-war-50239056.html
27. 'Ukrainian president signs decree on general mobilization of population', Reuters, 24 February 2022. https://www.reuters.com/world/europe/ukrainian-president-signs-decree-general-mobilisation-population-interfax-2022-02-24/
28. https://www.cnn.com/2022/02/26/europe/ukraine-zelensky-evacuation-intl
29. https://thereload.com/ukraine-distributes-10000-automatic-rifles-to-civilians-as-capitol-city-fights-russian-invasion/ ; https://time.com/6154068/ukrainian-citizens-fight-russian-troops/
30. Ukrainian president signs decree on general moblization of population', Reuters, 24 February 2022. https://www.reuters.com/world/europe/ukrainian-president-signs-decree-general-mobilisation-population-interfax-2022-02-24/
31. Staff writer, 'Reports Suggest Heavy Resistance to Russian Entery into Ukrainian Capital', *The Aviantionist*, 26 February 2022, https://theaviationist.com/2022/02/26/two-il-76s-shot-down-in-ukraine/; Staff Writer, 'Ukraine Claims To Shot Down A Russian IL-76 Transport with Paratroopers onboard', *Fighter Jet World Blog*, 26 February 2022, https://fighterjetsworld.com/latest-news/ukraine-claims-to-shot-down-a-russian-il-76-transport-plane-with-paratroopers-onboard/27632/; '2 Russian transport jets shot down

as attacks continue in Kyiv: Reports', https://www.theweek.in/news/world/2022/02/26/2-russian-transport-jets-shot-down-as-attacks-continue-in-kyiv-reports.html

32. Tim McMillan, 'Know No Mercy: The Russian Cops who tried to Storm Kyiv', *The Debrief,* 2022. https://thedebrief.org/know-no-mercy-the-russian-cops-who-tried-to-storm-kyiv-by-themselves/

33. Rice, 'The Untold Story of the Battle for Kyiv.'

Chapter 12: Defending Kyiv's Eastern Flank

1. Maryna Looijen-Nosachenko, 'Sumy: The gates of Europe 30 kilometres from the Russian Border', *New Eastern Europe,* 15 November 2022, https://neweasterneurope.eu/2022/11/15/sumy-the-gates-of-europe-30-kilometres-from-the-russian-border/

2. The 1st Tank Brigade's garrison is near Kyiv inside the Mizhrichyskyi Nature Reserve. It was forward deployed to Chernihiv on the night of 22 February 2022.

3. https://twitter.com/archer83able/status/1382285880581316610?lang=en.

4. Illia Pononmarenko, 'Exclusive: Voice message reveals Russian military unit's catastrophic losses in Ukraine', *Kyiv Independent,* 2 March 2022, https://kyivindependent.com/national/exclusive-voice-message-reveals-russian-military-units-catastrophic-losses-in-ukraine

5. David Axe, 'Ukraine's Best Tank Brigade Has Won The Battle for Chernihiv', *Forbes,* 31 March 2022, https://www.forbes.com/sites/davidaxe/2022/03/31/ukraines-best-tank-brigade-has-won-the-battle-for-chernihiv/?sh=193451f07db9

6. https://www.cnn.com/videos/world/2022/03/23/velyka-dymerka-firefight-ukraine-russia-ac360-vpx.cnn

7. Staff, 'Russian retreating from Chernihiv Region', *Ukrinform,* 20 November 2022, https://www.ukrinform.net/rubric-ato/3445517-russians-retreating-from-chernihiv-region-local-administration-chief.html

8. https://www.russiamatters.org/analysis/lessons-battle-kyiv

9. https://www.france24.com/en/live-news/20220303-mine-warfare-on-kyiv-s-eastern-front

10. Dmyro Syniak, 'Kruty became a stronghold of resistance, worthy of Ukrainian traditions…', Interview with the head of Kruty Municipality, Ukraine government post, https://decentralization.gov.ua/en/news/14818

11. Looijen-Nosachenko (15 November 2022).

12. Tweet from BMO News, 24 February, 2022, https://twitter.com/BNONews/status/1497008145893400577. Footage of night urban combat in Sumy.

13. https://apostrophe.ua/news/society/2022-02-28/boi-pod-sumami-artilleriya-i-bayraktaryi-unichtojili-100-tankov-i-20-gradov-okkupantov/260916

14. Greg Miller, Mary Ilyushina, Catherine Belton, Isabelle Khurshudyan and Paul Sonne, 'Wiped Out: War in Ukraine has decimated a once feared Russian brigade', *The Washington Post,* 16 December 2022, https://www.washingtonpost.com/world/2022/12/16/russia-200th-brigade-decimated-ukraine/

15. Miller et al, 'Wiped Out', *The Washington Post,* 16 December 2022).

16. Alina Lohvynen, Serhill Lysenko, 'Pavlo Fedosenko, Hero of Ukraine: After Victory, I want to march with my brigade from Kharkiv to Chuhuiv', *Ukrinform,* 6 June 2022. https://www.ukrinform.net/rubric-ato/3505811-pavlo-fedosenko-hero-of-ukraine.html

17. https://www.ukrinform.net/rubric-ato/3413585-russian-invasion-update-ukrainian-forces-destroy-convoy-of-fuel-trucks-in-sumy.html

18. Michael G. Anderson, 'How Ukraine's Roving Teams of Light Infantry Helped Win The Battle of Sumy: Lessons for the US Army', Modern War Institute at West Point, 17 August 2022. https://mwi.usma.edu/how-ukraines-roving-teams-of-light-infantry-helped-win-the-battle-of-sumy-lessons-for-the-us-army/

Chapter 13: Battle for Kyiv (March 2022)

1. Staff, 'Ukraine's Secret Weapon Against Russian: Turkish Drones', *Time,* 1 March 2022. https://time.com/6153197/ukraine-russia-turkish-drones-bayraktar/

2. Marson (20 September 2022).

3. Ibid.

4. 72nd (Black Zaporizhzhia Cossack) Mechanized Brigade

5. Staff, '80 Ukrainian Soldiers Managed to Hold Back Thousands of Russian Troops Attempting to Cross Irpin River to Enter Kyiv', *Défense Express*, 20 April 2022. https://en.defence-ua.com/events/a_mere_80_ukrainian_soldiers_managed_to_hold_back_thousands_of_russian_troops_attempting_to_cross_irpin_river_to_enter_kyiv-2610.html; Chris Huges and Alice Peacock, 'Russian troops storm woods as they attempt to enter Kyiv by crossing Irpin River', *Mirror*, https://www.mirror.co.uk/news/world-news/russian-troops-storm-woods-attempt-26485780

6. Charles K. Bartles, *A Russian Approach to a Battalion Hasty River-Crossing Assault*, (Foreign Military Studies Office: Fort Leavenworth, KS, 2018), pp 58–62.

7. Zabrodsky, (30 November 2022), p 31.

8. Ibid.

9. Staff, 'Western official: Russian tank commander run over and killed by his own angry troops', *The Times of Israel*, 17 February 2022. https://www.timesofisrael.com/western-official-russian-tank-commander-run-over-and-killed-by-own-angry-troops/

10. Liz Sly, 'Accounting of bodies in Buch nears completion', *The Washington Post*, 8 August 2022, https://www.washingtonpost.com/world/2022/08/08/ukraine-bucha-bodies/; Staff, 'Could Humans really do this?: Stories of civilians killed in Bucha Ukraine', *60 Minutes*, YouTube Video. https://www.youtube.com/watch?v=8crdog2b_Bg

11. Isabel Van Burgen, 'Russian Units Linked to Bucha War Crimes Likely Destroyed in Combat', *Newsweek*, 12 August 2022. https://www.newsweek.com/bucha-massacre-killings-russian-units-war-crimes-ukraine-1733168

12. Laurel Wamsley,'Rape has reportedly become a weapon in Ukraine, Finding may be difficult', *NPR*, 30 August 2022. https://www.npr.org/2022/04/30/1093339262/ukraine-russia-rape-war-crimes; Alanna Vagianos, 'Russia Is Using Rape As A Weapon of War Against Ukraine', *The Huffington Post*, 21 April 2022, https://www.belfercenter.org/publication/russia-using-rape-weapon-war-against-ukraine

13. Sun Tzu, *The Art of War*.

14. https://www.nytimes.com/2022/03/22/world/europe/ukraine-air-force-russia.html

15. Phillips Payson O'Brien, 'Why Ukraine Is Winning', *The Atlantic*, 19 October 2022.

Chapter 14: Battle for the Donbas (24 Feb–1 April 2022)

1. Anatolly Amelin, 'The Forgotten Potential of Ukraine's Energy Reserves', *HIR*, 10 October 2022 https://hir.harvard.edu/ukraine-energy-reserves/

2. Staff, 'The Russians are controlling Izyum', General Staff of the Ukrainian Armed Forces, 1 April 2022, https://mil.in.ua/en/news/the-russians-are-controlling-izyum-general-staff-of-the-ukrainian-armed-forces/

3. 'Who was Russian Colonel Nikolay Ovcharenko killed in Ukraine,' *Ground Report*, 23 March 2022, https://groundreport.in/who-was-russian-colonel-nikolay-ovcharenko-killed-in-ukraine/

4. Staff, 'Russian Offensive Campaign Assessment, 1 April 1', *Institute for the Study of War*, 1 April 2022, https://www.understandingwar.org/backgrounder/russian-offensive-campaign-assessment-april-1. The Russians are Controlling Izyum-General Staff of Ukrainian Armed Forces, Defense Industry Ukraine, April 1, 2022.

5. Stefan Korshak, Ukrainian officials: Dozens of RF mercenaries from Libya, Syria, Russia killed in Popasana', *The Kyiv Post*, 2 April 2022.

6. Sebastien Robin, 'Ukrainian Veterans Recall Pivotal Tank Battles in Volnovakha', *Forbes*, 9 November 2022, https://www.hrw.org/news/2022/04/03/ukraine-apparent-war-crimes-russia-controlled-areas

7. Robin (9 November 2022).

8. Marc Champion, 'Why Ukraine's Donbas Region Matters to Putin', *The Washington Post*, 12 September 2022. https://www.washingtonpost.com/business/energy/why-ukraines-donbas-region-matters-to-putin/2022/09/12/3bd4a4f4-3285-11ed-a0d6-415299bfebd5_story.html

9. Brendan Cole, 'Ukrainian Marine Commander Pavlo Sbytove, Killed Fighting Russian Invaders, *Newsweek*, 12 March 2022, https://www.newsweek.com/ukraine-marine-commander-pavlo-sbytov-killed-fighting-russia-invaders-1687453

Chapter 15: The Naval Battle for the Black Sea Coast

1. Mia Bennett, 'The Cost of the Bridge to Crimea', *The Maritime Executive*, 18 May 2022, https://www.maritime-executive.com/editorials/the-cost-of-the-bridge-to-crimea, https://www.theguardian.com/world/2018/may/15/putin-opens-bridge-between-crimea-and-russian-mainland
2. David Hambling, 'Ukraine Threatens Russia's Vital Bridge to Crimea (UPDATE: Bridge Down, Still Partly Operational)', *Forbes*, 5 May 2022, https://www.forbes.com/sites/davidhambling/2022/05/06/ukraine-threatens-russias-vital-bridge-to-crimea/?sh=3f724dcd5d77
3. Eric Jenson, 'Ukraine Symposium – The Kerch Strait Bridge Attack, Retaliation and International Law', Lieber Institute West Point, 12 October 2022. https://lieber.westpoint.edu/kerch-strait-bridge-attack-retaliation-international-law/
4. Odessa is now being spelled as Odesa on most media maps and in most articles.
5. Trojan War Epic by Arctinus of Miletus.
6. Luke Harding, 'Russian warship, go f--- yourself', *The Week*, 6 January 2023.
7. Sophie Williams and Paul Kirby, 'Ukraine war: Snake Island and battle for control in the Black Sea', BBC, 11 May 2022, https://www.bbc.com/news/world-europe-61406808
8. Ibid.
9. B. J. Armstrong, 'The Russo-Ukrainian War At Sea: Retrospect and Prospect', *War On The Rocks*, 21 April 2022. https://warontherocks.com/2022/04/the-russo-ukrainian-war-at-sea-retrospect-and-prospect/
10. Ibid.
11. Harding (6 January 2023).
12. https://www.bbc.com/news/world-europe-61406808
13. https://www.bbc.com/news/world-europe-61103927
14. Staff, 'Assessing Russia's first major naval loss of the war in Ukraine', *Navy Lookout*, 28 March 2022. https://www.navylookout.com/assessing-russias-first-major-naval-loss-of-the-war-in-ukraine/
15. Note, Ukrainian anti-aircraft missiles have damaged smaller Russian vessels. The anti-aircraft missiles locked on to the vessels' heat signatures.
16. H Sutton, 'Russian Navy's 5 Significant Losses in the Ukraine War So Far', *Naval News*, 4 May 2022, https://www.navalnews.com/naval-news/2022/05/russian-navys-5-significant-losses-in-the-ukraine-war-so-far/
17. Kostia Andreikovets, 'The Ukrainian Armed Forces launched more than 10 accurate strikes on the Snake Island, The Russian "pantsir-C1" system was destroyed', *Babel*, 30 June 2022, https://babel.ua/en/news/80586-the-ukrainian-armed-forces-launched-more-than-10-accurate-strikes-on-the-snake-island-the-russian-pantsir-c1-system-was-destroyed?utm_source=page&utm_medium=read_more
18. https://www.reuters.com/world/europe/russia-steps-up-attacks-ukraine-after-landmark-nato-summit-2022-06-30/
19. Staff, 'Russia Abandons strategic Snake Island, the early symbol of Ukrainian defiance', CBS, 30 June 2022, https://www.cbsnews.com/news/russia-snake-island-early-symbol-ukrainian-defiance/
20. Yaoslav Lukov, 'Snake Island: Why Russia couldn't hold on to the strategic Black Sea outcrop', BBC News, 30 June 2022. https://www.bbc.com/news/world-europe-61992491

Chapter 16: Ground Conquest of the Black Sea Coast

1. Translations of Ukrainian sources uses the term 'direction' instead of 'sector'.
2. *Ukraine Conflict Monitor*, Issue 10, Rochan Consulting, February 2022, https://rochan-consulting.com/issue-10_1-25-february-2022/
3. Jon McCure and Peter M. Graff eds, 'Zaporizhzhia on the frontline,' Reuters, 1 September 2022, https://graphics.reuters.com/UKRAINE-CRISIS/ZAPORIZHZHIA/mypmnznjqvr/
4. https://www.irishtimes.com/news/world/europe/we-hit-them-with-everything-we-had-ukrainian-town-fights-off-the-russians-1.4865429
5. Zaheer Akram Bora, '800 vehicles strong Russian military convoy "destroyed" by Ukrainian forces Bashtanka', *Northeast Now*, 2 March 2022, https://nenow.in/world/russian-military-convoy-destroyed-by-ukrainian-forces-bashtanka.html

6. *Ukraine Conflict Monitor*, Issue 17, Rochan Consulting, 24 March 2022. https://rochan-consulting.com/issue-17_2-4-march-2022/
7. Joseph Trevithick, 'Ukraine Strikes Back: Barrage Leaves Russian-Occupied Kherson Airbase in Flames', *The War Zone*, 16 March 2022, https://www.thedrive.com/the-war-zone/44780/ukraine-strikes-back-barrage-leaves-russian-occupied-kherson-airbase-in-flames,https://www.criticalthreats.org/analysis/russian-offensive-campaign-assessment-march-7; https://twitter.com/konrad_muzyka/status/1500876567509147650
8. *Ukraine Conflict Monitor*, Issue 20, Rochan Consulting, 17 March 2022, https://rochan-consulting.com/issue-20_1-7-march-2022/; https://rochan-consulting.com/issue-21_2-8-march-2022/
9. Carole Landry, 'Scenes from the Resistance', *The New York Times*, 15 March 2022.
10. Sravasti Dasguta, 'Ukrainian soldiers and volunteers defeated larger Russian force in strategically important town, report claims', *Kyiv Independent*, 17 March 2022,https://www.independent.co.uk/news/world/europe/ukraine-voznesensk-russia-soldiers-defeat-b2037837.html
11. Yaroslav Trofimov, 'A Ukrainian Town Deals Russia One of the War's Most Decisive Routs', *The Wall Street Journal*, 16 March 2022, https://www.wsj.com/articles/ukraine-russia-voznesensk-town-battle-11647444734, https://www.bbc.com/news/world-europe-60840081;https://www.cbsnews.com/news/russia-ukraine-voznesensk-battle-mykolaiv-defend-nuclear-plant-odesa-port/
12. Trofimov (16 March 2022).
13. Deep State Map Ukraine. https://deepstatemap.live/en#10/46.9353/32.6665
14. 'For Want of a nail', https://nationalpoetryday.co.uk/poem/for-want-of-a-nail/
15. *Ukraine Conflict Monitor*, Issue 19, Rochan Consulting, 6 March 2022, https://rochan-consulting.com/issue-19-6-march-2022/
16. *Ukraine Conflict Monitor*, Issue 11, Rochan Consulting, 26 February, 2022, https://rochan-consulting.com/issue-11_2-26-february-2022/

Chapter 17: The Battling Bastards of Mariupol

1. Staff, 'Battle ongoing near Mariupol', *Ukrainform*, 26 February 2022, https://www.ukrinform.net/rubric-ato/3412585-battle-ongoing-near-mariupol-mayor.html
2. Andy Hayes, 'Ukraine war: 20,000 flee Mariupol in biggest evacuation yet from besieged port city', Sky News, 16 March 2022, https://news.sky.com/story/ukraine-war-20-000-evacuated-from-mariupol-in-biggest-evacuation-yet-from-besieged-port-city-12566507
3. https://www.cnn.com/2022/03/19/europe/mariupol-shelter-commander-ukraine-intl/index.html
4. https://www.thetimes.co.uk/article/british-fighter-captured-by-russians-in-mariupol-mrgbph35h
5. The 1942 US and Filipino defenders of the Philippines against the Imperial Japanese Army and Navy.
6. https://www.reuters.com/world/europe/russia-says-remaining-531-azovstal-defenders-surrender-steelworks-siege-over-2022-05-20/
7. https://www.bbc.com/news/world-europe-60585603

Chapter 18: Russian Reorganization After Decisive Defeat

1. https://www.defense.gov/News/News-Stories/Article/Article/2985302/russia-possibly-repositioning-forces-to-donbas/
2. https://www.cnn.com/2022/04/11/europe/ukraine-donbas-battle-russia-cmd-intl/index.html
3. Zabrodsky, (30 November 2022), p 31.
4. Ibid, pp 45–47.
5. Ibid, p 31.
6. https://www.understandingwar.org/backgrounder/russian-offensive-campaign-assessment-april-9
7. Frederick W. Kagan, George Barros, Kateryna Stepanenko and Larolina Hird, 'Russian Offensive Campaign Assessment', *ISW*, 9 April 2022, https://www.understandingwar.org/backgrounder/russian-offensive-campaign-assessment-april-9,

8. https://www.understandingwar.org/backgrounder/russian-offensive-campaign-assessment-april-9,https://donpress dot com/news/09-04-2022-ocherednoy-polkovnik-vs-rf-byl-ubit-na-voyne-s-ukraincami;   https://74.ru/text/incidents/2022/04/08/71241086/; https://twitter.com/RALee85/status/1512556106853363718; https://kazanreporter. ru/news/ 48967_pohorony-pogibsego-na-ukraine-komandira-diviziona-motostrelkovoj-brigady-prosli-v-tatarstane; https://twitter.com/RALee85/status/1512142148208054276?ref_src= twsrc%5Etfw; https://www.businessinsider.com/ukraine-russian-officer-elite-decimated-; https://www.understandingwar.org/backgrounder/russian-offensive-campaign; https://www. facebook.com/GeneralStaff.ua/posts/287740683539017; https://www.facebook.com/General Staff.ua/posts/288811783431907

9. Zabrodsky (November 30, 2022), p 46.

10. Thomas Nilsen, '200th Motorized Rifle Brigade send mixed volunteer battalion to Ukraine', *The Barents Observer*, 4 July 2022. (https://thebarentsobserver.com/en/ security/2022/07/200th-motorized-rifle-brigade-sends-mixed-volunteers-battalion-ukraine-war

11. Greg Miller, Mary Ilyushina, Catherine Belton, Isabelle Khurshudyan and Paul Sonne, 'Wiped Out: War in Ukraine has decimated a once feared Russian brigade', *The Washington Post*, 16 December 2022, https://www.washingtonpost.com/world/2022/12/16/russia-200th-brigade-decimated-ukraine/

12. https://www.youtube.com/watch?v=eHhgVrKJJoA

13. https://www.mirror.co.uk/news/world-news/russian-commander-shot-himself-finding-26579585; https://www.express.co.uk/news/world/1587696/Russian-commander-suicide-financial-corruption-military-equipment-ukraine-latest-ont

14. Zabrodsky (30 November 2022) p 43; Per Skoglund, Tore Listou, Thomas Ekstrom, 'Russian Logistics in the Ukraine War: Can Operational Failure be Attributed to Logistics?', *Scandinavian Journal of Military Studies*, https://sjms.nu/articles/10.31374/sjms.158/

Chapter 19: Battle for the Donbas, Summer 2022

1. https://www.military.com/daily-news/2022/04/11/us-doubts-new-russian-war-chief-can-end-moscows-floundering.html

2. Dr Lester W. Grau and Charles K. Bartes, *The Russian Way of War: Force Structure, Tactics, and Modernization of the Russian Ground Forces* (US Foreign Military Studies, 2016), pp 130–139.

3. Grau, *The Russian Way of War* (2016), pp 135–140.

4. Ibid, pp 107, 125

5. Russian Offensive Campaign Assessment, 23 April, 2022, *ISW*, https://www. understandingwar.org/backgrounder/russian-offensive-campaign-assessment-april-23.

6. https://kyivindependent.com/national/explainer-what-to-expect-from-the-battle-of-donbas-russias-new-offensive/

7. Only about 10 per cent of well-trained tank crews can effectively engage tanks at 4,000m. Fire-and-forget Javelin Anti-Tank Missiles have a higher percentage of hitting their target at these ranges.

8. https://quotefancy.com/napoleon-quotes.

9. David Axe, 'Massive Bombardment Signals Russia's Renewed Offensive in Donbas', *Forbes*, 18 April, 2022, https://www.forbes.com/sites/davidaxe/2022/04/18/massive-bombardment-signal-russias-renewed-offensive-in-eastern-ukraine/?sh=ab4e3394236a

10. https://www.understandingwar.org/backgrounder/russian-offensive-campaign-assessment-april-11

11. https://www.defense.gov/News/News-Stories/Article/Article/3002606/defense-official-russia-adds-11-battalion-tactical-groups-in-ukraine/

12. *Heavy Opposing Force Operational Art Handbook*, TRADOC Pamphlet 350–14, 1994, 4–1 to 4–54.

13. Russian Offensive Campaign Assessment, 23 April 2022, *ISW*, https://www. understandingwar.org/backgrounder/russian-offensive-campaign-assessment-april-; Defense Official: Russia Adds 11 Battalion Tactical Groups in Ukraine, US DoD, 18 April 2022,   https://www.defense.gov/News/News-Stories/Article/Article/3002606/defense-official-russia-adds-11-battalion-tactical-groups-in-ukraine/

14. 'War of Attrition – Russian Invasion of Ukraine', *Kings and Generals*, https://www.youtube.com/watch?v=D-93q4GMFT0; Deep State Ukraine Map April 1–May 1, 2023, https://deepstatemap.live/en#9/49.2167/36.7850

15. Deep State Map, 10 May 2022. https://deepstatemap.live/en#10/48.6284/37.9385

16. War of Attrition.

17. Grau (2016), pp 130–139

18. 'The Battle of the Donbas', Austrian Army, https://www.youtube.com/watch?v=RpC1kXhW2Lw; The Battle of Donbas Phase 1, *Kings and Generals*, https://www.youtube.com/watch?v=K2N_fHKrWIg; Volodymyr, Dacenko, 'Evolution of Russian tactics in Ukraine: From failed blitzkrieg to assult infantry', Euromaidan Press, 1 January 2023. https://euromaidanpress.com/2023/01/31/evolution-of-russian-tactics-in-ukraine-from-failed-blitzkrieg-to-assault-infantry/

19. Volodymyr, Dacenko, 'Evolution of Russian tactics in Ukraine: From failed blitzkrieg to assult infantry,' Euromaidan Press, 1 Janaury 2023, https://euromaidanpress.com/2023/01/31/evolution-of-russian-tactics-in-ukraine-from-failed-blitzkrieg-to-assault-infantry/

Chapter 20: Twenty-first Century Lend-Lease and the Arsenals of Democracy

1. Claire Mills, *Military Assistance to Ukraine since the Russian Invasion* (House of Commons Library: London, 11 November 2022), pp 6–11.

2. Claire Mills, *Military Assistance to Ukraine since the Russian Invasion* (House of Commons Library: London, 11 November 2022), 10.

3. Katharina Buchholz, 'Where Military Aid to Ukraine Comes From', *Statista*, November 2022, https://www.statista.com/chart/27278/military-aid-to-ukraine-by-country/

4. Emma Nix, Akshat Dhankher, and Nancy Messieh, 'Ukraine Aid Tracker: Mapping the West's support to counter Russia's invasion', Atlantic Council, 13 May 2022, https://www.atlanticcouncil.org/commentary/trackers-and-data-visualizations/ukraine-aid-tracker-mapping-the-wests-support-to-counter-russias-invasion/

5. Jonathan Swan, Zachary Basu and Sophia Cal, 'Scoop: Zelensky pushes Biden on no-fly zone', *Axios*, 10 March 2022, https://www.axios.com/2022/02/28/ukraine-no-fly-zone-zelensky-biden-russia

6. 'Proposed no-fly zone in the 2022 Russian invasion of Ukraine,' *Wikipedia*, retrieved 28 November 2022, https://en.wikipedia.org/wiki/Proposed_no-fly_zone_in_the_2022_Russian_invasion_of_Ukraine,

7. Claire Mills, *Military Assistance to Ukraine since the Russian Invasion* (House of Commons Library: London, 11 November 2022), p 12.

8. Mark F. Cancian, 'Aid to Ukraine Explained in Six Charts', *CSIS*, 18 November 2022, https://www.csis.org/analysis/aid-ukraine-explained-six-charts

9. 'United States Security Assistance to Ukraine', Congressional Research Service, 21 October 2022.

10. Mark F. Cancian, 'Aide to Ukraine Explained in Six Charts', *CSIS*, 18 November 2022, https://www.csis.org/analysis/aid-ukraine-explained-six-charts https://www.csis.org/analysis/what-does-40-billion-aid-ukraine-buy

11. Mark F. Cancian, 'Aid to Ukraine Explained in Six Charts', *CSIS*, 18 November 2022. https://www.csis.org/analysis/aid-ukraine-explained-six-charts

12. 'Putin Would Nuke NATO to Defend Russian Speakers in Baltics, Ally Suggests', *Newsweek*, August, 18, 2022, Robbie Gramer, 'German Tanks in Ukraine Yesterday', *FP*, 27 September 2022, https://www.newsweek.com/russia-latvia-lithuania-estonia-kremlin-solovyov-1734782; Holly Ellyatt, 'Fears grow among Russia's neighbours that Putin might not stop at Ukraine', CNBC, 8 March 2022, https://www.cnbc.com/2022/03/08/baltic-states-in-europe-fear-putin-has-them-in-his-sights.html

13. https://www.whitehouse.gov/briefing-room/statements-releases/2022/03/16/fact-sheet-on-u-s-security-assistance-for-ukraine/

14. 'Germany to send Ukraine weapons in historic shift on military aid', *Politico*, 26 February 2022, https://www.politico.eu/article/ukraine-war-russia-germany-still-blocking-arms-supplies/

15. https://www.oryxspioenkop.com/2022/09/fact-sheet-on-german-military-aid-to.html

16. https://www.thedrive.com/the-war-zone/45050/soviet-era-t-72-tanks-to-be-transferred-from-nato-states-to-ukraine
17. MGM-140 Army Tactical Missile System (ATACMS) have a range of 185 miles/300km and Precision Strike Missile, 310 miles/500km. Both the towed M777 and M109 Paladin series self-propelled howitzers have a maximum range of 30,000m and fire the Copperhead laser guided anti-tank munition, https://www.19fortyfive.com/2022/04/u-s-himars-rocket-artillery-going-to-ukraine-would-be-a-game-changer/
18. FASCAM rounds scatter anti-tank mines that remain active for a fixed duration and then self-detonate.
19. Gustav Gressel, Rafael Loss, Jana Puglien, 'The Leopard plan: How European tanks can help Ukraine take back its territory', European Council on Foreign Relations, 9 September 2022.
20. One battalion of SP 155mm and four battalions of towed 155mm howitzers. France agrees to deliver French-made Caesar 15mm wheeled howitzers to Ukraine, 22 April 2022, www.armyrecognition.com. The Dutch are sending a battalion of SP 155mm, Autoevolution.com.
21. https://www.reuters.com/world/europe/germany-okays-sale-former-gdr-infantry-fighting-vehicles-ukraine-2022-04-01/
22. https://www.reuters.com/world/europe/czech-republic-sends-tanks-ukraine-czech-tv-reports-2022-04-05/; as of 12 August 2022, support for Ukraine from the Free World. https://www.forumarmstrade.org/ukrainearms.html
23. https://ecfr.eu/article/the-leopard-plan-how-european-tanks-can-help-ukraine-take-back-its-territory/
24. Miranda Murrey, 'Rheinmeatall wants to deliver 20 new Leopard 2 tanks to Ukraine-Handelsblatt', *Zawya*, 25 April 2022, Reuters, https://www.zawya.com/en/special-coverage/russia-ukraine-crisis/rheinmetall-wants-to-deliver-20-new-leopard-2-tanks-to-ukraine-handelsblatt-fp0op3a1
25. Anne Applebaum, 'Germany Is Arguing with Itself Over Ukraine', *The Atlantic*, 20 October 2022.
26. Both M1A1 and Leopard II are armed with the same 120mm main gun.
27. https://www.rferl.org/a/russia-eastern-ukraine-offensive-donbas-next-phase/31795550.html
28. https://www.dw.com/en/ukraine-war-how-to-repair-the-ukrainian-armys-modern-weapons/a-63215373
29. Gramer, 'German Tanks in Ukraine Yesterday'.
30. Anne Applebaum, 'Germany Is Arguing with Itself Over Ukraine', *The Atlantic*, 20 October, 2022.
31. David MacDougall, '"Free the Leopards!" Campaign aims to "embarrass" Germany into sending tanks to Ukraine', *Euronews*, 1 January 2023, https://www.euronews.com/2023/01/05/free-the-leopards-campaign-aims-to-embarrass-germany-into-sending-tanks-to-ukraine
32. https://kyivindependent.com/news-feed/zelensky-ukraine-needs-300-500-tanks
33. Dan Sabbagh and Phillip Olterman, 'US and Germany agree to send infantry fighting vehicles to Ukraine', *The Guardian*, 5 January 2023, https://www.theguardian.com/world/2023/jan/05/germany-tanks-ukraine-russia-war
34. Clea Caulcutt, 'At Last, Ukraine gets Western Tanks', *Politico*, 5 January 2023, https://www.politico.eu/article/emmanuel-macron-sending-western-tanks-to-ukraine-amx-10-rc-volodymyr-zelenskyy/
35. Staff, 'Military Support for Ukraine', The German Federal Government, https://www.bundesregierung.de/breg-en/news/military-support-ukraine-2054992
36. Staff, 'M2 and M3 Bradley Fighting', Vehicles Global Security, https://www.globalsecurity.org/military/systems/ground/m2.htm
37. Siobhan O'Grady and staff, 'Russian missiles rain down on Ukrainian cities; Britain to send battle tanks', *The Washington Post*, 14 January 2023, https://www.washingtonpost.com/world/2023/01/14/challenger-2-tanks-ukraine/
38. Adam Taylor, Willian Neff and Daniel Wolfe, 'For Ukraine, what's so special about Germany's Leopard 2 tanks?', *The Washington Post*, 25 January 2023. https://www.washingtonpost.com/world/2023/01/24/leopard-2-ukraine-germany-m1-abrams/

39. Bastian Giegerich, Yohann Michel and Michel Tong, 'Ukraine: can the German Leopards change its spots?', *IISS*, 13 January 2023, https://www.iiss.org/blogs/military-balance/2023/01/ukraine-can-the-german-leopard-change-its-spots

40. Fact Sheet on U.S. Security Assistance to Ukraine, 10 November 2022, US Department of Defense.

41. https://www.dailymail.co.uk/news/article-10697737/Russia-Ukraine-crisis-Australia-sends-20-Bushmaster-military-vehicles-Ukraine.html. The Bushmaster, nicknamed 'The Bushy', is an 11-tonne armoured military vehicle designed to carry and deploy up to ten soldiers on to the battlefield. The four-wheel-drive vehicles are built to withstand any environment and protect troops from bomb blasts, and were widely used by the Australian Defence Force during the conflict in Afghanistan. The Bushmaster can carry mortars and other heavier weapons and can also be equipped with machine guns and other military equipment. It can also carry enough fuel and supplies to operate for three days without resupply and has a central tyre-inflation system allowing it to function with punctures.

42. https://www.politico.com/news/2022/03/22/ukraine-weapons-military-aid-00019104

43. Claire Mills, *Military Assistance to Ukraine since the Russian Invasion* (House of Commons Library: London, 11 November 2022), p 9.

44. The countries joining the UK in this programme are the Netherlands, Canada, Sweden, Finland, Norway, Denmark, Lithuania and New Zealand.

45. 'Russian MP says 1.5 million military uniforms are missing', *Nocaya Gazeta Europe*, 2 October 2022, https://babel.ua/en/news/85759-the-ministry-of-defense-all-soldiers-at-the-front-were-provided-with-winter-uniforms 2022; https://novayagazeta.eu/articles/2022/10/02/where-did-they-disappear-to-russian-local-pm-says-1-5-mln-military-uniforms-are-missing-news; https://en.defence-ua.com/analysis/uncomfortable_questions_appear_in_russia_where_are_15_million_sets_of_uniforms_for_the_mobilized-4408.html; https://mediacenter.org.ua/strong-there-is-no-problem-anymore-with-providing-winter-uniforms-oleksii-reznikov-the-minister-of-defence-of-ukraine-strong/

46. https://www.defensenews.com/global/europe/2022/08/25/abrams-maker-gdls-announces-11-billion-tank-deal-for-poland/

Chapter 21: The Ukrainian Counteroffensive Shaping Operation

1. FM 3-0 Operations, (US Army Publication 2022), 6–4. https://armypubs.army.mil/epubs/DR_pubs/DR_a/ARN36290-FM_3-0-000-WEB-2.pdf

2. Isabelle Khurshudyn and Paul Sonne, '5 key takeaways on how Ukraine's counteroffensive reshaped the war', *The Washington Post*, 29 December 2022, https://www.washingtonpost.com/world/2022/12/29/ukraine-counteroffensives-kharkiv-kherson-takeaways/

3. Illia Ponomarenko, 'Ukraine targets Russia's ammunition depots, undermining its artillery advantage', *Kyiv Independent*, 8 July 2022, https://kyivindependent.com/national/1234

4. Isabelle Khurshudyan, Serhiy Morgunov and Kamila Hrabchuk, 'Inside the Ukrainian Counteroffensive that shocked Putin and reshaped the war', *The Washington Post*, 29 December 2022.

5. https://www.theguardian.com/world/2022/aug/21/ukraine-strikes-psychological-blows-game-of-drones-crimea;https://theconversation.com/crimea-ukraine-uses-new-tactics-to-attempt-to-take-back-strategic-territory-from-russia-188951; https://www.understanding war.org/backgrounder/russian-offensive-campaign-assessment-august-18

6. https://www.voanews.com/a/large-scale-explosions-rock-russian-ammo-depot-in-crimea-/6703567.html

7. https://www.19fortyfive.com/2022/08/putin-is-angry-ukraine-destroys-russian-satellite-system-and-ammo-depot/

8. https://www.reuters.com/world/europe/ukraine-says-it-has-destroyed-50-ammunition-depots-using-himars-war-with-russia-2022-07-25/; https://www.newsweek.com/russia-destroyed-himars-ammunition-strike-ukraine-donetsk-konashenkov-1733430; https://kyivindependent.com/national/1234

9. Isabelle Khurshudyan, Serhiy Morgunov and Kamila Hrabchuk, 'Inside the Ukrainian Counteroffensive that shocked Putin and reshaped the war,' *The Washington Post*, 29 December 2022.

Chapter 22: Ukrainian Counteroffensive Strategic Deception and Shaping Operation, Donbas and Kharkiv Sectors

1. https://www.youtube.com/watch?v=Q9-NER8aFJ4
2. https://kyivindependent.com/national/with-successful-kharkiv-operation-ukraine-turns-the-war-in-its-favor
3. https://kyivindependent.com/national/russia-masses-forces-in-south-ahead-of-counterattack
4. https://kyivindependent.com/national/russia-masses-forces-in-south-ahead-of-counterattack
5. https://deepstatemap.live/en#9.25/49.3703/37.4480
6. https://www.google.com/maps/place/Izyum,+Kharkiv+Oblast,+Ukraine,+64306/@49.123 6347,37.3235042,15.44z/data=!4m5!3m4!1s0x41209e482e572663:0x37d676a144d4cc74! 8m2!3d49.2121445!4d37.2665006
7. https://www.thefivecoatconsultinggroup.com/the-coronavirus-crisis/ukraine-counterattack
8. https://www.longwarjournal.org/archives/2022/09/ukraines-counteroffensives-in-kharkiv-and-kherson-and-the-road-ahead.php.
9. https://deepstatemap.live/en#9.25/49.3703/37.4480
10. https://www.youtube.com/watch?v=nWv2OY01fOI; https://www.defense.gov/News/News-Stories/Article/Article/3157239/ukraines-success-was-a-surprise-only-to-the-russians/
11. 14th, 92nd Separate Mechanized Brigades, 25th Separate Airborne Brigade, 80th Separate Airborne Assault Brigade, 107th MRLS Brigade, 40th, 43rd, 44th Separate Artillery Brigades, 26th Artillery Brigades, 15th Separate Artillery Reconnaissance Brigade and elements of the Main Intelligence Directorate; https://www.president.gov.ua/en/news/vidpovimo-teroristam-na-kozhnu-yihnyu-pidlist-na-kozhnu-rake-77801
12. Illia Ponomarenko, 'With successful Kharkiv operations, Ukraine turns the war in its favor', *Kyiv Independent*, 13 September 2022, https://kyivindependent.com/national/with-successful-kharkiv-operation-ukraine-turns-the-war-in-its-favor
13. https://www.youtube.com/watch?v=fiiAmiipj8g
14. *The Soviet Army Operations and Tactics*, FM 100-2-1, 4-7, 4-8.
15. https://www.youtube.com/watch?v=7u2Px-bC55c
16. https://www.thefivecoatconsultinggroup.com/the-coronavirus-crisis/ukraine-counterattack
17. https://www.thefivecoatconsultinggroup.com/the-coronavirus-crisis/ukraine-counterattack; https://www.oryxspioenkop.com/2022/02/attack-on-europe-documenting-ukrainian.html
18. https://twitter.com/JominiW/status/1569506286001070080/photo/1
19. Igor Kossov, 'Ukraine capture Russian ammo weapons, vehicles in Kharkiv Oblast', *Kyiv Independent*, 12 September 2022, https://kyivindependent.com/national/ukrainians-capture-russian-ammo-weapons-vehicles-in-kharkiv-oblast

Chapter 23: Russian Mobilization

1. 'Russian Mobilization – what does it mean for the war in Ukraine?', *Perun*, https://www.youtube.com/watch?v=6hXnQNU8ANo
2. Miodrag Soric, 'Russia's army: An overestimated power', *DW*, 29 September 2022.
3. 'Russian Mobilization – what does it mean for the war in Ukraine?', *Perun*, https://www.youtube.com/watch?v=6hXnQNU8ANo
4. Rob Lee, 'How the Battle for the Donbas Shaped Ukraine's Success', Eurasia Program, 23 December, 2022. https://www.fpri.org/article/2022/12/how-the-battle-for-the-donbas-shaped-ukraines-success/
5. Sam Cranny-Evans, 'Understanding Russia's Mobilisation', RUSI, 28 September 2022,https://rusi.org/explore-our-research/publications/commentary/understanding-russias-mobilisation
6. Staff, 'BARS Special Combat Army Reserve', GlobalSecurity.org, 31 January 2023, https://www.globalsecurity.org/military/world/russia/reserves-bars.htm
7. Staff, '"We Were Nothing To Them": Russian Volunteer Reservists Return from War Against Ukraine Feeling Deceived', Radio Free Europe, August 2022, https://www.rferl.org/a/russia-volunteers-ukraine-treatment-minimal-training-war/31985377.html
8. Nikolai Petrov, 'Volunteer battalions: From offense to territorial defence?', *Russia Post*, 19 August 2022, https://russiapost.info/politics/dobrobat

9. Staff, 'Russia's 3rd Army Corps Collapsed and Cannot Perform Given Tasks – The General Staff of Ukraine', *Defence*, 4 October 2022. Express https://en.defence-ua.com/analysis/russias_3rd_army_corps_collapsed_and_cannot_perform_given_tasks_the_general_staff_of_ukraine-4426.html

10. Tim Lister and John Pennington, Russia is recruiting thousands of volunteers to replenish its ranks in Ukraine. Prior experience isn't always required,' CNN, July 29, 2022. https://www.cnn.com/2022/07/29/europe/russia-recruits-volunteer-battalions-ukraine-war-cmd-intl/index.html

11. Nikolai Petrov, 'Volunteer battalions: From offense to (territorial) defence?' Russian Post, August 19, 2022. https://russiapost.info/politics/dobrobat

12. Staff, 'Russia forming 3rd Corps for war in Ukraine,' UKRINFORM, January 23, 2023.https://www.ukrinform.net/rubric-ato/3544612-russia-forming-3rd-army-corps-for-war-in-ukraine-isw.html

13. Twitters from battalion members and families. https://twitter.com/ChrisO_wiki/status/1590040745414918144

14. David Axe, The Last Russians Spent Month Forming A New Army Corps. It Lasted Days in Ukraine,' Forbes, September 15, 2022, https://www.forbes.com/sites/davidaxe/2022/09/15/the-russians-spent-months-forming-a-new-army-corps-it-lasted-days-in-ukraine/?sh=218b0256e60f

15. Russian Volunteer Units and Battalions, ISW July 16, 2022

16. Sam Cranny-Evans, 'The Chechens: Putin's Loyal Foot Soldiers,' RUSI, November 2, 2022.https://www.rusi.org/explore-our-research/publications/commentary/chechens-putins-loyal-foot-soldiers

17. Mary Ilyushina, 'Putine secretly pardoned convicts recruited by Wagner to fight in Ukraine', *The Washington Post*, 10 January 2023, https://www.washingtonpost.com/world/2023/01/10/putin-wagner-convicts-secret-pardon/

18. 'Russian Mobilization – what does it mean for the war in Ukraine?', *Perun*, https://www.youtube.com/watch?v=6hXnQNU8ANo

19. Janice Dickson and Adrian Morrow, 'Putin signs documents to illegally annex four Ukrainian regions, in drastic escalation of Russia's war', *The Globe and Mail*, 30 September 2022.https://www.theglobeandmail.com/world/article-putin-signs-documents-to-unlawfully-claim-4-ukrainian-regions-in/

20. 'Russian Mobilization – What does it mean for the war in Ukraine?', *Perun*, September 2022, https://www.youtube.com/watch?v=6hXnQNU8ANo

21. Emily Sherwin, 'Panic, protests follow Putin's partial mobilization', *DW*, 21 September 2022,https://www.dw.com/en/russia-panic-protests-follow-putins-call-for-partial-mobilization/a-63197427

22. Matthew Loh, 'So many mobilized Russian reservists had to buy their own military gear that thermal underwear now costs up to $340 and a hiking backpack costs as much as $600', *Insider*, 20 October 2022.

23. 'Russian Mobilization – What does it mean for the war in Ukraine?', *Perun*, September 2022, https://www.youtube.com/watch?v=6hXnQNU8ANo

24. Atle Staalesen, 'Mobilized Russian reservists get combat training along the border to NATO', *The Barents Observer*, 10 October 2022, https://thebarentsobserver.com/en/security/2022/10/mobilized-warriors-do-combat-training-along-russias-border-nato

25. Tim Lister, 'Russian Mobilization Problems…', CNN, 17 November 2022, https://www.cnn.com/2022/11/17/europe/russia-soldiers-desert-battlefield-intl-cmd/index.html

26. Doug Klain, 'Mobilization Can't Save Russia's War', *Foreign Policy*, 4 October 2022.

Chapter 24: Liberation of Kherson

1. Deep State Ukraine Map 5 September–10 November 2022.

2. Isabelle Khurshudyan, (29 December 2022) https://www.washingtonpost.com/world/2022/12/29/ukraine-counteroffensives-kharkiv-kherson-takeaways/

3. Isabelle Khurshudyan, Paul Sonne, Serhiy Morgunov and Kamila Hrabchuk, 'Inside the Ukrainian counteroffensive that shocked Putin and reshaped the war,' *The Washington Post*, 29 December 2022, https://www.washingtonpost.com/world/2022/12/29/ukraine-offensive-kharkiv-kherson-donetsk/

4. Deep State Ukraine Map 15 September – 9 November 2022.

5. Jonathan Landay, 'Ukrainian president visits Kherson celebrates Russian retreat,' Reuters, 14 November 2022. https://www.reuters.com/world/europe/ukrainian-president-visits-liberated-kherson-thanks-allies-support-2022-11-14/
6. Mick Krever, 'Ukrainian troops sweep into key city of Kherson after Russian forces retreat, dealing blow to Putin,' CNN, 11 November 2022, https://www.cnn.com/2022/11/11/europe/russian-troops-leave-kherson-region-intl/index.html
7. Shejane Farberov, 'Russians lose 31 armoured vehicles in Ukrainian ambush', *New York Post*, 3 February 2023, https://nypost.com/2023/02/13/russian-lose-31-armored-vehicles-in-ukrainian-ambush/
8. These are just estimates based upon open sources.

Chapter 25: Battle of Donbas and the Fight for Bakhmut, (August–December 2022)

1. *Ukraine News Letter*, Issue 236, 2–8 January 2023, Rochan Consulting, 1 February 2023.
2. 'Why Russia is Obsessed With Capturing This one Town', *The Infographic Show*, downloaded 3 January 2023, https://www.youtube.com/watch?app=desktop&v=BBJUrJffXYw
3. Olga Kyrylenko, 'Invincibility centre Bakhmut. What is happening at the most difficult axis of the front', *Ukrainska Pravda*, 8 December 2022, https://www.pravda.com.ua/eng/articles/2022/12/8/7379743/
4. Andriy Kuzakov, 'Ukrainian Troops Says Russian "Zombies" Repeatedly Attack Lines Around Bakhmut', Radio Free Europe, 21 December 2022.
5. Dr. Lester W. Grau and Charles K. Bartles, *The Russian Way of War* (Foreign Military Studies Office, Fort Leavenworth KS, 2016), p 94.
6. Ibid, p. 96.
7. *Ukraine News Letter*, Issue 236, 2–8 January 2023, Rochan Consulting.
8. Jomini of the West, Tweet, 4 Febuary 2023. https://twitter.com/JominiW?ref_src=twsrc%5Egoogle%7Ctwcamp%5Eserp%7Ctwgr%5Eauthor
9. Isaac Chotiner, 'How Russia's New Commander in Ukraine could Change the War', *The New Yorker*, 17 January 2023.
10. Deep State Ukrainian Map, 31 January 2022.
11. https://www.yahoo.com/video/heavy-fighting-luhansk-oblast-russians-073536320.html
12. Borys Sachalko, "'We Fight With Our Brains. They fight with numbers": Ukrainian Paratroopers on the Battle for the Donbas City of Kreminna', Radio Free Europe, 28 December 2022, https://www.rferl.org/a/ukraine-kreminna-battle-recapture-russia-supply-lines/32197165.html

Chapter 26: The Threat of Nuclear War: Potential Use of Tactical Nuclear Weapons

1. https://www.kcl.ac.uk/would-russia-have-invaded-ukraine-if-soviet-nuclear-weapons-had-remained-on-ukrainian-soil
2. Sources differ as to when the last nuclear warheads were transferred. The dates ranges from 1996 to 2001. https://www.icanw.org/did_ukraine_give_up_nuclear_weapons; https://www.nytimes.com/2022/02/05/science/ukraine-nuclear-weapons.html; https://www.kcl.ac.uk/would-russia-have-invaded-ukraine-if-soviet-nuclear-weapons-had-remained-on-ukrainian-soil
3. https://nuclearweaponsedproj.mit.edu/nuclear-weapon-effects-simulations-and-models/fallout-calculator
4. https://www.gmfus.org/news/despite-threat-it-faces-ukraine-was-right-give-its-nuclear-weapons; Budapest Memorandum 5 December 1994. Full Name: *Memorandum on Security Assurances in connection with Ukraine's Accession to the Treaty on the Non-Proliferation of Nuclear Weapons*, Budapest, 5 December 1994, https://treaties.un.org/doc/Publication/UNTS/Volume%203007/Part/volume-3007-I-52241.pdf; Jack Kelly, 'Despite the Threat it Faces, Ukraine was Right to Give Up its Nuclear Weapons', *Insights*, February 22, 2022.
5. Al Mauroni, 'Would Russia Use A Tactical Nuclear Weapon In Ukraine?', *Modern War Institute at West Point*, 16 March 2022, https://www.1kt.at
6. Army as a carrier of nuclear charge can use the following modifications of materiel: operational and tactical missile complex Iskander-M, self-propelled guns (203mm gun Pion/Malka, 152mm Hyacinth, 152mm howitzers Msta-S and Acacia, 240mm Tulip mortars), 152mm towed howitzers Msta-B, and others.

7. https://world-nuclear.org/information-library/safety-and-security/safety-of-plants/chernobyl-accident.aspx

8. https://world-nuclear.org/information-library/safety-and-security/safety-of-plants/chernobyl-accident.aspx

9. https://world-nuclear.org/information-library/country-profiles/countries-t-z/ukraine-russia-war-and-nuclear-energy.aspx, https://www.pbs.org/newshour/world/why-military-action-in-radioactive-chernobyl-could-be-dangerous-for-people-and-the-environment;https://www.reuters.com/world/europe/unprotected-russian-soldiers-disturbed-radioactive-dust-chernobyls-red-forest-2022-03-28/

10. Al Mauroni, 'Would Russia Use A Tactical Nuclear Weapon In Ukraine?', *Modern War Institute at West Point*, 16 March 2022.

11. Lawrence Freedman, 'Going Nuclear: On Thinking the Unthinkable (Part 2)', *Kyiv Post*, 25 September 2022.

12. Gregg Herkin, Avner Cohen and George M. Moore, '3 Scenarios for How Putin Could Use Nukes', *Politico*, 16 May 2022.

13. Lawrence Freedman, 'Going Nuclear: On Thinking the Unthinkable (Part 2)', *Kyiv Post*, 25 September 2022.

14. https://www.nbcnews.com/politics/national-security/will-biden-putin-goes-nuclear-experts-say-nuclear-response-unlikely-no-rcna32756

15. https://www.military.com/daily-news/2022/03/23/if-russia-uses-wmd-ukraine-fallout-could-trigger-nato-response-key-lawmaker-says.html

16. https://www.brennancenter.org/our-work/research-reports/natos-article-5-collective-defense-obligations-explained

17. https://www.cnn.com/2022/03/07/politics/what-is-nato-article-5/index.html

18. https://www.icrc.org/en/document/humanitarian-impacts-and-risks-use-nuclear-weapons;https://www.nato.int/docu/review/articles/2022/07/07/the-consequences-of-russias-invasion-of-ukraine-for-international-security-nato-and-beyond/index.html

19. Richard D. Hooker, Jr., 'What Ukraine needs to win the War', Atlantic Council, 21 August 2022.

20. 'The Atomic Bombing of Hiroshima and Nagasaki', *Atomic Archive*, retrieved 13 February 2023, https://www.atomicarchive.com/resources/documents/med/med_chp10.html

21. Gar Alperovitz, *Atomic Diplomacy: Hiroshima and Potsdam* (New York: Simon and Schuster, 1965).

22. John Ray Skates, *The Invasion of Japan: Alternatives to the Bomb* (University of South Carolina Press, 1994), pp 234–235.

23. Takaki, pp 70–100.

24. Murray and Millett, p viii.

25. Takaki, p 27.

26. Skates, pp 242–243.

27. Murray and Millett, pp 523–524.

28. Takaki, p 23.

29. Murray and Millett, p 520.

30. Murray and Millett, p 511.

31. Timothy Snyder, 'Putin's case for invading Ukraine rests on phony grievances and ancient myths', *The Washington Post*, 28 January 28, https://www.washingtonpost.com/outlook/2022/01/28/putin-russia-ukraine-myths/; Mykola Riabchuk, 'A Long Ongoing War. Putin's Imaginary Ukrainians and Mythic Russian Identity', *SciencesPo*, April 2022, https://www.sciencespo.fr/ceri/fr/content/dossiersduceri/long-ongoing-war-putin-s-imaginary-ukrainians-and-mythic-russian-identity; Chris Brown, 'A Kremlin paper justifies erasing the Ukrainian identity, as Russia is accused of war crimes', *CBC News*, 5 April 2022, https://www.cbc.ca/news/world/kremlin-editorial-ukraine-identity-1.6407921; Igor Berezhanskiy, 'They Consider Ukrainians To Be 'Subhumans' and Want to Murder Them: How Putin the Denazifier Sends Russian Nazis to War against Ukraine', *TCH*, 12 August 2022, https://tsn.ua/en/ato/they-consider-ukrainian-to-be-subhumans-and-want-to-murder-them-how-putin-the-denazifier-sends-russian-nazis-to-war-against-ukraine-2136544.html

Chapter 27: Twenty-first Century Holodomar: Putins Terror Campaign

1. Staff, 'Ukraine war: Captured Russian documents reveals Moscow's 10-day plan to take over the country and kill its leaders', AP News, https://news.sky.com/story/ukraine-war-captured-russian-documents-reveal-moscows-10-day-plan-to-take-over-the-country-and-kill-its-leaders-12759836
2. Staff, *Preliminary Lessons in Conventional Warfighting from Russia's Invasion of Ukraine: February-July 2022* (RUSI, 2022), pp 8,9.
3. The Katyn Massacre.
4. Staff, 'Katyn Massacre', *Britannica*, 12 January 2023, https://www.britannica.com/event/Katyn-Massacre
5. Staff, *Preliminary Lessons in Conventional Warfighting from Russia's Invasion of Ukraine: February-July 2022* (RUSI, 2022), p 8.
6. Andrian Propkip, 'Russian Air Attack on Ukraine's Power System', *Focus Ukraine*, 19 October 2022, https://www.cnbc.com/2022/10/14/russia-looks-to-deprive-ukrainians-of-water-and-electricity-supplies.html
7. Liz Sly, '66,000 war crimes have been reported in Ukraine. It vows to prosecute them all', *Washington Post*, 6 February 2023.
8. Ibid.
9. Luke Harding, '"Russian warship, go fuck yourself": what happened next to the Ukrainians defending Snake Island?' *The Guardian*, 19 November 2022.
10. Camille Gijs, 'Ukraine slams Moscow's humanitarian corridors to Russia as "absurd"', *Politico*, 7 March 2022, https://www.politico.eu/article/russia-humanitarian-corridors-are-absurd-ukraine-says/
11. Staff, 'Hundreds of thousands of Ukrainians forced to Russia US claims', *Politico*, 8 September 2022, https://www.politico.com/news/2022/09/08/ukraine-forced-russia-deport-united-nations-00055394; Staff, 'Hundreds of thousands of Ukrainians force to Russia, US says', NBC, 9 September 2023, https://www.nbcnews.com/news/world/ukraine-forced-deportations-russia-un-filtration-rcna46804
12. Associated Press, 'Hundreds of thousands of Ukrainians forced to Russia, US says,' NBC News, 8 September 2022, https://www.nbcnews.com/news/world/ukraine-forced-deportations-russia-un-filtration-rcna46804; 'Russia's "Filtration" Operations, Forced Disappearances, and Mass Deportations of Ukrainian Citizens', US State Department Press Statement, 13 July 2022.
13. A quisling is a traitor who collaborates with an enemy occupying their country.
14. Staff, 'Crimea bridge: Russia "to repair blast damage by July 2023"', BBC, 14 October 2022, https://www.bbc.com/news/world-europe-63255611
15. Justin Bronk, Nick Reynolds and Jack Watling, 'The Russian Air War and Ukrainian Reequipments for Air Defense', RUSI, 7 November 2022.
16. Ibid.
17. https://www.cnbc.com/2022/10/14/russia-looks-to-deprive-ukrainians-of-water-and-electricity-supplies.html
18. 'Lavrov defends Russian attack on Ukraine's infrastructure', Aljazeera, 1 December 2022, //www.aljazeera.com/news/2022/12/1/lavrov-defends-russian-strikes-on-ukraines-infrastructure.
19. Gerrard Kaonga, 'Russia Official Says No Choice But to Freeze and Starve Ukrainian Civilians', Newsweek.com/russia-ukraine-conflict-andrey-gurulyov-freeze-starve-electricity-latest-update-1753411
20. Staff, 'Russia turns to "terror" campaign after Ukraine failures: top US general', France 24, https://www.france24.com/en/live-news/20221116-russia-turns-to-terror-campaign-after-ukraine-failures-top-us-general
21. Koffler, Rebekah. *Putin's Playbook* (p 84). Regnery Gateway. Kindle Edition.
22. Claire Parker, 'What are war crimes, and is Russia committing them in Ukraine', *The Washington Post*, 23 May 2023.
23. United Nations Office on Genocide Prevention and the Responsibility to Protect, https://www.un.org/en/genocideprevention/crimes-against-humanity.shtml
24. Shaun Walker and Owen Bowcott, 'Russia withdraws signature from international criminal court statute', *The Guardian*, 16 November 2016, https://www.theguardian.

com/world/2016/nov/16/russia-withdraws-signature-from-international-criminal-court-statute

25. Michel Martin (host), 'The US does not recognize the jurisdiction of the International Criminal Court,' NPR pod cast, 16 April 2022, https://www.npr.org/2022/04/16/1093212495/the-u-s-does-not-recognize-the-jurisdiction-of-the-international-criminal-court

26. Ibid.

27. Jamie Dettmer and Tristan Fielder, 'European Parliament declares Russia a "a state sponsor of terrorism" as Putin launches fresh attack on Ukraine', *Politico*, 23 November 2022, https://www.politico.eu/article/eu-declares-russia-a-state-sponsor-of-terrorism/

28. Cory Welt, 'Russia's War Against Ukraine: Overview of US Sanctions and Other Responses', Congressional Research Service, 20 December 2022, https://crsreports.congress.gov/product/pdf/IN/IN11869

29. 'Russia's Greatest Defeat? Finland and Sweden Joining NATO and What it Means for Europe,' Perun, YouTube Videohttps://www.youtube.com/watch?v=S7qNd2U1i4g&t=2934s

Chapter 28: Rush to Join NATO

1. 'Finland & Sweden Accession', NATO, downloaded 16 February 2023, https://www.nato-pa.int/content/finland-sweden-accession

2. 'Russia's greatest defeat? Finland and Sweden joining NATO and what it means for Europe', Perun, YouTube Video. https://www.youtube.com/watch?v=S7qNd2U1i4g&t=2934s

3. Ibid.

4, 'Sweden's road to NATO', Sweden's Government Offices, 5 October 2022, https://www.government.se/government-policy/sweden-and-nato/swedens-road-to-nato/

5. Staff, 'Partnership Interoperability Initiative', NATO, 22 February 2022, https://www.nato.int/cps/en/natohq/topics_132726.htm

6. 'Sweden's road to NATO', Sweden's Government Offices, 5 October 2022, https://www.government.se/government-policy/sweden-and-nato/swedens-road-to-nato/

7. Sweden's road to NATO, Sweden's Government Offices, 5 October, 2022, https://www.government.se/government-policy/sweden-and-nato/swedens-road-to-nato/

8. *Deterioration of the security environment-implications for Sweden*, Swedish Government Publication, September 2023, https://www.government.se/contentassets/05ffb51ba640 4a459d7ee45c98e87a83/deterioration-of-the-security-environment---inplications-for-sweden-ds-20228/

9. John R. Deni, 'Sweden and Finland are on their way to NATO membership. Here's what needs to happen next', Atlantic Council, 22 August 2022, https://www.atlanticcouncil.org/in-depth-research-reports/issue-brief/finland-and-sweden-in-nato-looking-beyond-madrid/

10. Jim Garamone, 'Sweden, Finland Move Closer to NATO Membership', US Department of Defense, 5 July 2022. https://www.defense.gov/News/News-Stories/Article/Article/3083359/sweden-finland-move-closer-to-nato-membership/

11. John R. Deni, 'Sweden and Finland are on their way to NATO membership. Here's what needs to happen next', Atlantic Council, 22 August 2022, https://www.atlanticcouncil.org/in-depth-research-reports/issue-brief/finland-and-sweden-in-nato-looking-beyond-madrid/

12. Marc Pierinin and Sinan Ulgen, 'Two Turkey Experts on Why Erdogan Is Rejecting NATO Expansion', Carnegie Europe, 19 May 2022, https://carnegieeurope.eu/2022/05/19/two-turkey-experts-on-why-erdo-is-rejecting-nato-expansion-pub-87159

13. Ibid.

14. Selcan Hacaoglu, 'Turkey's Erdogan Puts the Brakes on NATO's Nordic Expansion', 16 May 2022, https://www.bloomberg.com/news/articles/2022-05-16/turkey-s-erdogan-puts-the-brakes-on-nato-expansion-in-nordics?utm_source=google&utm_medium=bd&c mpId=google&leadSource=uverify%20wall

15. Ibid.

16. Ibid.

17. Ibid.

18. Tristan Fiedler, 'Orban: Hungary will approve Sweden, Finland NATO bid next year', *Politico*, 24 February 2022, https://www.politico.eu/article/viktor-orban-hungary-ratification-finland-sweden-nato-membership-2023-postponed/

Chapter 29: Lessons Learned and the 2023 Offensives

1. James F. Dunnigan, *How to Make War, A Compressive Guide To Modern Warfare* (Quill: New York, 1983), p 11.
2. Zabrodskyi, pp 60–65.
3. Staff, 'NATO Secretary General warns of growing cyber threats', NATO, 11 November 2022, https://www.nato.int/cps/en/natohq/news_208889.htm?selectedLocale=en
4. Justin Bronk, Nick Reynolds and Jack Watling, *The Russian Air War and Ukrainian Reequipments for Air Defense*, (RUSI, 7 November 2022), p 35.
5. Justin Bronk, 'The Mysterious Case of the Missing Russian Air Force', RUSI, 28 February 28 2022.
6. Staff, 'General Staff: Russia has lost 80,860 troops in Ukraine since Feb. 24', *Kyiv Independent*, 13 November 2022, https://kyivindependent.com/news-feed/general-staff-russia-has-lost-80-860-troops-in-ukraine-since-feb-24
7. Justin Bronk, Nick Reynolds and Jack Watling, *The Russian Air War and Ukrainian Reequipments for Air Defense* (RUSI, 7 November 2022), p 35
8. Zabrodsky, *Lessons Learned* (2022), p 46.
9. The BOS have been modified over the years as explained in Chapter 5.
10. Zabrodsky, *Lessons Learned* (2022), p 46.
11. Ibid, pp 46–47
12. My 1970s flack vest and twenty-first century body armour carried such a warning.
13. Michael Peck, 'Ancient anti-aircraft guns are taking on a new mission amid Russia's war in Ukraine', *Insider*, 23 November 2022, https://www.businessinsider.com/old-anti-aircraft-guns-used-against-missiles-drones-in-ukraine-2022-11
14. 'Tanks are obsolete, apparently since 1919', Military History Visualized, https://www.youtube.com/watch?v=QPth_xqBXGY&t=753s
15. Anthony H. Cordesman and Abraham R. Wagner, *The Lessons of Modern War, Volume I: The Arab-Israeli Conflicts, 1973–1989* (London: Westwood Press, 1990), pp 31, 60, 61.
16. Miguel Miranda, 'The Kornet', *Military Today*, https://www.military-today.com/missiles/kornet.htm
17. Nicholas Moran, The Chieftain, 'No The Tank is Not Dead,' The Chieftain YouTube Video, https://www.youtube.com/watch?v=lI7T650RTT8
18. Ibid.
19. Ibid.
20. Staff, 'The size of the five largest NATO members vs Russia as measured by GDP', Reddit, 2022, https://www.reddit.com/r/dataisbeautiful/comments/t1ruy6/oc_the_size_of_the_five_largest_nato_members_vs/; https://www.nationmaster.com/country-info/compare/NATO-countries/Russia/Military
21. https://www.rusi.org/explore-our-research/publications/commentary/return-industrial-warfare,https://euromaidanpress.com/2022/07/09/challenges-to-russian-arms-resupply-tanks-combat-aviation-artillery-ammunition/; https://breakingdefense.com/2022/05/russian-attempts-to-restock-its-military-may-be-doomed-to-failure/
22. https://www.france24.com/en/live-news/20220707-ukraine-ammo-stocks-become-crucial-as-artillery-rages; https://www.rusi.org/explore-our-research/publications/commentary/return-industrial-warfare
23. https://www.google.com/search?q=will+russia+run+out+of+artillery+shells&client=safari&rls=en&biw=1219&bih=646&ei=n4z2YoXWDLXLkPIPwdWfUA&oq=Will+Russia+run+out+of+ammo&gs_lcp=Cgdnd3Mtd2l6EAEYATIHCAAQRxCwAzIHCAAQRxCwAzIHCAAQRxCwAzIHCAAQRxCwAzIHCAAQRxCwAzIHCAAQRxCwAzIHCAAQRxCwAzIHCAAQRxCwA0oECEEYAEoECEYYAFAAWABgoCJoAXAAeACAAQCIAQCSAQCYAQDIAQjiAAQE&sclient=gws-wiz#kpvalbx=_zI32YrLxF6OXkPIP8YOi4AE18
24. Natasha Bertrand, 'Exclusive: Iran is seeking Russia's help to bolster its nuclear program, US intel officials believe', CNN Politics, 4 November, 2022; Tanmy Kadam, 'Drones for Nukes? Russia Is Helping Iran With Nuclear Program in Exchange For Missiles & UAVs-CNN', *The Asian Times*, 7 February 2023.
25. Dr. John J Mearsheimer, 'The Causes and Consequences of the Ukraine War', Belfer Centre, Harvard Kennedy School for Science and International Affairs, 23 June 2022.

Index